JORDAN

A Whole New World

Katie Price is Jordan, one of the UK's top celebrities. She is a glamour model, TV presenter, mother and wife. She currently lives in Sussex with her husband Peter Andre and her two sons.

Praise for *Jordan: A Whole New World*:

'With Jordan's honest, no nonsense attitude evident on every page, this is a truly compelling read . . . this latest look at her life makes for seriously juicy reading' *heat*

'Intimate, riveting confessions show her in an unexpected and moving light . . . It's a full-on passionate love story' *Daily Mail*

'A real page-turner' *OK!*

'Compulsive reading' *More*

Praise for *Angel:*

'The perfect sexy summer read' *heat*

'A page-turner . . . it is brilliant. Genuinely amusing and readable. This summer, every beach will be polka-dotted with its neon pink covers' *Evening Standard*

'The perfect post-modern fairy tale' *Glamour*

Also available by Katie Price

Angel

Katie Price

JORDAN

A Whole New World

arrow books

Published in the United Kingdom by Arrow Books in 2007

1 3 5 7 9 10 8 6 4 2

First published in the United Kingdom in 2006 by Century
First published in paperback in 2007 by Arrow Books

Arrow Books
The Random House Group Limited
20 Vauxhall Bridge Road, London, SW1V 2SA

Addresses for companies within The Random House Group Limited can be
found at: www.randomhouse.co.uk/offices.htm

The Random House Group Limited Reg. No. 954009

A CIP catalogue record for this book
is available from the British Library

ISBN 9780099497851

The Random House Group Limited makes every effort to ensure that the
papers used in its books are made from trees that have been legally sourced
from well-managed and credibly certified forests. Our paper procurement
policy can be found at: www.randomhouse.co.uk/paper.htm

Typeset by SX Composing DTP, Rayleigh, Essex
Printed and bound in Great Britain by
Bookmarque Ltd, Croydon, Surrey

To Pete, Harvey and Junior
for giving me a whole new world . . .
and to Mum, Daniel, Paul and Sophie

CONTENTS

ACKNOWLEDGEMENTS

To my family and Pete's family for all their love and support. To my friends Michelle and Nicky Baker, Gary Turner, Gary Cockerill and Phil Turner, Clare Atkinson and Sally Cairns – let's be as close in the years to come. Rachel, Melodie and Danielle, Sarah Harding and Michelle Heaton – I'll try not to be so busy in future so we can meet up more! To Maggie and Rebecca for everything they've done for this book and to Random House – we got there in the end! To Claire and Nicola and everyone else at Can, thanks for all your hard work, I do appreciate it, even though I know we've had our moments . . . To Dave Laudett for all my singing lessons. To my accountant, Ali and bank manager, David. And to my fans thanks for being dedicated.

And finally another big thank you to my mum for helping with Harvey in a tremendously big way, and my brother Daniel for being patient with me and for my website – and this year let me spend more money!

CHAPTER ONE

AGAINST ALL ODDS

Sussex, February 2006

'I don't love you any more Katie.' I stared at Peter in total disbelief, unable to take in what he'd said, the words cutting into me like knives. 'It's not true, you don't mean it!' I cried out. 'You do love me, I know you do. And I love you. We've only just got married!'

'I've met someone else. I'm leaving.' His voice was cold as ice and his normally warm, handsome face was set into a hard and unfeeling mask. This couldn't be happening. I felt the room spin round and a feeling of dread grip me.

'Look at me Pete,' I begged him, believing that if he saw the love in my eyes he could never leave. But he turned away and started walking towards the door. I tried to run to him, but found I couldn't move. I was paralysed.

I knew if he went through the door that would be the end. I couldn't let him; he couldn't leave me. Without him there was nothing, my life would have no meaning at all. '*Please* don't go. I'm begging you. What about Junior and Harvey? They need you too.' He reached out to open the door. I summoned all my strength and screamed out, 'Oh my God no!'

* * *

'It's okay baby, you were dreaming.' I surfaced from my nightmare to find Peter cradling me in his arms. 'Pete, thank God, you're here!' I clung to him, tears streaming down my face. 'I had such a terrible dream. You said you didn't love me any more, that you'd met someone else – that you were leaving me.'

'Well I know we'd had a bit of a row yesterday about you bossing me around—' he said laughingly.

Then he looked serious when he saw my tears and held me closer to him. 'Hey, I'm never going to leave you ever. I love you more than anything else in the world.'

'*Promise!*'

'I don't need to promise. You know it's true. You are everything to me.' He gently kissed away my tears. 'Now try and get some sleep; we're going to be up in a few hours with the kids.'

I curled against him, my head on his chest so I could hear his heart beating, breathing in his scent and feeling his warmth. I was safe at last. Pete – my true love, the man who had come into my life and changed it for ever. I had wanted him from the first moment I saw him. Two years on I wanted him more than ever. As I snuggled against him and tried to go back to sleep I counted my blessings for the millionth time that I had met this wonderful man and that we were together. *For ever and ever* I murmured to myself, *I love you for ever, for always.* Then I smiled to myself as I thought, who in their wildest fantasies would have believed that I would have a reality TV show to thank for my amazing good fortune?

*

I fell in love with Peter Andre in the Australian jungle, surrounded by eight other celebrities, in between eating live bugs and swimming in snake-infested water, my every move watched by millions of viewers – if that isn't a surreal start to a relationship then I don't know what is!

From the moment I first set eyes on Pete as he walked through the door and into the drinks party given for all us celebs before we were all whisked off to the jungle, I thought, fucking hell he's gorgeous! Pretty boy – just my type! I remember looking him up and down, seeing that he was well-dressed in a black suit and a black shirt, which was unbuttoned and revealing his chest, and I thought, he's got a well-fit body, I wouldn't mind some of that – even though I knew I shouldn't be thinking like this as I was supposed to be with someone else. We only got a chance to say hello because there was so much going on around us. It was more than the physical attraction I felt for him, though that was almost overwhelming I can tell you . . . I just had this feeling inside me, like he could be the one. It was lust and love at first sight! All I wanted to do was to get close to him . . .

But it makes my heart miss a beat when I look back and realise that I very nearly lost him there too. During our two weeks together in the jungle filming *I'm A Celebrity Get Me Out Of Here!* Pete was totally honest about his attraction to me, but because I still had a boyfriend – Scott Sullivan – I felt unable to open up about my true feelings. As a result it must have looked as if I was playing games with Pete – flirting one minute, then pulling back the next. I hated behaving like that but could see no other way until I had ended my relationship with Scott, leaving me free for Pete.

I'm sure none of the other celebs felt like this, but I couldn't wait to get voted off the show so I could sort out my love life. I would text Scott immediately and tell him that it was over – simple, or so I thought. But as soon as I stepped out of the jungle to be met by my mum, I could tell that things were in a mess. She looked as if she was about to burst into tears. After hugging me tightly she whispered that Scott had flown to Australia to see me. 'What!' I exclaimed, thinking, what the hell is he here for? He's supposed to be in America. 'I don't want to see him! It's over between us.'

'We'll talk later,' my mum whispered. 'You've got no idea of the nightmare it's been.'

Mum had just dropped this bombshell and then I was faced by a wall of photographers. I had never felt less like smiling, but I posed away as if I didn't have a care in the world. Then it was off to be interviewed by Ant and Dec – at least I could finally set the record straight on how I felt about Peter. I took a large sip of champagne, feeling the alcohol rush straight to my head. Yes, I assured them over and over again, it was Peter that I wanted. I had completely fallen for him. But he was the one I was desperate to tell; I couldn't bear knowing that he was a short distance away, completely oblivious to how I really felt about him. I hated to think that just before I was voted off the show he had told me that he'd had enough of playing games with me and didn't want to know any more. What if I really had blown it with him? The tension was unbelievable. It was only slightly relieved when I did my *Romeo and Juliet* number during my ITV2 interview with Tara PT and Mark Durden Smith, rushing over to the barrier with the camp below and shouting out, 'Tell Pete, "Yes"!' When Pete was called to the bush telegraph and asked for his reaction to my message, he admitted that he really had feelings for me, but that I had hurt him. We needed to talk, he said. Too bloody right! But the waiting was eating me up.

As soon as my interviews were done I was given a medical, where I discovered that I'd put on half a stone, which well pissed me off! I was hoping to come out of the experience skinnier. I must have reverse metabolism, whereby the more healthy the food I eat the more weight I put on – no more beans and rice for me! Then I was free to go back to the hotel and civilisation. But I couldn't just get into a car: I had to wear a blanket over my head while a girl dressed as a decoy Jordan distracted the press. My manager had signed an exclusive deal with a magazine and newspaper, and I had to be kept under wraps – literally. I'd come back to reality with a vengeance and felt quite overwhelmed by seeing so many people all at once, being surrounded by cars and noise – even breathing in the petrol fumes made me feel giddy and disorientated because for two weeks my world had centred around a secluded campsite in the middle of nowhere.

On the journey back my mum revealed that I had been in the newspapers every single day, and it wasn't just for my jungle exploits with Peter. The tabloids had gone berserk over my hints that I had something to reveal about a certain footballer and myself in my forthcoming autobiography. An outraged Beckham was quoted saying I wasn't his type. No; dark-haired PAs with a line in masturbating pigs were much more up his street, as the world was about to discover . . . Another paper had dragged up my brief encounter with the Chelsea footballer Frank Lampard and blown it out of all proportion, claiming we'd had a wild affair when we'd never actually got that far. And all kinds of other people decided to cash in on my appearance on the TV show – someone I had met once claimed that we'd had a passionate affair, which was a complete pack of lies . . . It was almost too much to take in.

At the hotel the press madness was pushed to the back of my mind as I was reunited with my son Harvey. I had missed him so much and it was wonderful to see him again. He laughed and clapped his hands in delight at hearing my voice as I scooped him up in my arms, showered his face with kisses and held him close to me. 'Mummy's got some sorting out to do,' I told him, reluctantly putting him down and picking up my phone to check my messages.

Every single text was from Scott, begging me to see him. I texted back that I was really sorry but we were finished. I told him that I couldn't help how I felt, that I had fallen in love with Peter. I was sorry that he was hurting but that was it. Of course Scott replied immediately, again begging me to see him. But I had no intention of meeting him. I had made up my mind and nothing he said would change that; more importantly, I didn't want to ruin any chance I had with Pete. Mum had told me that Scott had flown over with his friend Dean, and I had the feeling that if I did agree to meet him it would become a photo opportunity with the press. I certainly didn't want Pete to see any pictures of me with Scott and think that there was still something going on between us. As far as I was concerned, Scott was history. It seems really harsh that I could go off him so suddenly and so totally but I didn't want him anywhere near me. Things had been going wrong between us, admittedly, but even so I never would have believed that I would want him out of my life so finally. It reminded me of the scenario I went through with one of my other exes – the pop star Dane Bowers – but in reverse, so that now I was the Dane figure and Scott was me. I suddenly realised how Dane must have felt about me when we split up, how even though I cried and begged him not to leave me – even taking an overdose and ending up in hospital because I was so devastated – it felt like he didn't give a shit. I had never understood until now how someone could be so cold and unfeeling towards the person they had once loved. But that was exactly how I felt about Scott. I didn't hate him and I didn't wish him harm; I just never wanted to see him again.

Scott was a really nice guy, and I've got nothing bad to say about him – we just weren't right for each other. It might sound big-headed to say it but I'd got him wrapped round my finger and that's never a good thing in a relationship. I also lost respect for him because he didn't seem to have any ambition. He was just no challenge. Worst of all, there was no sexual chemistry between us and towards the end of our relationship I'd used every excuse in the book to get out of having sex with him. Even if I hadn't met Pete, I would have broken up with Scott. Meeting Pete just speeded everything up. He was in a different league to Scott. If Scott was a boy, Pete was a man. I could tell that he was strong and that I wasn't going to be able to walk all over him. I loved the fact that I knew he'd been a bastard to girls in the past, because it showed he had that power over women. I liked the challenge of that and I wanted to make that power equal between us. I don't like a man who's putty in my hands . . .

It was another whole day before Peter was voted off the show, during which time I mooched around like a lovesick teenager and drove everyone around me crazy with my constant obsessing over him. All I could think about was being able to see him again and telling him once and for all that I was head over heels in love with him.

I had to do a shoot for a newspaper, and as I posed and pouted away I kept imagining what our meeting would be like. God, I wanted him so much, like I have never wanted anyone before. During a break when I was having my make-up touched up and when my mum was safely out of earshot, I whispered to her friend Louise, 'Don't tell Mum, but I'm going to marry this guy. It's perfect timing – it's a leap year and Valentine's Day is coming up. I'm going to propose. I've got to have him!' She probably thought I'd gone stark raving bonkers, but I really didn't care what anybody thought.

That night I sat in my hotel room listening to a compilation of love songs as I rifled through my wardrobe, trying on clothes and testing out make-up – I wanted to look stunning for Peter. I'd spent the last two weeks telling him how different l looked usually. I had kept saying, you just wait till you see me out of here, building myself up as if I was some amazing beauty – the natural look was all very well but I wanted to knock him dead. As far as I was concerned, even though he had told me that he loved the way I looked, I had hated seeing him with my hair in braids, without a scrap of make-up on. It's not exactly how you imagine meeting the man of your dreams! As I pulled on various different outfits and critically examined my reflection, I suddenly stopped what I was doing, riveted by the lyrics of the song playing on my stereo. It was 'Against All Odds' by Phil Collins.

My eyes filled with tears. Oh my God, I thought to myself, that's exactly how I feel about Pete. I played the track over and over again, fantasising about Pete. I was praying that he would be the next celeb to be evicted and my heart was beating wildly as I sat in the marquee watching the show the following day, along with all the other relatives and friends. I noticed Pete's parents sitting nearby and then the programme showed a series of clips with Pete and me. I was very embarrassed to see the one with Pete coming into my bed for a cuddle and then leaving with a big stonker! Everyone was looking at me to see my reaction and I looked over at his parents and smiled as if to say, 'How embarrassing was that?' And then to my huge disappointment Charlie Brockett got kicked out and I had to wait another whole day, not knowing what Pete thought of me. My mum introduced me to Claire Powell, Pete's agent, and I said to her, 'Have I got a chance with Pete? I really like him, have I blown it?'

Her reply wasn't necessarily what I wanted to hear:

'You're very different from the kinds of women he usually goes for, but just be yourself.'

In preparation for seeing Pete I begged Ariel, one of the production team assigned to look after us, to play the Phil Collins track to Pete when he was driven back to the hotel. 'Please,' I said, thrusting my personal stereo at her. 'Give this to him and tell him that I want him to listen to track seven.' The moment he came out of the jungle I wanted him to know that I was thinking about him. Later I discovered through Pete that Ariel had put the CD on in the car so everyone could hear it, including his mum and dad, which wasn't quite what I'd had in mind. But I liked the part when Pete told me that he'd had a tear in his eye as he listened to the song and that he thought it was a very romantic gesture on my part . . .

I also begged Claire to let me go with her and Pete's parents so that I could be one of the first people he would see when he came out of the jungle. Claire and Pete's parents chatted away during the car journey but I was in another world, lost in my dreams of Pete and what I would say when I saw him again. I was also feeling extremely self-conscious – I'd wanted to stun him with my sexy appearance but things hadn't quite gone according to plan. I'd had all my braids taken out and gone platinum blonde with new long extensions, but as soon as I left the salon I realised I hated how it looked. They hadn't blow-dried my hair straight, how I like it, and I thought I looked a complete mess. I wanted Pete to see me looking my best; instead I thought I looked ugly. And to cap it all I felt I was wearing the wrong outfit and the wrong make-up.

I was also extremely stressed because even on that car journey Scott was still bombarding me with texts, each one getting more and more desperate, culminating in him saying he was only five minutes away from the hotel and please could I see him? No, was all I would reply. And just before I'd set off from the hotel I even had his friend Dean phoning me up.

'Dean,' I said firmly, 'I don't want to see him. It's over.'

'Come on,' he said. 'He's flown all this way to see you; the least you could do is to see him for a few minutes.' But I wouldn't give in. Pete was the only man I wanted to see.

As soon as Pete came out of the jungle he threw

his arms round his parents and embraced them. And I was left standing behind them, feeling awkward, like an outsider. I willed him to notice me, thinking, *Please look at me – I'm here, please don't ignore me. I'm all yours.* But as I watched him crying with happiness, talking to his parents, I couldn't help feeling rejected. At last he saw me and came over and hugged me, though I could tell he was surprised to see my blonde hair. I had spent hours obsessing over what I would say when I finally saw him again. But as we were still being filmed it wasn't easy to express my feelings. As we embraced he whispered, 'I told you I wasn't lying about my feelings.'

I whispered back, 'I've finished with Scott, please tell me we can be together.'

He simply said, 'We'll have to talk.'

God it was frustrating, but as we were still on camera there was nothing for it. Then he was whisked away for his Ant and Dec interview. Afterwards there were drinks in the hospitality tent and I kept staring at Pete, longing for him to come over and talk to me, but it was impossible – he was surrounded by people and I knew he must be feeling pretty overwhelmed by all the attention as it was such a shock after being isolated in the jungle for two weeks. But finally I managed to speak to him across a crowded table – hardly the intimate setting I had imagined.

'Pete, I want to ask you something.'

'What?' he replied curiously.

'Well, here's a clue – Valentine's Day is coming up and it's a leap year.' I raised my eyebrows meaningfully but he just looked confused. Before I could explain further yet more people came up to him and started talking, congratulating him about his time in the jungle. I willed them to go away but it was no good; it was obvious I wasn't going to get Pete on his own just yet.

After a few more drinks it was time for me to take the helicopter back to the hotel, as you do when you're a celebrity! Though frankly I didn't give a toss about the luxury and the perks surrounding me. My mind was stuck on one track. I tried again.

'Here's another clue Pete: the letter "m".'

He still looked blank, then suddenly he clicked and said, 'It's not what I think it is, is it?'

'Yes!' I called back excitedly over the table. But I

still didn't know for sure if he really knew what I meant – even though I didn't know how much clearer I could be. God this was torture!

I was convinced that when we were both back at the hotel I would finally be able to see Pete, but his management clearly had other ideas.

'Hi, can I speak to Pete please?'

The woman at the end of the phone sounded very offhand.

'Pete's busy right now doing a shoot.'

'Well, will you please tell him that Katie has called again and ask him to call me back as soon as possible. It's really urgent.'

'Okay.'

I slammed the phone down in frustration. It was the fifth time I had rung and each time I was being fobbed off. Why wouldn't they let me speak to him – surely he could take a break for a few minutes and give me a ring? I couldn't understand why he hadn't called me back.

Foiled in my attempt to contact Pete by phone I resorted to writing messages and giving them to Ariel and Angie, the two young women assigned to

look after the contestants on the show, to take to
Pete's room. But I was rather wary of Angie as just
before the show started, and before anything had
happened between Pete and me, he admitted that
she had caught his eye and that he intended to ask
her on a date. In fact, minutes before all us celebs
were dropped in the jungle, I had seen Pete go over
to Angie and ask for her number and arrange to meet
her for coffee after the show. I felt a flash of jealousy.
Angie was very pretty, with dark hair and a great
body helped by her silicone boobs, but then I'm
hardly one to talk, am I? I remember thinking that I
hoped that was one date he wouldn't go on. Even
before I had spent those two weeks with Pete I knew
I wanted him. Now I was wondering whether Angie
was actually passing on any of my urgent messages
to Pete. He told me some time later that after he'd
had a spray tan treatment in his room, the beautician
had told him to wait in the bed and Angie would
come and see him – cheeky cow! Also he revealed
that Angie had been invited to have dinner with
him, his parents and his management in his hotel
room the night he came out of the jungle. So I
reckoned maybe, even though she claimed to have

passed on my messages and said that of course Pete would want to know me, she was being two-faced – wanting Pete for herself and telling me what I wanted to hear.

Whatever the truth, one thing was certain: I was being prevented from seeing Pete. Every time I called him or sent a message the answer was the same: no, I couldn't see Pete – he was under an exclusive contract with a paper and he couldn't talk to me.

It just didn't make sense. As the hours passed I grew more and more upset. It takes a lot to make me cry but I cried then – in fact, I was in tears pretty much constantly for the whole day. It didn't help that I had been drinking since the morning, knocking back wine and champagne, making my emotions even more extreme. That night there was going to be a wrap party to celebrate the end of the show. Surely I would be able to see Pete there? One minute I received a message saying he was coming and I was filled with excitement; the next I was told he wasn't coming and I was plunged into despair. We were running out of time. The next day we were all flying home – if I didn't get to talk to Pete now when would I get another chance? I didn't know where he was going to be staying; I didn't even have his mobile phone number.

I wanted to look stunning for him but as I'd been crying all day my eyes were horribly bloodshot and red-rimmed, which no amount of make-up could disguise. I wore a tiny black top, one of my famously short skirts and black heels. Finally a message came back to me that Pete would meet us in the foyer around half past eleven and we could go to the party together. At last, at last, I thought happily. But the next second the strap snapped on my top and I had no way of fixing it. I hardly wanted to meet Pete with one boob hanging out! Luckily Diane Modal, one of my fellow celebs, very sweetly lent me one of her tops – a black lace number. Then, just as I thought things couldn't get any worse, I got a message from one of the organisers saying that he would meet us at the party instead. Talk about keeping me dangling like a puppet on a string. Later I discovered that Pete's parents had seen me waiting in the foyer. I couldn't believe my bad luck; I was hardly making a good impression, drunk and falling out of my top. Pete had already told me that they were very religious with strong views on the right kind of girl for him – I don't think I would have been their ideal that night. Fortunately for me, in my drunken state, I didn't see them, otherwise I might have disgraced myself further in their eyes by going up to them and telling them that I was going to marry their son!

The party itself was a bit of a blur. I chatted away to Ant and Dec and Kerry McFadden, Queen of the Jungle – though God knows what I was coming out with, fuelled as I was with alcohol. Because I had been so desperate to see Pete I hadn't eaten a thing all day, and the booze had well and truly gone to my head. And all the time I kept asking Angie and Ariel when Pete would be turning up. Then they told me that he wasn't coming to the party after all but that I could see him in his room at half past twelve.

'Let's go,' I called over to my mum. 'I have to get back to the hotel to see Pete.'

'Calm down,' she replied, 'There's loads of time before we need to leave.'

But as far as I was concerned the party was over. All I could think about was that at last I would be seeing Pete. I kept checking my watch, willing the time to pass more quickly. Finally, after what seemed like hours but was probably only twenty minutes, we left the party and drove back to the hotel. As soon as we got out of the car Mum asked her friend Louise to take me up to Pete's room because I was in such an emotional state. As we travelled up to his floor in the lift my heart was pounding and I felt sick.

'Are you sure I look alright?' I kept asking Louise.

Finally we arrived at his room and I knocked at the door. *At last*, I thought, *I'm going to see Pete*. But the door was opened by his brother Danny and one of his friends called Reno.

'Pete's in the bathroom,' Danny told me.

Straight away I marched past the two men and into the bathroom; I was a woman on a mission and nothing was going to stop me now.

Pete had obviously just stepped out of the shower and simply had a small white towel wrapped around his waist. He looked unbelievably gorgeous and sexy, his beautiful brown skin still slightly damp. I'd had a taste of how fantastic his body was before, when I'd seen him in his swimming trunks, but that was with the cameras on us, when I couldn't be open about my feelings. This time I didn't hold back and I did what I had longed to do for the last two weeks; I walked over, put my arms round his neck, pressed my body against his and we kissed, passionately. Or at least I'd like to imagine it was passionate – I was so pissed I can't remember! I'd like to tell you that it was the best kiss I've ever had, but I can't. And later Pete was to reveal that I'd done a little more than just kiss him . . .

Then I broke away from our embrace. 'Pete, I've got to know,' I said seriously, hoping that I wasn't slurring my words too much, 'will you marry me?'

'Yes,' he replied.

Fireworks of sheer happiness exploded in my head and immediately I said, 'Get your brother in here now and tell him then.' I wanted everyone to know – probably had I been sober I would have been a little more discreet, well, just a little bit! But as I was pissed as a fart I wanted the whole world to know.

Pete opened the door and called his brother in.

'Tell him then,' I said to Pete.

'Tell me what?' Danny asked.

'Pete and I are getting married!' I exclaimed happily.

Danny looked at Pete as if to say, what the hell is going on?

'Yes,' Pete admitted. I didn't see that he raised his eyebrows at his brother as if to show that he wasn't serious, that he was only saying it because I was drunk. I, of course, was on cloud nine, delirious with happiness and champagne. I wanted to stay with Pete all night, just holding each other close. I didn't want to shag him; I just wanted to be with him, to feel his skin next to me, to feel his arms around me. I knew that this would be our last chance before I flew back to England. But to my complete surprise Danny said, 'You've got ten minutes then you've got to leave.'

I thought, why the hell is he speaking to me like I'm some stupid kid?

'Pete, why can't I stay?' I demanded.

'It's late. We'll talk in the morning,' was all he would say.

So ten minutes later, after a last embrace, I was shown out of the room and I tottered back to mine.

The next morning I woke up with a stonking hangover. But back then I was used to drinking a lot and hangovers were par for the course. After forcing down a boiled egg and toast for breakfast, I had to start packing. It was chaos in our hotel suite, with me and Mum falling over each other as we loaded up our suitcases and Harvey crying. My mobile phone rang and I frantically searched for it but couldn't find it in the confusion. Was it Pete, I wondered, praying that it was. I had given him my number the night before and I was willing him to make contact as I didn't have any numbers for him. A minute later the hotel phone rang.

'Hello,' I answered, still out of breath from charging round the room.

'Hi, it's Pete.'

'Oh, hi,' I replied, trying to sound casual, but inside my heart was racing and I was thinking, he's actually rung me and I'm sober!

'Do you remember what you asked me last night?' he asked.

'Of course I do. I asked you to marry me.'

'I was just checking you'd remembered.'

He went on to say that he would call me as soon as he got back to England – his flight was two hours after mine. His management had told him he couldn't travel back on the same flight as me, which I thought was completely pathetic. What did they think we were going to get up to? Have sex mid-air in front of everyone? All I wanted to do was talk to him.

'That was obviously Peter on the phone,' my mum called out to me, seeing the big grin on my face. Inside my mood was transformed. He had rung *me*, he had shown he was interested. This was progress. I couldn't wait to see him back in England.

Before we left for the airport I wrote Pete a note on a scrap of paper and asked Ariel to give it to him. In it I poured out my feelings, telling him that he completed me, that he was everything to me. I told him that I couldn't wait to see him again, how I knew he was the one for me. Talk about not holding back!

At the airport I was met by a gang of journalists and one of them shouted out, 'Katie, we've heard that Pete doesn't want anything to do with you. How do you feel about that?' I longed to shout back that they were wrong but I forced myself to stay silent. I knew the truth and that was all that mattered.

On the flight back I longed to talk to my mum about Pete, but because of the exclusive newspaper and magazine deal my manager had set up we had a minder, in the form of a journalist, to make sure I didn't talk to any other papers, which was deeply frustrating. I didn't want to say anything that the journalist could hear. I was already fed up with the terms of the deal as I hadn't liked having the blanket stuck over my head as I travelled back to the hotel. And once there I was barely allowed out of the hotel, and definitely not without the journalist tagging along.

So instead of confiding in my mum I listened to love songs and dreamed about Pete. I even had my Disney CD with me and Pete was singing one of the songs, 'Kiss The Girls'. I kept listening to that track over and over again, just to hear his voice – how sad am I?! Whenever the journalist was out of earshot I'd ask my mum if she thought Pete would call me, and if she thought he liked me, driving her absolutely mad with my constant questions. I tried to get some sleep, but I had too much going on in my mind. I wanted to see Pete so badly that it was like a proper ache inside me.

We landed at Heathrow at 2 p.m. and were greeted by a media scrum. I have never seen so much press in my life; it was crazy. They all wanted to know if I was going to see Pete again and how I felt about him. I smiled sweetly for the photos but had no intention of saying anything. I met up with my manager and as we travelled in the limo he showed me the huge pile of newspapers with stories in them about me and Pete and what had happened in the jungle. I tried not to show it but I was angry with him because he hadn't been out in Australia to meet me when I came out of the jungle to tell me what the hell was going on with the deals. He kept asking me about Pete but I didn't really tell him anything. Something stopped me from confiding in him, and I thought, *Actually, I don't know how much longer I want you representing me.*

I knew Pete was landing in two hours' time and I couldn't wait for him to call. In the meantime I had some urgent calls of my own to make and after reading some of the articles I was straight on the phone, making appointments to have my hair and nails done. I was absolutely knackered from the jet lag but knew I couldn't rest until I had them sorted. As any girly girl will know, it is impossible to function without those two things in order.

As soon as we'd driven back to Brighton and I'd had my hair cut and straightened, and as soon as my nails were perfect again, I felt back to my old self.

Then it was off to Hove, or Hove-Actually, as everyone who lives there calls it, to visit my nan. By now it was six in the evening and I knew Pete had landed two hours ago. I kept going on to my nan and my mum about Pete. 'Do you think he's going to ring? Why hasn't he rung me yet? Do you think he likes me?' Finally my mum gave a huge heartfelt sigh and said, 'Please, Kate, *stop*!'

*

By the time I finally arrived home it was eight o'clock and I was absolutely knackered. I got Harvey into bed and then sank down on to the sofa, too exhausted to move. Then my phone rang. It was Pete.

'Didn't you get my message?' he asked

'No,' I replied, and he said that as soon as he'd got to his hotel he'd called my mobile and left a message.

I was so happy to hear from him. He was as jet-lagged as I was and yet the first thing he had done was call me. Bingo! I thought, this is the start of something.

'I really want to see you,' he said. 'How far away are you?'

'About an hour away,' I told him, adding that I really wanted to see him too.

'Why don't you come and see me in my hotel then?'

I was so jet-lagged but I had to see him. I told him I would be with him in the next couple of hours. As soon as I put the phone down, adrenalin surged through me. I pleaded with my mum to have Harvey for the night. Luckily she agreed, and then I charged around getting ready. I put on my tight, low-rise jeans, a little pink top and my pink fluffy boots, feeling so much more confident than I had in Australia. Then I drove my Bentley up to London, listening to the DVD of *Gorillas in the Mist*, which I put on to keep me company, but which was hardly the most romantic soundtrack to my thoughts! As soon as I arrived at the De Vere Cavendish hotel in Piccadilly I called him to let him know I had arrived and he said he would send someone to meet me. *Oh*, I thought, a little disappointed that he hadn't rushed down to see me himself. I parked my car in the garage and went into the hotel through the back entrance; there the hotel manager met me and walked up the stairs with me to Pete's room. My heart was racing and I was bubbling over with excitement. I couldn't wait to see him. I just knew that this night was going to change my life for ever.

When we arrived at Pete's room the manager
knocked at the door. Pete answered and my escort
said good night and left. Now it was just the two of us,
alone for the first time.

CHAPTER TWO

A WOMAN
IN LOVE

With my heart beating wildly I followed Pete inside.
He had lit dozens of candles and placed them all
round the room, turning the luxurious hotel suite
into an intimate space. I thought it was very romantic
of him. Then I took a good look at Pete; I had never
seen him look so gorgeous, so desirable, so
goddamned sexy! He looked clean and fresh, as if he
had just stepped out of the shower, and whatever
aftershave he was wearing was irresistible. He was

casually dressed in a tight black T-shirt that showed off his amazing six-pack and muscular arms and black tracksuit bottoms. His feet were bare and I couldn't help noticing that he even had beautiful feet – I've got a bit of a thing about feet and can't stand ugly ones, even though feet were the last thing on my agenda at this moment. *Ah yes!* I thought to myself, *I've got to have him!* He poured us a glass of wine – I didn't know then that he rarely drinks, so looking back I can only imagine that he must have been as nervous as I was about our first time alone together.

As we sat on the sofa together he told me how good I looked and I returned the compliment, thinking, *Phwoar, phwoar, fucking phwoar!* We sat there for ages talking about everything that had happened to us – I told him how upset I had been when I couldn't see him after he came out of the jungle, how desperate I had been to tell him that I had ended my relationship with Scott and what my true feelings were for *him*. In turn he told me how much he had been longing to see me and how much he had hoped that I did have feelings for him. Neither of us could quite believe that we were on our own together at last – that there were no cameras watching our every move and that we weren't wearing microphones! But even though we talked so easily I was very nervous now that I was finally alone with him. It felt like a first date. Suddenly I felt self-conscious and shy, with butterflies in my tummy, which was silly really when I had spent the last two weeks with him slobbing it in the jungle, in my bare necessities, eating like a pig out of a tin and washing in a pond! I guess I just wanted him to like me so very much. He kept looking at me but I couldn't quite bring myself to look him in the eye, so I'd sneak a glance and then look down. Our surroundings in the hotel were so different to the jungle that it almost felt like I hadn't met him before. I almost forgot the two weeks we had spent together and it felt like we were starting all over again. To calm my nerves I knocked back the wine and, as it took hold, my feelings of insecurity gradually left me.

Suddenly Pete moved closer towards me and said, 'Come here and give me a cuddle.' We embraced and then we were kissing and I thought, *this feels so right.* He was a fantastic kisser – slow and gentle at first, then becoming more passionate – and I could feel desire building up in me. He tasted really good –

believe me, girls, if you could try him too he would sweep you off your feet! I've always believed that you can tell what kind of a lover a man will be from how he kisses, and if Pete's kisses were anything to go by I was in for one hell of a treat. He was the best kisser I've ever experienced. But even as I lost myself in his kiss I was still nervous, and at first I could feel my mouth shaking because I so wanted him to enjoy the way I was kissing him back. As we kissed he pulled me on top of him and I thought, *I don't care if we end up having sex now, because I want him so much, I can't wait.*

As if reading my mind, Pete whispered, 'Let's go into the bedroom.' As we kissed again on the bed I thought, *I've got to make love with him.* I burned for him, my whole body longed for his touch, I wanted to feel his hands caress me, I wanted to touch him, taste him, I wanted him inside me. We pulled off each other's clothes and then we were touching each other, as I had longed to do. My eyes widened as he peeled off his boxers, revealing his huge cock. My joke in the jungle about him having an acorn-sized one had thankfully been wildly off the mark! Less of an acorn, more of an oak! It was long and thick – it was definitely dickalicious! His whole body was just perfect; I had never seen a man who I desired as much as him at that moment. My golden rule of waiting a month before sleeping with a man belonged to the past. I couldn't resist Pete a second longer.

We were driven by pure lust and our lovemaking seemed to last for hours. But, turned on as I was, I couldn't help thinking, *Am I making the right moves? Does he like it like this? And will he want to know me in the morning if we have sex now?* But then my desire would take over and I'd think, *Yes! This feels so right, there's no way I can hold back* – plus the wine had given me extra confidence. We couldn't get enough of each other: we touched, caressed, kissed, licked, sucked each other's bodies and then finally he was inside me . . . After the best, most satisfying, sweetest fuck of my life, we collapsed in each other's arms, hot, sweaty, exhausted and completely satisfied.

We held each other all night, and I woke up to find Pete's arms still around me, holding me close to him. I turned round to face him and kissed him awake. I didn't want to leave the bed even for a second – I didn't care that I hadn't washed, I didn't care that I hadn't cleaned my teeth. Usually I don't like to kiss anyone first thing because of morning breath, but nothing was going to stop me kissing him. He looked so handsome in the daylight, desire surged through me and then we were making love again, me on top, riding this beautiful sexy man. He certainly knew all the right moves and so did I! But afterwards, as I lay down next to him, sadness gripped me: now we had found each other, I didn't want to leave him. I had a shoot to do for *OK!* magazine and he was appearing on *CD:UK* to promote his re-released single, 'Mysterious Girl'. We held each other tightly. All I wanted to know was, when was I going to see him again? Any idea of playing it cool and not showing how keen I was, of taking the relationship slowly, seemed like madness. I had to be with him; I was like a woman possessed.

'Pete,' I told him, 'the only way this is going to work is if we never leave each other's side.' It might sound crazy, seeing as we had only known each other for three weeks, but I believe that when you meet *the one* you know, and I knew with all my heart that Pete was the one for me. This was no time for playing

Taking some precious time out to relax at home.

My mum enjoying some pool time with Harvey.

Harvey has become used to taking his regular medication.

My mum held a fancy-dress murder mystery party and all of our friends and family came. It was on the day of the party that I realised I was pregnant with Junior.

Pete with his brothers, Michael and Daniel, and my stepdad Paul (*back*).

Pete and I took all of our friends and family away on a fantastic cruise to celebrate our engagement.

All the girls together!
From left: my friends Michelle, Sally and Shauna and my sister Sophie.

Gathered with my family, ready to celebrate the engagement.

Peter's dad, Savva Andrea; mum, Thea; and his sister, Debbie all joined in our celebrations aboard the cruise ship.

Pete and I with his good friend, Reno Nicastro.

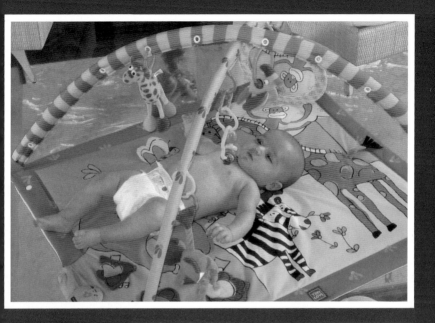

A new arrival!
Our beautiful baby
boy, Junior was born
on the 13th June 2005!

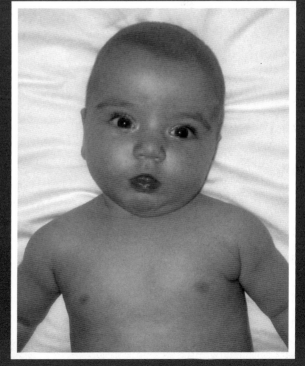

Pete and Harvey hang out with Pete's brother, Michael.

On the night before the wedding, our close family got together at Highclere Castle. *From left to right*: Peter's mum, Thea; Pete; my mum, Amy; my stepdad, Paul; my brother, Daniel and his wife, Louise; me and Pete's dad, Savva Andreas.

games. It was all or nothing. From that night I knew that was it; I didn't ever want to leave his side. I wanted to be with him for ever.

Thank God he felt the same way, and he was just as open and passionate in expressing his feelings for me, telling me how much he wanted me and how he had fallen in love with me. He also begged me not to hurt him, asking me if I really meant what I said. He told me he was worried because I had been with someone when I met him and, as I'd left Scott for him, perhaps I'd end up leaving him for someone else.

'I'm never going to leave you! And I'd never do anything to hurt you,' I replied, the very idea seeming crazy, especially as I didn't even want to leave him to go to work!

All the same it was like a physical pain saying goodbye. Straight away I was on the phone arranging for a huge bouquet of flowers and a note to be presented to him when he appeared on TV. 'You are my everything,' my message said. Even when he was on TV I wanted him to know that I was thinking of him.

*

As soon as I was in the car on the way to the shoot I was desperate to text him, but he still didn't have a mobile so there was no chance of that, something which I found incredibly frustrating. Just a text to know that we were in each other's thoughts would have made me feel so much better. I could think of nothing but him as I posed for my *OK!* pictures. My body still tingled deliciously from our lovemaking and I longed to be with him again. Everyone from the magazine kept asking me how I felt about him and when I was going to see him again. Little did they know what we'd been up to all night long and first thing this morning! Though they might have guessed, seeing how I was walking like John Wayne after our marathon session! During a break in the photographs I watched *CD:UK* and saw Cat Deeley presenting Pete with my bouquet. *God, how will he react?* I wondered, hardly daring to watch. Then to my delight Pete looked straight at the camera and, in answer to my message, said, 'I'll see you later,' sending a shiver of longing down my spine.

We did indeed see each other later, back at his hotel room. I was barely through the door before Pete was kissing me passionately and slipping off my clothes. *Yes, yes, yes!* I thought to myself, kissing him back and caressing his gorgeous, toned body. I loved touching his smooth tanned skin, loved the way he felt, loved the way he tasted. I also loved the fact that his body hair was kept to a minimum – we're talking back, sack and crack! As he took off his boxers, revealing his trimmed pubic hair, I thought, *Perfect*, because I can't stand hairy balls! As we all know, girls, it's better off! And if you don't believe that you are in denial . . .

Making love that afternoon was even better than the night before because now I was sober and really able to appreciate his body. And it was perfect – there wasn't a blemish on his skin, not a dimple, not a pimple. Every part of him was delicious and he smelt gorgeous all over. I love a man who smells good, not like some of my exes have . . . Yet again I was forced to eat my words about the acorn comment as I went down on him. I could barely fit it all in my mouth – my eyes were watering and I had goose bumps all over my body, knowing how much he was being turned on and feeling so turned on myself. Then I moved up his body and I was on top of him – it was the most erotic and intense lovemaking I had ever experienced . . .

Afterwards we lay in each other's arms and Pete told me he knew I was special.

'Usually, when I've been with a girl, I just want her to leave straight afterwards. I can't bear them touching me, wanting me to hold them. But with you it's different, I want you to hold me, I want to hold you, I never want to let you go!'

'Oh my God, Pete!' I exclaimed. 'That's exactly how I feel about you!'

We gazed deeply into each other's eyes. There was no doubt in my mind I had found the love I had been looking for all my life.

* * *

All I wanted to do was spend my time with Pete and gradually introduce him to my family and, more importantly, to my twenty-one-month-old son Harvey. But there could be nothing gradual about it where Harvey was concerned: much as I was head over heels in love with Pete, I wanted to be with my son and I couldn't just shut myself away in a hotel room with Pete. There was someone else in my life and Pete and I were going to have to face it head-on. But I was very anxious about introducing Pete to Harvey. If I'm honest, I was afraid that the fact I was a single parent might scare Pete off. Maybe he wouldn't want to get involved with me because I had responsibilities. After all, the other men I'd been involved with in the past hadn't exactly had a good track record when it came to Harvey and me. First there was Dwight Yorke, Harvey's father, the premiership footballer who didn't want to know when I fell pregnant during our disastrous on-off relationship. His first response was that I should have an abortion, and then when I went ahead with the pregnancy he denied that the child was his. Even after Harvey was born, Dwight still claimed not to be sure that he was his son, demanding a paternity test. Anyone could see that Harvey was mixed race and obviously Dwight's son – never mind how he dare suggest that I had been sleeping with other people when I was with him! Then there was Dane Bowers, who I had been in love with before I met Dwight, who told me that if I had an abortion we just might be able to get back together at a time when I was incredibly emotionally vulnerable.

Even the Chelsea footballer Frank Lampard, with whom I'd shared a few intimate moments, said that if I wasn't having a baby maybe we could get together. We had met out clubbing during my wild partying days in 2000, just after I had split up with Dane Bowers and was going off the rails, drinking too much and going out all the time. He was going through a pretty wild patch too and for a brief time me and a group of friends would always end up drinking back at his house after we'd been clubbing. Frank was very flirtatious with me and really tried it on, but kissing and the odd blow-job was as far as it went. Back then when he'd had a drink he was just one of the lads and that wasn't enough for me. On the few occasions we met when he was sober he was completely different, probably just as I seemed to him – quite shy and sweet – and I liked him. But as we only met up when we were both drunk we never did get the chance to get to know each other. And by the time I was pregnant with Harvey, it was too late to wonder what might have been. Now it seems that, just like me, those wild days are behind him and he's settled down and grown up and I wish him well.

And all those men I'd been with before I had

Harvey hadn't exactly instilled confidence in me about how men feel about single mothers. No wonder that when Harvey was born I had sought solace in the arms of a much younger man, though in fairness I didn't realise how young Matt was as the cheeky sod had lied to me! He, at least, whatever his other shortcomings, was kind and gentle with my son, but he was a boy of nineteen! After Matt, I chose to be with Scott, another 'boy', who was also very good with Harvey. But neither of those relationships were good for *me* – I need to be with a man but my confidence in them had been so damaged.

And now I'd found Pete, who was a million miles away from the other men I had been out with. Even though I was nervous about him meeting Harvey, in my heart I couldn't believe that Pete would reject me because of my son. I loved him and I knew he loved me, and I had to trust that he would accept Harvey as a part of me and my life. But the early days were very stressful as I tried to keep Harvey away from Pete, which was really hard because I wanted to be with Harvey and I wanted to be with Pete. I had endless arguments with my mum, as I begged her to have Harvey to stay the night so that I could spend my days with my son and my nights with Pete. I wanted to see how our relationship would develop while we spent time alone, but then I didn't want Pete to think that I was a bad mother for spending time away from my son. I felt torn in two and realised I couldn't go on like this; Pete would have to meet Harvey.

I was very anxious about their first meeting – I wanted Pete to show affection to Harvey, so that I would know he was the right man to have near my son, and I wanted Harvey to be in a good mood, so Pete wouldn't reject him. Initially it was a little awkward. I think Pete felt equally anxious about getting things right with Harvey and he was wary of picking him up and giving him a cuddle. But as they saw more of each other Pete became more relaxed with him and it wasn't long before he was treating my son with such warmth and affection and, later, love. Soon he felt confident enough to play with him, make him laugh and help calm him down when he had a tantrum. He needed reassurance from me at first to know that he was doing the right things, but he rapidly got the hang of communicating with Harvey and I knew I had made the right decision getting them to meet. Mind you, it was essential because any free time Pete and I had when we weren't working we spent together, and I didn't just want to see Pete at night in anonymous hotel rooms. I wanted him in my life twenty-four seven.

When Pete and I met he was living in Cyprus, where he owned a successful gym. He was doing well and also had property in Australia and owned a nightclub with his friend. He had left his music manager in 1998 and walked out on his music career because he'd had enough of the gruelling recording and promotion schedule. He suffered something of a breakdown brought about by the fact that from the age of sixteen, when he landed his first recording contract, he had been working flat-out, often fifteen hours a day, seven days a week, and it got to the point where he felt he just couldn't carry on. He'd been incredibly successful and for several years was the number one solo act in Australia – he'd even toured with Madonna and Bobby Brown. By the time he came to the UK at the age of twenty-one and released 'Mysterious Girl' and set so many girls' hearts racing with his six-pack – mine included – he'd already had five years of success in Australia. Much as I admire him for his pop career I'm so glad I met him when I did – it might have been difficult having a relationship when he was at the height of his success and shagging all those girls. When we met he told me he was more content and more at peace with himself than at any other time in his life. He had left his brother Michael in charge of running the gym and told him that he'd be back from Australia in three weeks. He'd decided to go on *I'm A Celebrity* because he figured he had absolutely nothing to lose. Of course, as it was, the two weeks in the jungle turned out to be a life-changing experience for us both . . .

Just before I took part in *I'm A Celebrity* I had bought a new house. I had grown to dread returning home to my small village just outside Brighton because too many people knew I lived there and every day I would have people driving past and shouting out abuse, telling me to get my tits out. It made me feel very insecure and no longer safe when I was at home, and it was hardly the environment in which I wanted to raise my son. I managed to find what I hoped would one day be my dream house in the middle of a private estate, deep in the beautiful Sussex countryside.

Before I had Harvey the tabloids always made me

out to be a wild party girl who practically lived in hip clubs such as China White. But while I did do more than my fair share of partying, I have always loved the peace and quiet of the countryside. The house needed a lot of work but I loved its location – it was set in stunning grounds and surrounded by fields. There was enough land for me to build stables for my six horses and the private road meant that I felt safe. I was also planning to install state-of-the-art security, with a high perimeter fence, entry-phone system and CCTV – such is the life of a twenty-first-century celeb. I wished I didn't need to surround my house with such devices but it was essential, I had already had a couple of nasty experiences with stalkers and it wasn't pleasant. A few years before a woman had sent me threatening letters, and when I was pregnant with Harvey I had to get an injunction against another man who had bombarded me with letters in which he claimed that we were having a relationship. They had started turning up at my mum's house, where I was staying, which freaked us all out.

While I was in Australia my mum had arranged for my furniture and clothes to be moved into my new house, and I couldn't wait to show it to Pete. I very much hoped that he would see it as his home too. Within a week of returning from Australia he had moved in with me, even though we pretended that he hadn't. Luckily he loved the house, even though for months it was like living on a building site – I was having the interior ripped out, rebuilt and decorated, and there was dust absolutely everywhere. My bedroom and Harvey's room were the only two that were anywhere near ready, which was fine by us as once Harvey was tucked up in bed we were free to get to know each other even better. My bedroom became our playroom and every night became an erotic voyage of discovery.

There was no doubt in my mind: in Pete I had found my perfect sexual partner. I have always had a very liberated attitude towards sex and love experimenting with different positions, different sex toys, different scenarios, to discover what turns us both on. But in the past I've often had to hide my adventurous side with the men I've been with. Warren, my *Gladiator*, was far too inhibited in the bedroom to fully satisfy me – I'll never forget the look of shock on his face when he opened the goody bag I'd bought him from Ann Summers as a Valentine's

Day surprise – anyone would think he had never seen a vibrator and a set of handcuffs before! My pop idol, Gareth Gates, was too young and inexperienced to know how to satisfy me, though hopefully I taught him a few tricks! Dwight only seemed to care about *his* pleasure. And, while I was adventurous with Dane, it very quickly became solely on his terms – *he* wanted to film us having sex, *he* wanted me to dress up in sexy underwear, *he* wanted us to have a threesome. Because at times he was emotionally distant and because I feared I would lose him, I did all those things to please him, rather than please myself.

But with Pete, I have no inhibitions and neither does he – he's willing to try anything and both of us can let our sexual imagination run riot. For the first time I have met a man who can match me fantasy for fantasy and I have the most satisfying, pleasurable sex of my life with him. He's definitely the most experienced lover I've ever had and sometimes that winds me up and I end up thinking, *You cheeky bastard, just how many women have you had?* because he's obviously had plenty of practice to perfect his technique. But then I console myself by

51

thinking it's good that he's been with so many women, because hopefully he's got that wildness out of his system and he's not interested in sleeping with anyone else. And it's good for me that he's been around because he knows exactly how to please me. And please me he does: he gives me orgasms like no other man ever has . . . I also love the fact that he likes a good old erotic story being told in the bedroom – something I've always loved, but not always been able to indulge in. It's such a turn-on thinking of a fantasy to share with your lover, arousing their desire with your words and then satisfying it . . .

CHAPTER THREE

CHANGES

It wasn't just my personal life that had changed dramatically following my two weeks in the Australian jungle, I also had some major decisions to make about my career and in particular how I was managed. I'd been with my manager for nearly two years. I had signed up with his agency just before I fell pregnant with Harvey and for the majority of that time it was an arrangement that suited me – my modelling was going from strength to strength and even after I had Harvey I was as much in demand as ever. As well as being my manager he quickly became a good friend. But after a while I started to get frustrated with him. He kept promising, as so many others had before him, to get me lined up with a record deal as I longed to start my singing career. But nothing seemed to be happening. By December 2003 I was also tired of doing personal appearances at nightclubs. They had been great for a while and I can't deny that I appreciated the money they earned me. But every other week it seemed I would be flying to some club or other and it was starting to get me down. Inevitably I would end up drinking too much to give me the courage I needed to go up on stage in front of the screaming crowd. I'd had enough of getting girls to get their tits out and being shouted at to flash mine. It was starting to feel tacky. I had told my manager that I was unhappy with doing all these PAs and being away from Harvey so much. But I can't say anymore about this as we're locked into a legal battle. I couldn't have been clearer but while I was filming *I'm A Celebrity*, he lined up yet more club appearances for when I returned home, which was expressly against my wishes and was the very last thing I wanted to do. The public had got to know a different side of me while I was in the jungle and my autobiography was about to come out, which would also show the real me. I didn't need to do the PAs any more.

While we were in Australia my mum met Claire Powell, who had been Pete's manager for ten years. She impressed Mum with her forceful character and go-getting attitude, and Mum thought it might be good for me to have a female manager for a change. When we were alone in our hotel room Mum told me that she thought it might be time for me to change managers, but she told me to keep my options open because my brother Daniel was also meeting potential managers back home in England. When Mum introduced me to Claire I was also impressed – she was very good at talking the talk and I liked her, she seemed a really nice woman. She told me that she had all sorts of plans to help me get my music career off the ground. I was filled with excitement at those words – maybe at long last, I had found the right person to help me realise my lifelong dream of becoming a singer. But she said that I'd have to sign up with her quickly as she couldn't act on any of her plans for my music career until I had.

But to be honest the deciding factor in my decision that I should change management was my feelings for Pete. I thought, *If I don't sign up with her and sign with someone else, our itineraries would be different and we'd end up never meeting up*, and I couldn't bear the thought of that. I was so crazily in love with Pete that I let my heart rule my head and I went ahead and signed the contract without having my solicitor check it over to ensure my interests were fully represented.

I had been in the business ten years – when was I going to learn? I wish I'd looked at it more carefully. Even though a lot of good things happened in my career during 2004 I still shouldn't have signed it. Later we ended up at loggerheads over it and had to draw up another one. But I was a woman in love and that was all I could think about. I was on a different planet and everything was just Pete, Pete, Pete!

I soon discovered that even as Claire had been so keen to sign me up she had warned Pete to stay well away from me in the jungle. Apparently she had told him that if he wanted any chance of a singing or acting career he should steer clear of me, that I wasn't the 'kind of girl' to be seen with! How ironic was that?! It had been Claire who had been responsible for keeping me away from Pete when he came out of the jungle. She had left her sister Vicky in charge of Pete and given her strict instructions not to let me or anyone else see Pete while she flew back to England. Even now I can't quite bring myself to forgive Vicky. What she did put me through hell. I was fucking fuming, I found out from Pete that he'd hardly received any of my many messages, and none of the ones he did receive asked him to call me back urgently. So he'd had no idea of how anxious I was to speak to him. She'd been the one I spoke to when I kept phoning Pete's hotel room at half-hourly intervals, in tears, begging her to let me speak to him. I can't quite believe that she had not passed my messages on to Pete when it was obvious that I was desperate to speak to him.

I hadn't known any of that when I signed up with Claire and, even if I had, it probably wouldn't have made a difference. I still would have signed, because of Pete. But I'm sorry I lost a good friend in my old manager. When he wasn't accompanying me on my work commitments we'd had a great laugh together, socialising. I'd loved going out clubbing with him and his friends and I did miss his company. What a pity we ended up in litigation. It only goes to show that nothing in my life is ever straightforward. I didn't get stressed about it though – I had Pete, so nothing else really mattered to me, and when you have a son who has as many problems as mine everything else seems pretty insignificant . . .

* * *

For the ten years I had been modelling I had always been known as Jordan. Glamour-girl Jordan was out-rageous, sexy and provocative – she was the one who made me famous. I was Jordan when I was modelling and often when I went out clubbing, but I was never Jordan twenty-four seven. The press seized on the whole Jordan/Katie thing, though, and loved to go on about how devilish Jordan had taken over sweet little Katie Price and ruined her, with her boob job, her wild party antics and her man-eating. Those stories cracked me up: of course I was different when I was working, and of course I was different when I went out clubbing and had a drink. But I hadn't got a split personality! Everyone is different at work from how they are at home, it's just that in my case it's more noticeable. I've got a sexy and outspoken reputation to live up to and I know perfectly well what will grab people's attention and get me on the cover of men's magazines and in the newspapers.

Up till my appearance on *I'm A Celebrity* the public only really knew me as Jordan and probably thought that was the only role I could play. That was the Jordan the press loved to describe as a plastic surgery-obsessed, fame-seeking bimbo, oh, and don't forget, slapper. I think I surprised a lot of people when I pitched up in the jungle without a scrap of make-up on, ready to throw myself into the bush-tucker trials however gruesome or frightening they were. I wasn't tottering around in high heels and tiny skirts plastered in make-up – I was myself. The only thing I couldn't be entirely honest about while I was being filmed in the jungle were my true feelings for Pete.

When I read the newspaper coverage of my time in the jungle it was clear that everyone was amazed to discover that there was more about me than being paid to get my tits out. So when I came back to England I had already decided to see what other work possibilities there were for me – I figured I could be Jordan and Kate Price . . .

* * *

But back to February 2004, which was such a mad time. Pete and I were insanely (or, should I say, insanialy!) busy doing shoots, being interviewed in the press and on TV, and Pete was recording his new album and promoting 'Mysterious Girl', which had shot to number one. We were also being filmed by our management for what would later become the ITV documentary series *When Jordan Met Peter* and *Jordan and Peter Laid Bare.* At first I didn't realise this was the plan and thought they were only film-ing Pete. But even when they started filming me I didn't care; I certainly didn't stop to think about who owned the copyright to all this material and what would happen to it – something that would later concern me. Oh no, I didn't give a shit about anything other than being with Pete, and if being with him meant being in front of a camera then so be it.

I was more concerned that during this time Pete and I had to keep our relationship a secret. I wanted nothing more than to shout from the rooftops that Pete and I were in love; I didn't care what anyone else thought, I had found the love of my life! But my new manager had very different ideas and she convinced Pete and me that it would be a good idea to keep our relationship under wraps for a while so that we got the chance to get to know each other better out of the media spotlight. I think she was probably thinking of the business possibilities rather than the romance, as it was a clever way of building up the press interest in us. Reluctantly I agreed. I had after all just signed up with her and thought I should trust her on this one, however frustrating it was. She wouldn't let us be seen on our own in public, so intimate romantic meals were vetoed. Even at Pete's thirty-first birthday on 27 February we had to go out as a large group to the hip Chinese restaurant Hakkasan, though I longed to be alone with him. But we were allowed to hold hands in front of the press when we came out of the restaurant!

Sure it gave our sex life an extra edge knowing that our relationship was secret, but after a while we just wanted to be a couple doing normal things. We talked about all the things we wanted to do together, like go out for dinner, go to the cinema, even go out shopping! If we ever travelled in the same car together we panicked in case anyone saw us. It was a little stressful. I also hated reading interviews where Pete had said that I wasn't his girlfriend. I felt that he would have girls going up to him and trying it on with him, believing that he was single and available. I consoled myself by thinking that *I* was the one he was going to be spending the night with – because even though we were keeping our relationship secret we spent every single night together. Also I hated not being entirely open in interviews when I was asked about how I felt about Pete. I'm usually so honest, perhaps too honest! And it didn't feel right pretending that we weren't lovers.

I kept asking Pete every day, 'Will you marry me?'

'No,' he replied. 'Wait until I ask you!'

But I was driving myself mad, thinking I *so* wanted to be married to him. I was totally obsessed. I had never felt like this before. Ever. And it wasn't just the intoxicating sexual chemistry between us that was affecting me. I had found the man of my dreams and all my cynicism about men – my feeling that I only ended up with bastards who hurt me or that I would never find a man capable of loving me as much as I loved him – had been blown away by Pete. As well as wanting to be married to him, even in those early weeks I wanted to have his baby, which I thought would seal our love for each other and complete us as a family. Although looking back I'm very glad we had a good few months to get to know each other before I fell pregnant.

I love everything about Pete. I love him for his character, for his warmth and generosity, for his passion, for the way he makes me laugh, for the way he is so open about his feelings, for the way I know I can trust him more than any other man I've been with (though not quite one hundred per cent – more of that later . . .). I love him for his kindness and gentleness but I know I can't take the piss – if he says no he means it; he is very strong and I could never walk all over him. I love that we have never played any games with each other – there's never been a 'will he ring or won't he?' situation. It's been honest from the start, a relationship of equals. I love him for his talent, for his creativity and for his ambition and drive. I've been in too many relationships in the past where I'd end up not respecting the man I was with because he didn't seem to want to do anything with his life.

We're also very similar; both of us are insecure and both of us get jealous – in the way that we want each other so intensely and we don't want to lose each other. When he goes out it's not him I don't trust, it's other women coming on to him, and he feels the same about other men coming on to me. We know what winds each other up and we respect each other. He really is my lover, my best friend and my soul mate. I'm sorry if this sounds too good to be true and you're reaching for the sick bag, but believe me I've kissed enough frogs in my life to deserve a prince! And I love that he knows me and understands me better than any other man ever has. I love the fact that he didn't know me as Jordan, that he met me as Katie Price. I never had that feeling I've had in other relationships that he was only interested in me because I was famous.

And I loved the fact that he was so cool about my success. As soon as we were back in England it became clear to him that I was more famous than him, but that didn't bother him at all – if anything he was proud of me. It was such a contrast to how some of the other men I'd been with had reacted to my success. When I was with Dane Bowers he thought that he was the best thing going and he never had any respect for my career. He was very successful when he was in his boy band but his solo career flopped and it was downhill from there. Whereas I'm still here . . . He hated me modelling and never thought I'd make anything of myself, but he must be eating his words now. And you can't imagine the great satisfaction I get from knowing that – I fucking love it! If there is revenge (and after all he did put me through hell during the last months of our relationship), it's knowing that I'm the successful one and knowing that he knows that. I'm sure that sometimes he must wonder whether we could have got back together, but if you're reading this, Dane, no you couldn't have, because as far as I'm concerned you had nothing going for you apart from a voice box.

But Pete didn't love everything about me, and during those early weeks of our relationship I had to make some changes to my life. If I hadn't I would have lost him. Before I met Pete and before I had Harvey, drink played a big part in my life; whenever I went out clubbing, or to parties, more often than not I would end up getting drunk. Inevitably I would change: I'd become louder and I'd flirt outrageously with men and be a bit of a prick tease. There have been times when my drinking has very nearly got out of control – I'm thinking of the months following my traumatic break-up with Dane Bowers when I hit the bottle big time, using alcohol to try and numb the pain I was feeling. Thank God I was able to pull myself together before I became dependent on alcohol. But from the moment I became a successful glamour girl I used drink to give me confidence – whenever I appeared on TV to be interviewed I would always have to have a large glass of wine first. And I always had to sink a number of glasses before I went up on stage for my personal appearances in nightclubs. I was so nervous that I just couldn't have imagined doing those things sober. But meeting Pete changed all that for good.

One night early in March 2004 Pete and I went to a private members' club in London with his brother Michael, his friend Reno and my friend Sandra. I was looking forward to having a few drinks and letting my hair down. I'd dressed to thrill in one of my little outfits – a red chamois leather skirt with a matching red top, revealing plenty of cleavage and leg – and I felt pretty damn good. The club was practically deserted, which encouraged me to be bolder as it didn't seem like anyone was watching us, and before long I'd had several large glasses of wine plus several vodkas and was well on the way to becoming drunk. Pete isn't teetotal but he rarely drinks. He'll have the odd glass of wine or a Jack Daniel's, but ever since his breakdown in the 1990s he's stopped drinking heavily. That night he'd had one Jack Daniel's, then he switched to Diet Coke and stayed sober.

There was a microphone on the stage and I kept pestering Pete: 'Come on Pete, sing us something, *please.*' I was too drunk to see how much I was annoying him, and when he wouldn't give in to my demands I took to the stage and started belting out a few numbers myself – a little compilation of some of my favourites: 'Get Here', 'How Do I Live Without You?' and, just to wind Pete up, one of my favourites, with those cracking lines about you going your way and me going mine – no doubt making a complete and utter tit of myself. But I didn't care; I was in that selfish state of drunkenness where you don't think about anyone but yourself.

I woke up in the morning with a thumping head-
ache to discover Pete sitting on the bed looking at me
with a very serious expression.

'What's the matter?' I asked, suddenly feeling very
anxious.

'You were different last night,' he replied abruptly.

'Yeah, I'd had a few drinks, that's all. Everyone
changes when they've had a drink,' I replied, the
anxiety building within me.

'Well, I didn't like the person you became last
night. She wasn't the woman I'm in love with.'

Whoa, I thought, *this is serious stuff.*

He went on: 'It's your choice, Katie. If you want to
keep drinking, then go ahead and do it; I'm not going
to tell you to stop drinking. But I'm warning you now
that we won't last because I don't like the way you are
when you're drunk.'

In the past when men have told me they don't like
something about me – usually it's been about my
glamour modelling – I quite honestly haven't given a
damn what they thought and I would never have
changed my behaviour for them. No man has *ever*
told me what to do! But Pete was a different story
altogether; he wasn't telling me to stop drinking in so

many words, but I knew he would stick to his guns and if I carried on drinking I would lose him.

'I'd never do anything when I was drunk, Pete,' I tried to reassure him. 'I'm just loud and a big flirt, but I'd never go off and shag a bloke because I was drunk!'

He looked very unimpressed and started getting dressed. I wanted him to get back into bed with me, to give me a cuddle, to reassure me, to tell me that he loved me. For the first time there seemed to be some distance between us. This was not good. I lay back on my pillow, my head still pounding, and suddenly everything seemed very simple: I'd found someone who I really wanted to be with, so why did I want to fuck it up, just because I wanted to be able to get drunk?

'Pete,' I called out, 'I'm going to stop drinking.'

He came over and sat next to me on the bed.

'Are you sure?'

'Listen,' I pulled him towards me. 'There's really no competition; I want you. I can live without getting drunk again. I can't live without you.'

Since then I've had the odd glass of wine with a meal but that's it, except for three or four occasions when I've got a bit pissed. I've even stopped having a drink before going on TV and discovered that I didn't fall to pieces. I sung on Westlife's Christmas show without alcohol and survived an interview with Frank Skinner stone-cold sober. So I've proved to myself that I don't need drink to perform. I haven't missed those drunken club nights one little bit and I definitely haven't missed the hangovers! As far as I'm concerned, Pete doesn't drink so what's the point of me drinking? Our first night together was the one and only time we've been drunk together. My hell-raiser, party-girl image belongs to the past. Sorry, paparazzi, there'll be no more shots of me falling out of clubs and falling out of my tops, pissed as a fart! (Though I'm telling you now that she'll be back if Pete is ever a naughty boy . . .) But I promise you I haven't become boring. I still know how to have a good time, I still say outrageous things when I go out, it's just that now I can actually remember what I said in the morning!

But drinking wasn't the only thing that went out of the window when I met Pete. Take a look at Katie Price in action pre-Pete, circa 2003 . . .

*

I took a long sip of my drink and stared deeply into the eyes of the handsome man who was staring at me. I flicked back my hair and gave him a sexy smile. I knew I looked good and was enjoying his gaze on me. I was wearing one of my famously tiny outfits – a skirt that was barely there, a tight, low-cut top, showing plenty of cleavage and heels. I was out with a group of girlfriends in China White and having a wild time. All night I'd been willing the handsome footballer – though sometimes it could be a singer or an actor – to come over to our table and was delighted when he did, offering to buy me a drink.

I had no intention of taking things further – I just wanted the thrill of the flirt, knowing that I could have him if I wanted. By the end of the night I would probably have kissed him and got his number. I can admit it now because it's so far behind me – when I was in relationships in the past I was a huge flirt. I loved going to clubs with my girlfriends, *without* my boyfriend. I loved having the attention of famous men coming up to me, chatting me up and flirting with me; I loved flirting back. The truth was that I was always on the lookout for someone better. I hadn't yet found the man who completed me and

I knew it. Before I met Pete I always felt restless after a while in relationships. For instance, I'd say to Scott that I had a business meeting in London and would be staying over. He would always want to come up with me but I'd refuse, saying it was business and he'd be bored, when all the time I was planning to go out clubbing and flirting. I'd return to Brighton the next day, hungover and probably with a new number on my mobile from one of the men I'd met the night before. I would never let my boyfriends anywhere near my mobile in case I got a text from one of my admirers, or in case they found a bloke's number that they didn't recognise.

That girl who flirted and teased is gone as well. There is no question that I am looking for anyone else. Pete is that someone better I have been looking for all my life, and I would never risk my relationship for a bit of flirtation. I'm sure I will go out clubbing without him, with my girlfriends, but it will be a very different experience from before. I won't be doing any flirting and I don't want men coming up and trying it on with me; I don't need their attention to make me feel good about myself any more.

I'm so different that I can leave my mobile phone

lying around the house and Pete can pick it up and take a look at my numbers and texts because I've got absolutely nothing to hide. I've got rid of all my sneaky numbers of men I used to flirt with. I would never have believed I could have changed so much, and so much for the better.

Before I met Pete I went out a lot – to London clubs and to parties – though I cut down dramatically when I had Harvey. But when we got together we discovered that we'd both lost our taste for going out all the time. Thank God we met when we did – I think if we'd both been in our partying phase we might well not have lasted. As it is, our idea of a good night out is dinner with friends, either at a restaurant or at our house. We still go to clubs together but I'm no longer on the lookout for that someone better – he's right beside me . . .

CHAPTER FOUR

HARVEY

Since my son Harvey was born there has never been a time when I haven't worried about his health. I always hope for the best, but I always have to be prepared for days like these . . .

'Harvey,' I said gently, bending down to give him a kiss, 'Mummy's back.' I had just returned home from a shoot and my mum had just dropped Harvey off with Pete after his day at nursery. Quite often Harvey would fall asleep after the long drive back and Mum would carry him in from the car and lay him on the sofa. As soon as I arrived back home the first thing I always did would be to give Harvey a kiss and a cuddle. But tonight Harvey didn't respond. Instantly I could tell something was very wrong. When I touched him he was burning hot and his breathing, which is always quite loud because of his size, sounded especially laboured. I felt an awful rising sense of panic as I called his name again and tried to wake him, but he still wouldn't respond; he felt floppy and it looked as if he was foaming at the mouth.

'Oh my God, Pete!' I called out frantically. 'There's something wrong with Harvey, come quickly!'

Pete came racing into the room straight away, looking concerned.

'You stay with him while I get the thermometer.'

I rushed to the bathroom, grabbed it from the cabinet and raced back. Then I gently placed it under Harvey's arm to take a reading. His temperature was a frightening 39.8°.

'That's so high!' I exclaimed. 'I'm going to call the doctor.'

While we waited for her to arrive I stripped Harvey

down to his nappy and sponged him with tepid water to try and lower his temperature. We managed to wake him up but he wasn't himself – he wasn't alert, he was still floppy and he refused to drink anything. Feeling more and more frightened by the minute, I sat next to him and talked soothingly to him. Harvey had often had high temperatures in the past but nothing like this. One of the many medicines he has to take is cortisol – this is to boost his weak immune system and help his body fight off infections – and I knew that when he was ill he needed to have an emergency injection of a double dose of cortisol immediately. As soon as the doctor arrived I told her about Harvey's condition and all the different medicines he was on and I tried to explain about the cortisol shot. But I could tell that she wasn't used to dealing with a child with Harvey's condition and that made me feel even more anxious. In the end she phoned Harvey's registrar at Great Ormond Street and they decided we should call an ambulance immediately and not risk me driving Harvey to the children's hospital in Brighton. Before the ambulance arrived she gave him his cortisol shot, but Harvey still seemed really out of it and I was very scared.

It was the first time I'd ever seen Harvey in an ambulance and it was a shock, especially when they put an oxygen mask on him. I tried to stay calm for Harvey's sake and not break down in tears, but it was very hard seeing him like this. Pete was in tears, thinking it was his fault that he hadn't realised Harvey's temperature had rocketed. But it definitely wasn't – as far as Pete knew Harvey was doing what he always did after nursery, having a sleep on the sofa, and I didn't blame him at all; I was just relieved that I'd got back when I did.

Once we got to the hospital the doctors managed to bring Harvey's temperature down. He had a virus and had to be kept in hospital for a few days. As anyone who has ever had a sick child like Harvey will know, every time you take them to hospital it's heart-wrenching and you never really get used to it – even though for us it had become an all-too-regular occurrence. Harvey ends up in hospital at least once every couple of months, and when it's not an emergency dash to Brighton there are frequent trips to Great Ormond Street Hospital for him to have yet more tests. Watching my little boy surrounded by doctors and nurses and being given injections, having his blood tested, being put on a drip, is so upsetting, because even though I know the doctors are trying to make him better I hate seeing my son in pain. I would give everything to take the pain away from him. I especially hate it when he has to have blood tests or be put on a drip, because the doctors can never find a vein that easily – he must take after me in that respect. Every time they put the cream on to numb the spot where they are going to put the needle in Harvey gets so upset because he knows what's coming and he cries and cries. It's got so bad that I've had to say, 'Please don't put the cream on, just try and get the blood out as quickly as you can.' They usually end up having to get the blood from the side of his foot, which must be so painful for him. It takes four adults to hold him down because he's so strong and he gets hysterical. I hate having to watch him go through this and would much rather be the reward waiting for him when it's all done, so he doesn't think that I'm the one standing by and letting him get hurt . . . Welcome to my world . . .

When Harvey was born no one had any idea that there was anything wrong with him at all. He was a beautiful, happy and seemingly healthy baby, and it wasn't until his six-week check that the health visitor realised that there was something very wrong with his eyes. After a frantic visit to a specialist eye hospital my worst fears were realised: Harvey was blind; his optic nerves had failed to develop properly and the doctors told me that he would probably never be able to see. I was devastated by the news – I thought it was the worst thing in the world that could have happened to my son. I hated thinking of all the experiences he would miss out on by not being able to see. How, I wondered sadly, would he be able to do any of the things sighted children take for granted, like swimming, playing football, riding, going to the cinema . . . if he couldn't see? How would he ever be able to live independently, to have a job?

But although Harvey is registered blind, I have gradually realised that he can see a lot more than we know and he definitely has some sight. For example, if he is playing with his toys and he throws one across the room, he'll walk over to that exact spot and pick it up – we think he can see the colours there. And when he's playing he'll pick up each of his toys and look at them closely, exploring every detail. The limited vision he has is made worse by the fact that he is short-sighted in one eye and has something called a nystagmus (a rapid, involuntary to-and-fro movement of the eyes) in the other, which makes it extremely hard for him to focus. But to compensate for his vision his other senses, such as smell, touch and hearing, are extremely sensitive and he uses them to explore the world, whereas other children would just rely on their eyes.

Like any parent who has a child with a disability, I imagine, you learn to accept it, to make the best of things. I would be no good to Harvey if I went around brooding about what he can't do. But there are times when it still gets to me, like a physical pain, when I think of all the things he is missing out on by not being able to see like I can. How much can he see of the people who love him? I wonder. Can he see my face, or his nan's face or Pete's or his baby brother's? Can he see any of the beautiful sights around him – the sunset, the field full of bluebells, like the one by our house in the spring, the sea? Can he see *The Jungle Book* film which he loves hearing the sound-track to? The Shetland pony I bought him for his third birthday? I don't know, because even though he's three and a half he's still not talking, so he can't tell me about his world. I hope one day he will.

I have to keep reminding myself that he doesn't know any different, and just because he experiences the world in a different way from me, it doesn't mean that experience is any less rich for him. Meeting and talking to other parents who have visually impaired children or to people who are visually impaired has helped. Through my involvement with Look, the charity which received the money I earned from *I'm A Celebrity*, I met a young man called Stephen who has been visually impaired from birth. The fact that he seems so confident and happy in himself gives me optimism for Harvey. He refuses to use his cane, he has a job, he goes to Greece on holiday with a friend, he sails on long ships. And he's like a role model for the kind of life Harvey could lead. When I asked him what he could see, he said quite crossly, 'I can't really describe it because I don't know what you can see. This is what I've always been able to see and how do I know it's different from what you see?'

Because Harvey has such a catalogue of devastating health problems, incredible as this may sound, his visual impairment almost seems like the least of them. Harvey has a rare disorder called septo-optic dysplasia (SOD), which is characterised by abnormal development of the optic nerve and pituitary deficiencies. Symptoms may include blindness in one or both eyes and hormone deficiencies, and there may be developmental problems with the front part of the brain and the child may have abnormal sleep patterns.

But this wasn't diagnosed until Harvey was nearly a year old. Initially the doctors thought that there was only a problem with his eyes. But when he was around nine months old my mum and I became very concerned that his development seemed slower than it should have been – even given the fact that children with visual impairments always develop at a slower rate than sighted children because so much early learning is visual. He also seemed to be thirsty all the time and gaining weight rapidly, which didn't seem right. The mums at the Look support group, whose own children had SOD, were convinced that Harvey had the same condition and urged us to see our doctor and get Harvey referred to the specialist at Great Ormond Street. It was crucial to get an early diagnosis, as brain damage can occur if the right medication isn't given to correct the hormone deficiencies. However, the specialist didn't think Harvey had SOD and so didn't think it was a good idea for him to have an MRI scan. That would have shown the midline split in his brain and would have shown whether the pituitary gland was present. He was worried about the side effects of giving a general anaesthetic to such a young child. But there were already concerns about his thyroid gland (which produces hormones that are extremely important for the regulation of the body's metabolism) and Harvey was being regularly tested for his levels of thyroxine (a hormone produced by the thyroid gland), because if that drops below a certain level brain damage may occur.

But we continued to be extremely concerned about Harvey's development. In the end we booked a private appointment with Dr Dattani at Great Ormond Street, who is a world-renowned specialist in SOD. As soon as he saw Harvey he said he was certain that he had SOD, but he needed him to have the MRI scan. He also told us that we must get a referral to him from Brighton, because the cost of us seeing him privately would be so high. We got the referral and Harvey had the MRI scan, which showed that his pituitary gland wasn't present – he definitely had septo-optic dysplasia and was deficient in all the hormones that the body needs to function healthily. He is deficient in growth hormones; he has an underactive thyroid; he has diabetes insipidus, as he's deficient in the hormone that controls his water balance; finally, he has cortisol deficiency, which affects his stress responses and makes it harder for him to fight off illnesses and infections. He lacks the ability to respond quickly to traumatic events that the rest of us have – for instance, if he had an accident and bumped his head, he would need to have a cortisol injection to help his body deal with the shock as he can't produce enough cortisol naturally. He is a child with many, many complex and potentially life-threatening problems, and he's my baby boy. And if you thought it was complicated reading about his condition, just imagine what it is like living with it . . .

We knew other children who had SOD and were deficient in some of these hormones and we knew that because they took medication many of them were leading independent lives, working and going to university, so we hoped that Harvey would be able to do the same. But then we had another blow: Harvey's development continued to be slow and we started to suspect that he may have suffered brain damage. We probably won't know the extent of the damage until he is around five, but we suspect that it has affected the part of the brain that deals with his ability to communicate. He knows I'm his mum and he understands everything you say to him and never forgets what you tell him, though like all children he chooses when to listen! But he can't talk yet. He can say, 'Mummy,' but he never calls for me by saying it. If I walked in the room he wouldn't say, 'Mama,' though he does recognise me because he smiles when he knows I'm there. I do find it hard not to get upset when I see him with other children who don't have his condition. My friend's daughter is just a few months younger than him but she's talking, running, dancing and doing all the things you'd expect a happy, healthy three-year-old to do. I try not to show it but it does hurt when I see her throw her arms round her mum's neck and say, 'I love you Mummy.' I would so love Harvey to do that, but he's never called me Mummy and given me a hug, and sometimes I wonder if he ever will. When Junior was born I said to Pete, 'I can't wait for Junior to call me Mummy and to ask for a hug.' Harvey will give me a hug, but I have to ask him to do it.

Recently, though, Harvey has started taking my hand and leading me to what he wants, such as a drink or a snack. I was over the moon when he did this for the first time – probably how other parents feel when their child says its first word. To me it was almost as good as him talking because he'd gone from barely being able to express himself at all to clearly directing me to what he wanted; it was major progress. And while he can't yet talk he has the most amazing sense of rhythm – if you play music or sing to him he taps out the exact beat of the song, and he loves doing it.

He's on a large amount of medication, all of which he'll be on for life, and he regularly has to go into hospital so that the doctors can check his levels of medication are correct. Every day, every six hours, he has three different medicines, which I give him orally. Every evening I also have to give him an injection of growth hormones, which I hate doing because I'm totally needle-phobic, but I have to

My big day finally arrived! My pop star friends Sarah Harding (*left*) from Girls Aloud, and Michelle Heaton (*right*) from Liberty X were on hand to help me.

The girls get ready on the morning of the wedding at Highclere Castle.

My cousin Faye and my friend Sally
were also among the bridal party.

The countdown to the
ceremony continues.

My make-up artist,
Gary gets to work.

As Gary moved onto
my mum's make-up,
I started to get ready.

I was so happy at the
thought of walking down
the aisle to marry Pete.

The finishing touches are made to my hair and make-up.

With my dress on, I'm ready to go. Nick and Royston finish my mum's hair and Gary checks my make-up for a final time.

All set and raring to go!

The happiest day of my life!

overcome my phobia because this is something my son needs.

He is also unusually large for his age. He barely eats yet he weighs five and half stone – the weight of an average eleven-year-old child – and he has to wear clothes for sixteen-year-olds, which I have to alter to fit him. I can just about pick him up, but it is a huge strain and I have damaged my back. He's only three and a half; he's still my baby and I want to be able to pick him up and cuddle him.

Getting Harvey to eat properly is a nightmare. Visually impaired children can have a real problem with food because they can't always see what's on their plate; they are extra sensitive and don't like soft or slushy food – they only like food which has a hard texture, which they can pick up and feel, and Harvey is no exception. He used to like yoghurts and bananas but now he won't touch them because of how they feel. He only wants to eat food which has a hard texture and looks bland, so he will eat Weetabix and toast for breakfast but for lunch he will only eat food which is covered in breadcrumbs – things such as chicken nuggets and fishcakes, though you can get him to eat things like cheese if you coat them in breadcrumbs. It has been impossible to get him to eat vegetables and he only eats potatoes if they are roasted, and they have to be crispy not soft. He won't eat any fruit except raisins. And quite often he wouldn't eat anything at all, so we couldn't understand why he was gaining so much weight. Later in 2005 his weight was worrying us and the doctors so much that he ended up in Great Ormond Street for six weeks while the doctors tried to find the cause.

Harvey took longer than other children to walk but he is walking now. If we go out shopping, though, I can't rely on him walking for long and, like any child, if he doesn't want to walk, he won't. He'll just sit on the floor and when he does that he's so heavy that he's almost impossible to lift. Then he got to the stage where he was too big for a normal buggy. The hospital told me that I could get a special buggy but initially I resisted. I argued with my mum over it, saying, 'I don't want him to stand out any more than he does. He already looks different; I don't want people looking at him as if he's disabled.'

In January 2005, when we were flying back from Australia after our holiday, the airline wouldn't let us take the buggy through the departure gate; instead they offered us a wheelchair. I hated pushing Harvey on to the plane in that. I know it may sound illogical given that he is disabled, he's registered blind and he's even got a disabled badge, but I can't help wanting to keep things as normal for him as possible. I hope I'm not upsetting anyone who has a wheelchair-bound child; this is just my way of dealing with my own situation. And in the end Harvey got so heavy that I gave in and he now has the special buggy.

When I wrote my first book, *Being Jordan*, where I talked about Harvey's blindness, I was touched by the number of letters I received from people telling me how much they sympathised with me and how they wished me well, and reading those kinds of things can really help when I'm having a bad day, when I'm feeling stressed out by Harvey's problems. But I've also received hate mail about my son. I've had letters full of racist abuse, saying such vile things as, '*You've got a black ugly baby who looks like an ape.*' It's bad enough having people staring at Harvey when we go out shopping as if he's some kind of freak, never mind reading those hateful words. All I can say is there are obviously some very sad and very sick people out there, if they get their kicks from writing such things about a little boy. I don't let it get to me because I think they're the freaks, because they actually spent time writing that letter and posting it . . .

When Harvey was a baby and probably up until he was just over a year old he was the most angelic and placid child. True, he would wake up a lot in the night, but he was easily pacified and was always very contented during the day. He would be happy playing with his toys in the living room, lying under his baby gym or having a cuddle, and I could pretty much take him with me everywhere. He would come along to shoots with me and happily play with his toys. But then he changed and, although he would still be a contented happy child most of the time, his behaviour became much more challenging. He can get very frustrated – probably because of his visual impairment – and when he does he lashes out, hitting me, or he headbutts the floor or picks up something hard and hits himself on the head with it. Because he's so big it is very difficult to control him and calm him down.

Lately we have even wondered if he might be autistic. Sometimes it's as if he's in his own little world and you can't get through to him, no matter what you do. He is also obsessed with his routine and I can't deviate from it. Every morning he has to have his bath and then his breakfast at the same time. He likes having doors shut in whatever room he is in and he can spend hours and hours flicking his toys very close to his face. I know all children like and need routine to a certain extent but Harvey has taken it to extremes. A few months ago Pete and I watched the film *Rain Man*, on Pete's suggestion, which stars Dustin Hoffman as an autistic man going on a journey with his brother, Tom Cruise, who is trying to understand his behaviour. A lot of it rang true about Harvey – the obsession with routine and the head-banging. We probably won't know if he is autistic until he's five or when he can talk. It may be that the symptoms he exhibits – such as flicking objects very close to his face or needing routine – are because of his visual impairment and that he behaves in this way to make sense of the world around him.

He also has extremely sensitive hearing, and any high-pitched or very loud noises really distress him.

Because he has to rely on hearing rather than sight he is especially sensitive to sounds. He hasn't yet learnt to block out background noise and concentrate on what is happening in front of him. So noise can sometimes be overwhelming for him – when we're outside and he's walking along he will actually have his fingers in his ears because he doesn't want to hear something that will disturb him. I try to keep the noise down to a minimum in the house but I can't control the environment when we go out, and if there is a loud noise close to Harvey he becomes very upset. It's yet another thing we all have to watch. It's made eating out in restaurants quite difficult, as even the sound of the crockery being put on the table can set him off and cause him to become hysterical, because he can't see what's happening. Quite often, if we do eat out, we will give Harvey headphones and let him listen to music to drown out the other noises around him and calm him, but even that doesn't always work and he can get very upset and start throwing himself around. When that happens I feel very stressed because I'm so aware of people staring at us. Pete's always really calm and says, 'Don't worry about it, just eat your meal,' whereas I'm bolting down my food, trying not to choke and desperate to get the hell out of there! I got so fed up with people staring at Harvey in those situations that my mum and me had the idea of having a set of cards printed with details of his condition on them to hand out, saying, 'If you want to make a donation to Look or find out more, here is the website and phone number' – anything to stop those critical looks. Hopefully it would make those people think twice before they stared at another disabled child in that way.

My family, and particularly my mum, have been my biggest source of support in helping me care for Harvey. I can't imagine how I would have coped without them. Having Harvey and becoming a mother has been one of the most amazing and fulfilling things I have ever done, but it's definitely been one of the hardest as well and has tested me more than anything else ever has in my life. I'm usually a really impatient person, who doesn't like being kept waiting and who likes things done their way, but with Harvey I'm a different person. I've discovered I can be very patient, not only when it comes to dealing with his mood swings but also in playing with him and teaching him how things work.

None of the doctors are really sure what Harvey's long-term prognosis is. He may well have a normal life expectancy, so long as his medication is balanced correctly, and he will definitely have to take medication for the rest of his life. He may have delayed puberty, though they can give him drugs to trigger this. I try to take every day at a time with him and enjoy all the good things. It just makes me more determined to give him the best possible life. It was a one in a million chance that I gave birth to a son with such a rare genetic condition, but to me he is one in a million and I love him to bits. I'm so lucky that I'm now with Pete, who loves Harvey too and who is a wonderful father to him. I'm not facing this as a single mum any more; I've got someone to share the highs and lows of caring for my little boy.

CHAPTER FIVE

MEET THE PARENTS

As soon as I got to know Pete it was obvious how incredibly close he was to his parents and how much their approval mattered to him. *Fair enough*, I thought, *I'm very close to my family too*, but the difference was that I didn't need their approval in the same way. In fact, quite often in the past Mum and I had argued quite furiously about some of the men I'd had relationships with because she definitely hadn't approved of them. I also knew that back then Pete's parents would have liked nothing better than for Pete to marry a nice Greek Cypriot girl. I'm sure they wouldn't have seen me as the ideal daughter-in-law. With my blonde hair, silicone boobs and a child from another relationship, I was probably everything they wouldn't want their son to be with. And the whole family thing was a big source of stress in those early blissful weeks of our romance. Because while my mum knew all about my love for Pete – me having gone on and on about him continually and generally driven her mad – at first Pete didn't even reveal to his parents how he felt about me. When I challenged him about it he replied that for him it was a really big deal to introduce a girl to his parents and that he needed time to win his parents over to accepting that it was *me*. 'You've got to remember, Katie,' he told me, after one of our many discussions on the subject, 'all they know about you is what they saw in the jungle on TV, and along with all the good stuff they also saw you being horrible to me and playing games with me. They're bound to be wary.'

So during the first few weeks of our romance Pete simply told his father, who is more open-minded about these things than his mum, that we had become good friends and were spending time together. But he certainly didn't let on how serious our relationship was, nor did he mention that he was living with me. He kept telling me that he wanted to be honest with his parents, but that he wanted to pick the right time. I told him I understood but inside I thought, *Hang on a minute, there's nothing wrong with me! And I'm going out with* you, *not your parents!* Nothing in my life ever seems to go smoothly – there always seems to be an obstacle in the way – but I reasoned that if I wanted Pete, then I would just have to do it his way and hope that it worked out.

I also knew that his family was completely different from mine – from a completely different culture, being Greek Cypriots – and with a completely different set of values. The biggest difference of all was that Pete's parents are very religious and are Jehovah's Witnesses and devout Christians. Pete was brought up as one, though he stopped following the faith in his late teens, finding the strict rules on no sex before marriage a little too hard to keep up and not wanting to be a hypocrite. Pete says that he loves the way he was brought up and he feels the witnesses taught him all about respect and values. I haven't been brought up with any religious beliefs and I don't believe in God, but as that wasn't an issue between Pete and me, I hoped it wouldn't be one between his parents and me. They are also much older than my own parents, who are in their early fifties; Pete's parents are in their seventies and so are closer to my nan in age.

Although Pete wanted to get his parents used to the idea that I was in his life gradually, we were so in love that he couldn't keep his true feelings secret for long. Pretty soon his dad had guessed that we were a whole lot more than good friends, and in April 2004 he invited us over to Cyprus, though he reminded Pete what he'd said about women in the past – how he had said that he'd never have a relationship with a woman who already had a child, that he didn't like blondes and didn't like silicone implants. And now he had ended up with someone who had all three!

Much as I wanted to meet his parents I was very nervous, because I so wanted them to like me. I've always got on well with my boyfriends' parents in the past, but there was so much at stake here and I didn't want anything to go wrong. Everything seemed on track – Pete was busy singing my praises to his parents and telling them how much in love we were – then a couple of weeks before we were due to go Pete got a call from his brother Chris, who had some very unwelcome news for us.

'Someone's been telling my parents some awful lies about you,' Pete said as I walked into the living room.

My heart sank. 'Go on then, tell me.'

'Apparently you're a porn star who does top-shelf modelling, you're a drug addict and Dwight Yorke paid for your house.'

I looked at Pete and we both burst out laughing – the lies were so ridiculous.

'They just missed out serial killer,' I joked. But then I thought, *What if Pete's parents believe them?* And the smile was wiped off my face.

I was furious that anyone would have told his mum such a pack of lies; I could only imagine that it was some girl who fancied Pete and wanted to get into his pants. It took three and a half years to get Dwight Yorke to pay maintenance for Harvey and the idea that he bought my house is laughable – my house was bought by me and by me alone! As for the porn-star comment – I've never done top-shelf modelling, but even if I had I don't see a problem with that, it wouldn't make me a bad person. And as for the drug-addict comment – I'll set the record straight once and for all: I admit that I've tried one or two things. I hated the experience and it didn't do anything for me, except make me feel weird and it was a total waste of money. I've never been tempted since. End of.

But much as I tried to laugh off the lies, they did upset me. His parents didn't know me and even though I couldn't imagine that they would take these comments seriously, especially after seeing the kind of down-to-earth girl I was from the jungle, it wasn't exactly an ideal introduction. And then Pete's mum had a conversation with him where she said something along the lines that she didn't want him to be with me, that I was no good and that he was never to bring me to their house. He was free to choose who he wanted to be with but I wouldn't be welcome in their house. *Could it get any worse?* I wondered despairingly when Pete relayed what she'd said. But he reassured me, saying that he had told her how he felt about me and how much she was bound to like me when we met. And he promised that whatever they thought and whatever they'd been told they would still make me welcome.

Even so, I was crapping myself on the flight over to Cyprus. I so wanted to make a good impression, I'd even agonised over what clothes to pack and what to wear during my stay and when they met me for the first time. In the end I'd worn tracksuit bottoms and a T-shirt. It's the kind of outfit I'd wear during the day anyway. I didn't want to look overly dressed up. I just wanted to be me. As far as I was concerned, I wasn't a bad person; I had nothing to hide and nothing to prove.

I was also anxious about how they would react to Harvey and how he would react to them. He's not the easiest of children and at that time he was suffering really badly with his sensitive ears. I knew the slightest sound would set him off and he would end up having a tantrum, throwing himself back and crying, and because of his size he's very hard to handle. I felt under pressure because I wanted to show that I was a good mother and I didn't want them to judge me. I also wanted them to be able to see beyond Harvey's disability and see what a lovely child he was. So all in all it wasn't the most relaxing flight I've ever had. Plus I couldn't help feeling annoyed at the way that it was such a big deal for me to meet Pete's parents. I felt like saying, 'Pete, you're a thirty-one-year-old man. Surely you can make choices for yourself. Why do your mum and dad have to approve of me before you can go any further?' But as if to reassure me, Pete did say, 'I'm going to fight for you because I genuinely want to be with you. Don't let me down because I respect my parents and I've never had to fight for a girl to get my mum's approval, you're the first one.' The first and the last, I hope!

At the airport we were met by Pete's dad, Savva, who gave me a hug and immediately made me feel welcome. He has a warm, friendly face and exactly the same sense of humour as Pete. He was friendly to Harvey as well, but it was awkward for me because Harvey doesn't really respond to people he doesn't know and I could tell that Pete's dad didn't really know how to deal with him. But as we got in the car and drove to the apartment I allowed myself a little sigh of relief as I thought, *That's the first obstacle over with – one more to go.*

But my nervousness increased again as we got

closer to the house, as I thought maybe his mum really would hate me. But then I thought, *Stuff it, I know what I feel about Pete and I know what he feels about me, and even if it takes time to get his parents' approval, I'm prepared to wait. I'm not going anywhere, so they'd better get used to me!*

Fortunately Thea, his mum, couldn't have been nicer to me from the moment we met, and if she thought I was the devil in disguise, she didn't show it! I quickly discovered that she is a very loving and warm person, who always wants the best for everyone around her. Straight away she was offering me food and drink. At first I said I wasn't hungry, but she kept offering and I knew it was her way of showing hospitality, so even though I really wasn't hungry I thought I'd better eat, just to be polite.

But, nice as everyone was to me, I felt very out of place and awkward and extremely self-conscious. Because Pete's mum's English isn't very good I couldn't really explain to her about Harvey's condition, and it made me feel tense because I wanted her to understand why he behaved in the way he did. Then, just as I'd feared, Harvey's ears started to hurt him and he cried. And as I comforted him I thought, *Please don't let them think I'm a bad mother.*

We were staying at Pete's three-storey, three-bedroom apartment, which is his parents' home while they oversee the building of Pete's new beach house in Cyprus. Usually it's the family's holiday home and is simply but comfortably furnished – his parents live in a huge house in Australia. They are very well-off: Pete's father was a property developer before he retired and he still owns property in Australia and London. I knew the sleeping arrangements were slightly worrying Pete, as this would be the first time he had ever shared a bed with his girlfriend in the same house as his mum and dad. We had Harvey in with us in his travel cot and, rather embarrassingly, he was rocking and banging around in his cot during the night. I imagine Pete's parents, sleeping in the room below us, thought we were at it, when I can promise you we weren't!

Even though our visit seemed to be going well, in all honesty I could have done with a little more support from Pete. He wouldn't really show his feelings for me in front of his parents – he didn't hug me or kiss me or hold me in public and that hurt a little. I'd gone from one extreme to the other – usually he was constantly showing his affection, holding me, kissing me and telling me how much he loved me, but now he kept me at a distance. And I thought, *Please make me feel a bit wanted Pete. And if you want your parents to like me, then show them how much you're into me.* I especially wanted physical affection from him because he had told me that his parents had never seen him show affection towards a girlfriend before and I wanted him to prove to his mum and dad that I was different. I wanted to challenge him about it but then I thought, *Just go along with what he wants for now.*

Before our visit I had even asked Pete what I should wear in front of his parents because I wanted them to like me. But I wasn't too pleased with his answer 'Don't have your tits out when you're there,' he said, 'and try and dress a bit more modestly.' I suppose I had asked but I absolutely hate it when a man tells me what to do. It's not as if I go around with my boobs on display during the day, I'm nearly always casual in tracksuit bottoms and vests. I felt like saying 'don't be a Dwight.' Dwight Yorke had always told me to dress up and look more like a lady and I hated it. *I am what I am*, I thought, *don't try and change me, and I want your parents to see who I am because there's nothing wrong with me!* So throughout the visit I was incredibly self-conscious about what I wore, just in case Pete thought it wasn't acceptable for his parents. One day we went to the place his family had been visiting for years, where there are amazing caves and it's great for swimming – hardly anyone else was there. It felt like being on our own private beach, but I couldn't help feeling self-conscious when I stripped off to my bikini to go swimming and thinking that everyone would be looking at my body – it's a girl thing. But then I thought, *What else am I supposed to wear to go swimming?*

I also had to really watch what I said and be careful not to swear. I can say anything I like in front of my mum, it really isn't an issue. Along with swearing, I can talk about anything. I can talk about sex, willies, sex toys – you name it, we can discuss it with absolutely no embarrassment. But Pete would never swear in front of his parents and wouldn't dream of talking about sex.

We were in Cyprus for three days and the visit went well, better than I had expected. But I could sense that his mum was worried that I was going to use Pete. I don't think his mum and dad had heard of me before I met Pete and so at that time she didn't know how successful I was in my own right. She was no doubt remembering all those girls who had wanted to be with Pete at the height of his fame, just because he was a famous pop star. And maybe she thought that I was the same. I could have let it bother me, but I thought that once they came over and stayed in my house and saw the way I lived and saw that I had a successful career they would realise that I am not after Pete for anything. They would see that I'm with him because I love him, and I don't need to be with him to get publicity or money because I've got plenty of my own. If anything, in most people's eyes, I'm more successful and – no disrespect to Pete – he's had his time and is now making a comeback, whereas I haven't needed to make a comeback yet. I wasn't big-headed. I thought they would either like me or they wouldn't and I shouldn't have to try and sell myself. The fact that I was with their son should have been enough to tell them the kind of person I was.

And as for the lies they had been told about me, instead of stressing about them while I was there, I tried to turn them to my advantage. I thought, *They don't know anything about me, they think I'm the worst of the worst, so it can only get better, because how can it get any worse than them believing I'm a porn star, druggie and freeloader!*

But blimey, the whole parent thing was a minefield. My mum was cautious about Pete in Australia when I first met him and she warned me about him, saying, 'Be careful of Peter when you're in the jungle because apparently he's going to try it on with you or Alex Best.' So when we did get together she was a little unsure of him at first, worrying that maybe he wanted to be with me for the publicity. But when she got to know him back in England she could see how happy he made me, and all my mum wants is for me to be happy. But it did take a while for my mum to accept him totally – she kept her distance at first. Pete says he was glad because in the past mums of the daughters he's been involved with have been all over him, wanting things to work out with their daughters, and he really respects my mum for wanting to protect me. It was still stressful though, introducing him to my family. I so wanted them to like him and get on with him and I didn't want him to say anything that would upset them or make them question why I was with him. So although it was hard at first, I did understand why Pete wanted his parents to approve of me.

At the end of May 2004, just after Pete had proposed, we invited his parents over to stay with us in Sussex and celebrate our engagement. Pete had set the record straight and explained that Dwight hadn't paid for my house, and I felt more relaxed, as you always do in your own home. *Now*, I thought, *they can see the real me.* But I still thought, *Are they going to criticise the way I live?* Then I thought, *Surely there isn't anything to criticise about my house.* Alright, it's not perfect yet because I'm doing it up, but I'm a lot better off than a lot of people out there. And again, I didn't want to have to sell myself – I thought they could see for themselves how I live.

After a few more meetings I felt that I was getting on well with his parents, I could be more relaxed in their company and not worry that I was going to offend them with anything I said. They could see how deeply Pete and I were in love. And I think, even though they ideally would have wanted him to marry a Greek girl, they were happy that he and I were together and had found such a love. And so they should have been, if you ask me, because the woman Pete was with just before he met me treated him quite badly. He was actually planning to marry her. He told me he wasn't in love with her, but his brothers kept telling him he should marry her because he was never going to find the love he was looking for. They told him it was better to settle for a woman who loved him and who wanted to look after him, than keep searching for a love he might never find. I guess that's their Greek view on life. Luckily Pete broke off the relationship leaving him free and single and still looking for love, ready for when he met me . . .

CHAPTER SIX

THE EX FACTOR

'Katie, come here, there's something I want to show you,' Pete called out as I was relaxing in the bath.

'Can't it wait? I'm having a bath,' I shouted back.

'No, you have to come now or you'll miss it.'

Sighing, I pulled myself out of the bath, grabbed a towel and walked into the bedroom, where Pete was lying on the bed watching a music channel.

'I wanted to show you Kimmy, one of my exes who's in this Missy Elliot video.'

I turned to look at the TV and watched the girl dancing and writhing around to the music, then I saw red. As I stood there, dripping wet, something in me snapped. 'Actually Pete, I'm not fucking interested in seeing your ex.' And I stormed back to the bathroom. As I tried to push her image out of my head, and the image of her and Pete together, I couldn't help feeling down. I almost wanted to say to him, 'Well fucking well go back to your ex then!' Because this wasn't the first time I'd had to see one of Pete's exes. Sometimes it felt as if I could never escape from the girls he'd been with – they seemed to pop up everywhere.

One Saturday night in 2004 we were chilling out in front of the TV, watching the series *Hit Me Baby One More Time*, which I'd been looking forward to and suddenly Pete pointed out that one of the women taking part was yet another of his exes from the pop group The Honeys. That really put a downer on my night and I ended up feeling miserable and insecure. Then I really had to grit my teeth in the run-up to Live8 in July 2005, when Mel B was plastered all over the papers as there was the chance that the Spice

Girls might re-form. Several years ago Pete had an affair with Mel. Apparently she had been very taken with him and wanted to fly him here, there and everywhere to be with her. He admits she got him wrapped round her little finger, which is far too much information for me . . .

What makes this ex harder to deal with is that I was friendly with Mel B for a while, and before I went into the jungle she kept inviting me over to her house, which, typically for me, I never managed as I was working so hard. Then when I returned from Australia I received an email from her manager, asking me to give Mel a call, which I did. I wasn't too happy about what she had to tell me. She told me to be careful of Pete, saying that he could be a little possessive and insecure. I thanked her for her advice but felt very pissed off. She was right about Pete, he can be like that, but I had thought he was only like that with me; I hated to think he must have been like that with her as well.

But these women I've just mentioned are the tip of the ex-ice berg. Pete has been with so many girls and I hate it — I hate thinking about what he did with them. I have found this the hardest thing to deal with in our relationship and it's what we have argued over the most.

I wish we'd met years ago so there weren't all these exes with their intimate knowledge of the man I love, and I know Pete feels the same about my past. I can't help feeling jealous of all the many girls he's had before me, however irrational that is. And my God, he's had a lot! I don't think even he knows how many. To give you one example, one of the girls in the 2003 series of *Big Brother* claimed to have shagged Pete. When I asked him about her, he replied that he honestly didn't recognise her face, but that didn't mean she was lying. He admitted that he'd been with so many girls that he couldn't even remember all of them. I suppose it's not that surprising – he shot to fame as a very gorgeous seventeen-year-old pop star and had girls throwing themselves at him, so I guess I can't blame him, but it bloody winds me up.

He told me that whenever he recorded a music video he would always choose the girls he wanted to be in it with him and he would always have his eye on one particular girl and she'd be the one he'd end up shagging afterwards.

'That's nice!' I told him, not best pleased by this revelation. 'So every music video of yours I watch I can imagine you shagging the girl!'

He replied, 'At least I'm being honest Katie.'

True, but it doesn't make watching those old videos any easier, imagining him kissing her, caressing her and the rest . . . and I end up getting more and more upset. I feel that I can't celebrate his past in the way I want to because whatever music video or concert video he shows me, there's a girl in there who he's shagged. And it's a real shame because he had such a successful career and I would love to watch these videos and enjoy seeing him at the height of his success.

When he recorded his single 'Insania' he told me it was the first time ever in his career that he hadn't chosen the girl who appeared with him, and the first time ever he didn't flirt with her, or do anything else.

'Ask Claire,' (our manager) he told me, 'if you don't believe me. She's managed me for years and she knows what I was like then and what I'm like now.'

'Good, and I should think so too!' I retorted. 'Get bloody used to it!'

Of course, he did shag one of the girls in his recent

music video for 'The Right Way', but as it was me I don't hold it against him.

I would love to say that I trust Pete one hundred per cent to be faithful to me, but the more I've found out about his past, the harder I've found that to do. It's not just the number of women he's slept with, it's also discovering that he was serially unfaithful. He was a total womaniser. Apparently he was so bad that on occasions he'd see one girl in the morning, one in the afternoon and one in the evening.

'Katie,' he told me during one of our ex discussions, 'it was really hard juggling all those girls!'

'Well,' I replied, 'I've never been unfaithful so I wouldn't know!' The most I've ever done when I was in a relationship was to have the odd sneaky snog with another man when I was out clubbing, but that's as far as it went, and even then I'd feel really guilty and it's not something I'm proud of.

Hearing about Pete's past exploits arouses so many feelings in me – I feel insecure because I worry he'll be unfaithful; it makes it harder for me to trust him because he was so conniving; and, if I'm really honest, it makes me feel sick because he had so much sex and it didn't mean anything to him. He told me that when he was just starting out as a singer he and his friend would go out with the sole intention of getting laid or getting a blow-job, and every single time they went out they'd hit the shag-pot. On my blue days I think, *What's so special about sex with me then?* He's been with so many girls that they must think, *What's the big deal about him and Katie? Because I've had him . . .* And when you read some of these stories you'll understand my feelings.

When Pete was living in New York one of his girlfriends had an identical twin sister, something that obviously tickled his fancy because when he found out that the sister wanted a holiday he said to his girlfriend, 'Why don't you invite her over here?' I'm sure his girlfriend thought that was so sweet of him. What she might not have found so sweet is that while she went out shopping Pete was busy shagging her twin! And it wasn't just a one-off. He said to me that he'd liked bits of both of them, but he wished they were one person – it's not exactly a defence, is it?! Recently, this ex-girlfriend emailed him saying 'remember me?' I thought it was well out of order,

Pete and I have been together for two years now and it is public knowledge that we're married and have a child, so why email him?

Another example – when Pete was with a different girlfriend in LA he lived in an apartment block where there was a very pretty receptionist who caught his eye. So one day, while his girlfriend was at work, he went down to reception and spun a sob story about how he'd forgotten his key and could she please come up with him and let him in using hers? Well, she duly came upstairs with him but she ended up doing a lot more than simply letting him into his apartment . . . And from then on, whenever his girlfriend went out, he'd call the receptionist and she'd nip up to his apartment and give him a quick blow-job or a shag and the girlfriend never had the slightest suspicion of what he was up to.

When you meet Pete you simply cannot imagine that the friendly, warm, lovely, charming man in front of you could have been so devious. I think I would find it almost too much to bear if he had always been like that, but in the nineties everything changed for him. He had a breakdown and after that he was a different person. He stopped singing and told me that he gave up drinking because he was afraid of losing control. He stopped being a serial womaniser and instead tried to be faithful.

'Oh,' I said cheekily when he told me about how he had changed, 'So you're not just faithful now then because you're with me!'

Part of me, the really egotistical part, would love to know that I had changed him, that I had tamed him. And maybe I have, because when I questioned him about whether he was faithful to the woman he went out with before me – the woman he might have married – he replied, 'Not really, not towards the end.' But to me it doesn't matter whether it's the end or the beginning of the relationship: while you're with that person you should be faithful all the way to the end.

Thinking about Pete's past makes me recall my own. I remember how much I trusted Dane Bowers and how he betrayed me with his infidelity. His family was forever telling me that he was different when he was with me, that I had changed him and how he would never cheat on me. But cheat he did. That no longer has the power to hurt me, except that I think my relationship with Dane did have some similarities to my relationship with Pete – it was very passionate, it was very intense, I was deeply in love and I thought we would always be together. I know that Dane was usually unfaithful after he'd had a drink, but Pete hardly drinks and all the times he was unfaithful he was sober, so in a way that makes me even more paranoid because if he's got the balls to cheat when he's sober just imagine what he'd get up to if he was drunk! But I know he's not like Dane – he is so much the better man, and even though I can feel anxious I have never felt so truly loved as I do now. And of course some of my fear left when Pete proposed, though that comes later . . .

Unfortunately Pete's exes aren't confined to history. Throughout our relationship his past has had a nasty habit of spilling into our present and I've actually had to meet some of the women he's been with. Not only was it deeply upsetting meeting these women who had been intimate with him, I was also shocked by the way some of them looked. I was expecting to see some stunners, but none of these women were particularly special and it reinforced my impression that when it came to sex in the past, Pete wasn't at all fussy about who he went with – if something was offered to him he took it, no matter what the person looked like. I know looks aren't everything, but I wish Pete could have been a bit more choosy . . . I'm not saying that all my exes have been winners in the looks department but I actually had relationships with them, it wasn't just about sex.

In January 2005 we had planned to go on holiday to one of our favourite destinations, the Maldives, but then the devastating tsunami struck and we had to fly to Australia instead. I had been hoping for two weeks of complete relaxation where it would just be Pete, Harvey and me and I wouldn't have to see anyone else. Just before we flew there I'd had all my extensions taken out to give my hair a rest and it was really short. If I'd been able to lie on a beach unobserved it wouldn't have mattered, but as soon as we flew to Australia I knew I'd have to have extensions put back in – I simply didn't feel confident meeting Pete's friends with short hair, and I was already feeling uncomfortable about myself because I was pregnant and feeling fat. So – surprise,

surprise – a day after we arrived I had to book myself
in at the hairdresser's. That night Pete and his good
friend Reno wanted us all to go out for a curry. I was
very reluctant to take Harvey because his ears were
going through a very sensitive patch and I knew the
sounds in the restaurant would upset him and he'd
probably end up getting upset. But Reno said he
could organise a babysitter – someone who worked in
his music studio, who also babysat for his children.
Great, I thought, problem solved. But later in the
afternoon the babysitter came into the hairdresser's,
ready to collect Harvey, and as I watched the way she
was with Pete – all flirtatious and giggly – I knew
straight away that something had happened between
them. I'm a girl and I know exactly how a girl reacts
in those situations. It was obvious to me that the pair
of them had been intimate. So when she moved away
I went over to Pete.

'Pete, have you done anything with her?' I
demanded.

He looked shocked and said. 'What?!'

I said, 'Tell the truth, have you done anything
with her?'

He sighed and replied, 'Yes, but it was ages ago.'

'Did you fuck her?' I exclaimed, feeling the anger building inside of me.

'Yes, but I told you it was ages ago.'

That did it! I was furious. 'Right then, you can tell her she's not looking after Harvey. I'm taking him with me.'

Inside I was thinking, *You fucking arsehole. If you think I'm going to let a girl who you've fucked look after Harvey, you've got no idea!* I was in such a foul mood from then. I couldn't believe that Pete was so insensitive as to imagine that it was okay for this girl to look after Harvey. My mood was made worse by my insecurity about my appearance – I felt fat and my hair hadn't been finished so it was still too short.

Pete tried to calm me down. 'Come on, forget it. She's here now.'

'I don't give a shit, Pete,' I snapped back. 'Put it this way: when our baby's born, how would you feel if I got someone I'd fucked to look after him while we went out for dinner?'

'Of course I wouldn't like it,' Pete replied. 'But what happened between us was years ago.'

'I don't care,' I shouted back. 'The fact is that you were intimate with her.'

We ended up having a massive row. My hormones were making me feel incredibly emotional and I actually wanted to fly straight home. I knew I was right to feel so upset and anyone in my position would feel the same. But Pete didn't seem to get it. Dinner was a disaster as Harvey cried the whole time and Pete kept asking what was wrong with me. I didn't want to talk in front of his friends but back at the house, when Harvey was finally in bed, I told Pete how I felt.

'I think I want to go home. I just don't think I can handle this, Pete. Everywhere we go I seem to meet a girl you've been with and they're put in my face; it's not fair. I've never put any of my exes in front of you Pete.'

By way of an answer he took me in his arms, stroked my hair and kissed me. He told me how special I was to him, how much he loved me and I believed him. As I took in his words some of the bitterness I felt started to leave me, but it was hard, so very hard, because this wasn't the first time that I had come face to face with one of his exes . . .

A few months earlier we had been over to Cyprus for a visit and had gone out for dinner with his family. While we were eating a woman came over to the table and said hello – she was introduced as a close friend of the family. Straight away I could tell from the way she looked at Pete and reacted to him that there had been something between them. So after the meal I questioned Pete. 'Have you done anything with her? Tell the truth.'

He admitted that they'd been on a few dates, but it was never going to go anywhere because she already had two children and his parents wouldn't have been happy about him having a relationship with her, even though she was Greek.

'But,' he insisted, 'we didn't have sex. Well, we did everything but have full sex.'

'Great,' I replied through gritted teeth. 'So every time we come to Cyprus I'll have to see her.'

And if those two weren't enough then there was the air hostess . . . Pete and I were going out for lunch with Pete's brother and sister, Michael and Debbie, and we were going to meet a very good friend of theirs, let's call her Lisa. As we travelled to the restaurant Lisa called Pete and I could hear her being really loud and flirtatious on the phone. When Pete finished the call I said, 'Please tell me you haven't done anything with *her*, Pete.' Pete said no and there was an explosion of laughter from the back of the car. Debbie said, 'No way! He would never have done anything with her. You wait till you meet her and you'll understand why.'

But as we sat down for lunch with Lisa I got that familiar feeling again. As Debbie had implied, she wasn't the most attractive girl, but that clearly hadn't mattered to Pete in the past. She was really flirting and staring at him with a lovestruck, soppy expression. I felt so angry I barely touched my meal, wishing that we could just get the hell out of there. On the way home I asked him again if anything had happened between them.

'*No*,' he said wearily.

'Swear on your life,' I insisted, knowing that Pete was incapable of lying if I made him swear on his life.

'Okay, yes,' he admitted. 'But it was ages ago and it was just a kiss.'

I wasn't going to pursue the conversation in front of his brother and sister but I really wasn't convinced that he was telling the truth. When we flew out to the Maldives later that year and were met in the first-class lounge by Lisa I was certain that there had been something more between them than a kiss. Sure enough, when I brought up the subject in the Maldives – because I just had to know – Pete admitted that he'd shagged her more than once. Yet again I wanted to go home, it made me so angry. He tried to tell me it hadn't meant anything other than sex and he tried to laugh it off, saying that he'd got cheap flights out of her. But that really didn't make me feel any better about it and I told him straight, 'To be honest, Pete, your past puts me off you and makes me think that I don't really want to be with you. It makes me feel hate inside because it feels like what we have isn't that special because you've been with so many girls.'

Yet again Pete reassured me and I tried to push the thought of him and Lisa to the back of my mind, but I couldn't help getting in the last word: 'Is there anywhere else you're going to take me where we're going to meet someone you've shagged?'

So there was the girl in Australia, and every time I went there I would probably see her; there was the girl in Cyprus, and every time we went there I would have to see her; and there was the air hostess, who we would see every time we flew. That's three too many for me already. And I know damn well that when you see your ex again you always remember what you did with them, and I really don't want him reliving those memories. He never tells me when we meet these girls but I can always sense it. We were even flicking through a magazine once and he stopped to look at a picture of an Australian actress.

'Don't tell me you've been with her too?' I asked in exasperation.

'Yes, I have actually.'

Aghhhh!

I've found the best way of dealing with my worry about whether Pete is faithful to me is to know where he is all the time. Because we've got the same management, I know his itinerary and, vice versa, he knows mine. When I said this to him, he replied, 'Believe me, if people want to cheat, they will find a way.' Let's hope neither of us ever test out that theory because that would be the end of our relationship for sure . . .

During our many arguments on the subject I tell him, 'It's only because I really love you that I get so upset by your past.' I want to know that what we have is special, that he's never felt like this about anyone else. And during those early months of our relationship I couldn't help wanting to know that I was the best lover he'd ever had – though I tried not to ask too many questions in case I got the wrong answer back! But then if we did start discussing each other's sexual exploits, I could always reassure myself by saying, 'I can't be that bad in bed if you're still with me.' And of course when we got married that helped to lay some of my fears to rest . . .

I'm sure some of my insecurity stems from the fact that I'm so different from all the girls Pete has ever been with. Before we met, and fell in love, he had a definite 'type' that he'd go for, as I can see for myself from the exes I've met. They were all mixed race or Mediterranean girls, with dark hair and brown eyes, and I don't think he'd ever been with a girl who'd had a boob job before. Blonde-haired, green-eyed, siliconed me is a first for Pete! And sometimes I'll find myself looking at a Mediterranean beauty and wondering if Pete fancies her . . . and then I'll try and pull myself together and think, 'Come on, he's with me! Fake hair and fake boobs and he loves me!'

* * *

Just as I find it difficult and upsetting to deal with Pete's past, he also finds mine just as tough and just as painful. Whenever we argue about his exes he always throws Dwight back in my face, saying, 'Don't have a go at me about this. I have to look at your son who looks like his dad every day of my life.'

'Don't take it out on Harvey, it's not his fault,' I reply.

'Of course I wouldn't, I love that child, but I have to deal with the fact that you had a child with another man . . .' And there's nothing I can say to that.

And just as I have to endure his exes appearing on TV, he has his fair share of seeing mine. Whenever it happens he'll groan and say, 'Oh no, there's another one of your exes,' as Gareth Gates or Dwight Yorke pops up. I hate it as much as he does, but what's done is done.

Pete is just as jealous of my past as I am of his – he wouldn't even read my first autobiography, *Being Jordan*, because he didn't want to know all the juicy details of my other relationships. Which is ironic as I've slept with far fewer men than he has women, and I've never had a one-night stand! I admit I've got a quite a colourful past, but compared to Pete I've been bloody angelic! Sometimes I wonder what it must be like to have had one-night stands and sometimes I wonder, if I hadn't been a well-known model and there wasn't the risk that someone might go to the papers, whether I might have been tempted. You read all those stories about girls who go on holiday and have a no-strings-attached shag and a laugh and a tiny part of me envies their carefree attitude to sex. But then I think that I'm glad I didn't have one-night stands; I'm glad I respected myself.

Unfortunately my 'holier-than-thou, I-don't-do-one-night-stands halo' slipped as soon as I got Pete alone in that hotel bathroom in Brisbane, when I was finally allowed to see him after he came out of the jungle. I didn't just kiss him. Oh no, fuelled by my intense desire for him and the several bottles of champagne I'd guzzled, I went much further and quite a bit lower. I slipped off his towel, fell to my knees and gave him a blowie. I wanted him so much that it was the one time when I thought, *I don't care if I am acting like a slag, I just want him.*

I'm sure Pete had a very nice time in that hotel bathroom but he holds it against me now. He seems to think I was like that with all the men I've been with, which isn't true – I always made them wait. I told him it was totally out of character and that I'm not into one-night stands, but he won't believe it. I can't help that my desire for him got the better of me! Most of the time we can laugh about it, especially since I can't remember all the details . . .

And even though he does get jealous of my past relationships he really has no need to, because the past is where they well and truly belong. And with the exception of Dwight he never has to meet any of my ex-lovers. I can honestly say I never think of the men I had relationships with before Pete. I've no wish to hear from them or see them. I don't hate them; they just don't mean anything to me any more.

I didn't even feel bad about ending my relationship with Scott so publicly; I had to follow my heart and my love for Pete was all I could think about. Any sympathy I might have felt for him disappeared when I discovered that he sold a story about me – even though he had promised he never would – and went out with that wannabe me, Jodie Marsh. She'd built a career for herself out of slating me and the thought of the two of them together was kind of gross – not that I thought about it for more than a nanosecond. I did think that it was ironic that he ended up with her because he had told me that he thought she was rank. I can't help thinking he was foolish because she was so obviously just going out with him for the publicity. And he clearly wasn't all that taken with her because when they were on holiday together in Barbados he texted me, saying, *You probably won't reply, but how are you and how is Harvey? I still think of him.* I didn't want to give anything away about myself any more so I replied, *I'm sure your so-called bird wouldn't appreciate you texting me!* I thought, *Scott, you're such a kid, thank God we split up when we did.* He was sweet but absolutely no challenge and no good for me at all.

As for Dane Bowers, the only time I think about him is when I occasionally wonder if he ever reads about me or watches any of my TV programmes. He always thought that he was the successful one in our relationship and always looked down on my work, dismissing me as a two-bit model who was never going to get anywhere. Well, I'm pretty pleased with where I've got to, but I don't imagine Dane is quite so pleased about where he's ended up . . . Dane who?

In a bizarre coincidence, Pete met Dane when he

was touring in England. Dane's band, *Another Level*, were supporting Pete, and he can remember Dane watching him rehearse and telling him how much he loved the way he sang and performed. I'd like to imagine that deep down Dane is gutted that he not only supported Pete but also that I ended up with him. So Pete got everything: the looks, the body, the talent and the girl . . .

Pete has no need to worry that I ever fantasise about my exes – most of them just deserve the finger, because most of them treated me like shit. I felt when I met Pete that the slate was wiped clean. He made me forget all the bad times I'd had with men. And even though we have argued about our pasts and I'm sure we will in the future, I can say that I trust him more than I've ever trusted any other man. But no one can expect me to completely trust a man after what I've been through in the past. And there are positive things to come out of the fact that we've both been around the block. I think we've been able to learn from our many experiences, discovering along the way what we want and what we don't want, which has made us even more certain that we are right for each other. I know that the relationship we have with each other is unique, that we have never felt like this about anyone else. Even if we said we loved the people we were with before, it was a love that never felt like this . . .

CHAPTER SEVEN

CHAPTER SEVEN

WHO'S THE DADDY?

My son Harvey has been one of the most wonderful things that has ever happened to me, even with all the complications of his medical condition. It's ironic that he was the result of one of my most turbulent and disastrous relationships – the one I had with the footballer Dwight Yorke. But even though relations between Dwight and me have been difficult at times, to say the least, I've always been perfectly happy for him to see his son. I wanted to give Harvey the chance to have a relationship with his father but it's never been easy, and ever since Harvey was born there have been arguments about how much access Dwight should have and how much money he should pay.

It took three and a half years for Dwight to pay maintenance for Harvey and for him to pay my mum's wages – which he had promised he would do as she gave up her career to look after Harvey and to enable me to carry on working. I can't imagine what took him so long. It made everything so much harder and more acrimonious than it needed to be. I was fortunate to be in the position of being able to support Harvey without his money, but Harvey's special needs mean that I do have to spend a lot of money on special toys and equipment for him, and a con-tribution from Dwight earlier in Harvey's life would have been extremely helpful. Also it made me angry because I used to think, *Why won't he put his hand in his pocket for his son? It's not like he can't afford it.* But at least he is paying now. Though it's still not as much as I would have wanted.

We finally managed to agree that Dwight would see Harvey every Wednesday, usually at my mum's house. But for a start he often wouldn't turn up when he was supposed to, cancelling at the last minute, which upset me for Harvey's sake. Though as my mum is always quick to point out when we argue about Dwight – and we often do – this was due to his football commitments. My answer is that there was nothing to stop him getting a later flight down to see his son if he had training in the morning. After all, what's more important to him – seeing his son, or kicking a ball around?

In 2004 Dwight took me to court to try and get more access to Harvey. I felt extremely worried about the prospect of him getting more – not because I'm being unreasonable but because I believed that, given Harvey's many medical problems, Dwight simply wouldn't have been able to cope. I think Dwight would be the first to admit this. Until Dwight proved to me that he could look after Harvey on his own, then I didn't trust him.

Also, Harvey's condition means that he can become unwell with a high temperature very suddenly – within half an hour – and you need to know exactly what to do in those circumstances otherwise it could be very dangerous for him. Whenever I go away with Harvey, Great Ormond Street always contacts the nearest hospital and briefs them on Harvey's condition. Then they translate his medical notes into that language. That is how serious it is.

'Okay,' I told Dwight when we met round my mum's on one of his visits, 'if you're serious about wanting to spend more time with Harvey then you've got to prove to me that you can look after him. You need to spend the whole day with him, on your own.' I told him that on his next visit he should arrive at my house early enough in the morning to give Harvey his first lot of medication, which he has at eight o'clock. He would then bath him, get him dressed, give him breakfast, play with him and generally entertain him through the morning. He would give him lunch, followed by his second dose of medication at two o'clock. He'd spend the afternoon with him, give him tea and bath him, and then at eight o'clock he would have to give him his third dose of medication and the growth hormone injection, then put him to bed. 'If you do that then that will go some way to proving to me that you can look after him.' And I told him he would need to do that more than once.

But it seems to me that Dwight has and probably always will have different priorities, and the night before he was due at my house he went to some football do. Eight o'clock came and went, as did nine. Finally he rolled up at ten o'clock, stinking of alcohol. I had got Harvey up and given him his medication. Dwight was already proving that he wasn't up to the job. He played with Harvey for a while, then I suggested he take him for lunch at Pizza Express, saying there was a park nearby they could go to afterwards. I thought the trip would be a good test for Dwight. I was feeling extremely angry with him for being late. There he was, taking me to court to get more access to Harvey and he couldn't even turn up on time to the one thing we had arranged. When I'm feeling particularly negative about Dwight, I think of him as just being a sperm donor. To me he's Harvey's father only in name: he hardly sees him, it took him ages to pay any money towards him, so what exactly is the point of him being known as Harvey's dad? Anyone can fill a pram but it takes a man to be a father.

Pete and I gave them a lift to the restaurant because I certainly didn't want to be on my own with Dwight in the car. Maybe Dwight felt awkward, but I don't think that excuses the fact that he was sat next to Harvey but didn't pay him any attention, even though he hadn't seen him for ages. He was on the phone to his assistant and they were talking and laughing about me. Suddenly I lost it and shouted out so that the woman he was talking to could hear: 'If you've got a problem with me, then tell me to my face, I'm sick of you talking about me behind my back. See how you'd cope with a disabled son!' I was so angry – with Dwight for being late, and for having to deal with him at all, and hurt for Harvey that his dad paid him so little attention.

Pete stepped in and said to Dwight, 'And I'm sick of doing your job.'

'What do you mean?' Dwight replied.

'I'm doing your job,' Pete answered. 'You don't see your son for ages, you don't bother to turn up when you say you're going to.'

'It's easy for you to say in your situation,' was Dwight's reply.

'What are you trying to say?' Pete demanded. 'That you should be in the front with your ex and I should be in the back with your son?'

'No,' Dwight replied, 'but what do you expect me to do?'

'You should put your son before your career,' Pete told him bluntly.

Dwight just shrugged and said, 'That's your opinion.'

Just before we dropped them off I said, 'Please make sure that Harvey has his coat on if you go outside.' Harvey has such a weakened immune system and the last thing I wanted was for him to get another cold, which could make him very unwell. But when I picked Harvey up from the park some time later he wasn't wearing his coat, and nor had Dwight changed his nappy, which needed doing. *Honestly!* I thought angrily to myself, *the man doesn't have a clue; he has absolutely no common sense.* I couldn't imagine ever leaving Harvey with him for a weekend – I would be out of my mind with worry. There's no way Dwight could cope with him and he must know that too.

There was another dispute before Christmas which Dwight lost. Dwight was furious and didn't turn up for his Wednesday visit the week before Christmas, claiming that he didn't want to come to the house when Pete was there. *Great*, I thought, *take your anger out on your son*. On Christmas Eve, when I'd given up thinking he was going to send a present, we received four boxes of clothes for Harvey. Yes, the clothes were lovely, but it's hardly the most exciting gift for a two-and-a-half-year-old. All the clothes were far too small for Harvey and I thought to myself, *If you really knew your son and bothered to see more of him then you would know what size he is.*

Sometimes I wish that Dwight wasn't part of my life. But I don't ever want Harvey to turn round and say to me, 'Why didn't you let me see my dad?' It's not me who stops Dwight seeing Harvey; it's down to him. I believe he should see Harvey regularly so he can bond with him. I don't want to be in the position of saying to Harvey, 'You're seeing your dad today,' and then Dwight fails to turn up. Harvey doesn't understand that yet, but one day he might and I would hate him to get hurt. I don't think Dwight has really seen enough of Harvey to establish a relationship with him, and because of Harvey's condition you really do need to spend a lot of time with him to get to know how to communicate with him. I think Harvey probably knows his teachers at his special school better than he knows Dwight, and he doesn't yet recognise his voice. I've never seen Dwight cuddle his son or give him a kiss. But maybe he feels awkward doing that in front of me, because my mum says that he genuinely loves Harvey to bits and that he does cuddle and hold him when he is with her. In fact, Dwight is one of the things my mum and I argue over most furiously. She thinks it's very important that Dwight sees Harvey and is always telling me to be more reasonable and not to be so hard on Dwight, something I don't take very kindly to. In fact, she and my stepdad Paul, and my brother Daniel all get on well with Dwight. Of course, it's easier for them because they're not the ones who had such a shit time with him – they are not the ones he abandoned when they were pregnant . . .

Mum says that there has been a real change in Dwight's attitude towards Harvey and, whereas for the first couple of years of his life she admits that Dwight could have seen more of him and made more of an effort, she now says that she thinks Dwight does take his responsibilities as a father seriously. But this is something he needs to prove to me, because I haven't seen this side of him and I don't think it's enough just to pay money. She even goes so far as to say that she believes Harvey is the most important person in Dwight's life. She told me that when Dwight comes to see Harvey at her house he takes him out to the park, and Mum says that he is happy to play there with Harvey all afternoon, pushing him on the swings or walking him round the park. He'll also take Harvey swimming in Mum's pool. And now Mum does leave them alone together and Dwight does have to feed Harvey and change his nappy. And so he bloody should, he's his dad!

I always felt that Dwight needed to see more of Harvey and the fact that he lived in Cheshire wasn't ideal. The way I saw it was that he had many opportunities to move to a London club that would mean he could see more of Harvey, but he didn't take them up. Then in April 2005 he went to Australia to play football, meaning that he would see even less of his son. He saw Harvey seven weeks before he went to Australia, even though he knew he would be out of the country for months. Surely if he knew he wasn't going to see his son for seven months he could have fitted in another visit? Apparently he managed to find the time to go clubbing in London, so would it really have been too much to expect him to make the trip to see Harvey?

When he comes back from Australia it would be nice if I could see that he was making more of an effort with Harvey – for Harvey's sake – because so far I haven't seen this new side to Dwight that Mum goes on about. He is supposed to phone me up and check on Harvey but he always phones Mum instead. She reckons he's scared of me, but I would tell him how his son was and I would have more respect for him if he called me.

At least I've got the example of what happened to me with my stepdad, Paul. My real dad walked out on us when I was three and, though I saw him every other weekend in my childhood, by the time I was a teenager I rarely saw him. To me Paul was my dad. He gave me the unconditional love I don't feel I got from my real dad; Paul was the one who was always there for me. And I don't feel I missed out at all because my real dad wasn't around. As Pete grows closer to Harvey I can see the same pattern developing. We encourage Harvey to call Pete 'Daddy'. Pete is the one who shares the role of looking after Harvey with me – he hugs him, baths him, feeds him, gives him his medicine, tucks him in at night, plays with him, makes him giggle, comforts him when he cries, looks after him when he is sick, makes him feel safe, makes him feel loved. I couldn't ask for a better father for my son.

My feelings for Dwight have softened, though. For so long I felt angry with him because I felt he didn't make enough effort to see Harvey and I think I was still very hurt from the way he treated me during our ill-fated relationship, when he was unfaithful, and by the way he treated me when I was pregnant, denying the baby was his and then demanding a paternity test when Harvey was born. My mum has always maintained that Dwight is still in love with me and I think maybe he is, though he never showed it when we were together. When I saw him in March 2005, which was also the last time he saw Harvey before he flew to Australia, I felt genuinely sorry for him. For the first time I believed that he bitterly regretted how he'd treated me in the past and was truly sorry for his behaviour. He looked at me with eyes full of emotion for once and said, 'So you are getting married in September then?'

'Yes,' I replied.

He answered, 'Well, good luck for everything.'

But I don't think he really believed it would happen, because right up until a few weeks before the wedding he would call my mum to ask after Harvey and whether the wedding was really going ahead. He even worked out that he would be on the plane to Sydney at the time I married Pete. I know that he would have married me. He had already asked me in 2003, and even now I had Junior I think he still would have taken me back . . .

CHAPTER EIGHT

A PROPOSAL

Initially Pete and I tried to obey our management's instructions that we should keep the full extent of our relationship a secret from the world. No one knew that Pete had moved in with me. But as the weeks went by it was becoming harder and harder to pretend that we weren't head over heels in love. One evening we went out for dinner at a local pub – just us, no one else – and when photographs of our intimate dinner appeared in a magazine, showing

Pete and me kissing and cuddling, I was so glad. Even if we were pretending that we were taking things slowly and gradually getting to know each other, the photographs told the true story of how we felt about each other and showed us to be a couple who were madly in love. *See*, I wanted to say to everyone, *he's mine! So hands off!*

I was the happiest I have ever been in my life. Everything about our relationship was going so well – emotionally and physically I felt so incredibly close to Pete. We spent all our time together, but I never had that feeling I've had in other relationships of wanting to go off and do my own thing. And we didn't take each other for granted. If anything, spending time together made us want each other more. At last I had found a man who loved me in the way I had always longed to be loved, and a man who I loved with all my heart, soul and body. Sex was amazing – we fulfilled all each other's fantasies but still had plenty more up our sleeves. I loved Pete being as adventurous, passionate and downright naughty as me – inside the house or outside, in my large garden, where there were plenty of bushes and trees to hide our alfresco romps. We bought a trampoline, which was supposed to help us get fit but we found a far more interesting use for it one evening when no one was around, which certainly managed to put a spring in both our steps!

And as we were always arguing about who should pay when we went out for dinner or when we went shopping – that's to say that I always wanted to pay because I've always been independent, and he wanted to pay as well – we decided to open a joint account into which each of us would put money every month, and we agreed to split the household bills. Having a joint account was a first for me – it really must be love! I don't think Pete had realised how successful I was until he came back to England, but he's never had a problem with the fact that I earn more money than him. He's proud of my success – he definitely doesn't feel threatened by it. Since *I'm A Celebrity* he's earned very good money doing music gigs and PAs. As well as that source of income he's got his business interests in Cyprus and Australia, and he is starting up a property-developing business in Australia with one of his brothers. And while he accepts that I earn more money than him for our magazine shoots and TV show, he has very strong views that he wants to be able to support his family – that's the way he is and that's the way he's been brought up, so whatever happens he will always want to work. I've never had the feeling with him that I had with some of my exes, that they were quite happy to live off me and do f*** all . . .

But it seemed that not everyone shared our happiness, and we had a very unpleasant surprise when a letter arrived at the house from a stalker, saying that he was watching me and threatening to kneecap Pete. We'd both received hate mail in the past – when Pete was at the height of his fame in Australia he'd even received death threats – and at first we threw the letter in the bin and tried to forget about it. But then we received another one – this time it was delivered by hand to the house, which shook us both up. He had obviously been watching us, because he commented on what I'd been wearing the day before and said that he was watching Pete even more closely. Knowing that he had been on my property did scare me and we phoned the police and tightened up security around the house.

*

Apart from that nasty stalking incident everything to do with our relationship was perfect, except for one thing – I was still waiting for him to pop the question and it was torture! I was desperate for him to ask me to be his wife. I was still asking him to marry me every day, but he kept saying, 'Wait!' As my birthday in May approached, a small part of me wondered whether this might be the time that Pete would finally get down on one knee. But the day itself turned out to be a disaster, and at one point I even wondered if we had a future together . . .

The day before my birthday had been the last day of my book-signing tour for *Being Jordan*. After the morning signing I had lunch with Diana, the publicist, and Nicola from my management company. As it was my birthday the following day and as it was our last signing, we thought we should celebrate with a glass of wine. However, that glass became a bottle, then another. The wine went straight to my head and, before I realised it, I was drunk. I'd barely touched alcohol since February and so my tolerance had probably gone down. I had another book-signing in the afternoon and I don't know how I got through it as I was having real trouble focusing. Nicola kept saying, 'Shush Katie, you're being really loud!' But I was pissed enough not to care, even though I knew that Pete really didn't like me getting drunk because, like everyone, my personality changes and he would hate seeing me in this state. I wanted to sober up before I saw him again but unfortunately I couldn't, and even on the plane on the way home I was singing at the top of my voice . . . oops.

Back at the house there was no sign of Pete, which was a bit of a relief, even though I did wonder where he was, but not for long. I was still too drunk to phone him or text him – all I could do was pour myself a glass of water, take off my clothes and pass out in bed. Meanwhile, poor old Pete was hopelessly lost in the countryside, trying to get to a dog breeder from whom he had arranged to buy me a puppy. He didn't manage to find the place until midnight and the owner was not best pleased. Instantly the guy was on the defensive and, recognising Pete, he said, 'What makes you think that you can turn up when you feel like it to pick up one of my dogs?' Pete replied that he had phoned earlier and spoken to the man's wife, explaining that he was lost, and she said it would be okay if he was late. But the guy wouldn't have it and kept having a go at Pete, who then said if that was his attitude he would forget the dog. Pete left, pretty angry that he hadn't been able to pick up my birthday present. All he wanted to do was get home, but the next thing he knew this guy drove right up behind him on a narrow country lane, as if he wanted to push him off the road, and then another car came towards him, trying to block Pete in. Not liking the situation one little bit, Pete called the police. The men left before they arrived, leaving a rather shaken Pete to explain what had happened.

I imagine that when Pete got home he was looking forward to receiving a bit of TLC from me, but there was no chance. I didn't even wake up when he got into bed beside me. The next morning he was appearing on the ITV show *The Ministry of Mayhem* and he had to get up at half past four. After that we would have to drive up to Birmingham, where he had a PA in a nightclub. I had promised to go with him, so I had to drag myself out of bed as well. I was really pissed off that he was working on my birthday, and my stonking hangover was not improving my mood one little bit. I felt sick and shaky, not with it at all. I needed to be lying in bed, recovering, not traipsing up to London. Pete had the hump with me because he knew I'd been drinking the day before and he was annoyed that I hadn't called him to see where he was. There was a bit of an atmosphere between us, and I couldn't help feeling that this wasn't the birthday I had hoped for so far. There was no sign of any present or even a card, though as we were getting ready Pete told me to make sure I was wearing something halfway smart as he was taking me out somewhere. *Perhaps things will improve*, I thought to myself as we drove up to London.

After the TV show, by which time my hangover was starting to ease off, we were driven into the centre of London and dropped off at the Savoy, where Pete told me he was taking me for lunch. It was lovely that he was treating me, but to be honest posh restaurants like the Savoy and me don't really go together. I like places that are a bit more down to earth, where you get a good bit of grub on your plate! It was all very nice and classy, but I kept thinking I was going to break something and couldn't relax. And even though I knew it was an expensive meal, something kept niggling at me – where was my card and where was my present?! It's a girl thing – we all want that little something to open on our birthdays. We were just finishing off our main courses when our driver appeared at the window, tapping his watch, as if to say hurry up! Pete told me that we had to pick up the dancers on our way to his PA. Suddenly I felt cross again. I thought, *It's my birthday, I don't want to rush my meal!* And it did sort of spoil what should have been a romantic lunch.

After a short drive in the car Pete said we had to pull over and pick up the dancers and, knowing that we had a long drive ahead of us, I told him I'd better nip in and have a quick wee. But as I got out I realised we were outside a theatre. We weren't picking up the dancers; Pete had tickets for *The Lion King*. I was thrilled when I discovered that he'd booked us a box, and in the private room outside there was a bottle of champagne chilling. 'Happy birthday,' Pete said, kissing me. *Things are definitely looking up!* I thought to myself. Then the performance started and I absolutely loved it. I had never been to the theatre before to see a show –

apart from the odd local panto – and I was bowled over. But, even though I'd now been treated to a lovely lunch and a trip to the theatre, I was still thinking that surely he would have got me a present, even a small one. But then I told myself, *Don't be so selfish!*

All I wanted to do after the show was go home and chill out together, but after the matinee we had to get in the car, pick up the dancers and hit the motorway. Pete and I were sitting at the back of the Voyager and, as I told him how I'd loved my treats and how much I loved him, Pete suddenly looked serious and said softly, so no one else could hear, 'Are you sure you want to be with me?'

'Yes, of course!' I cried instantly, horrified that he would even ask such a thing.

He replied, 'I keep thinking that maybe you're not over your Jordan thing yet, and maybe you still want to do your partying.'

I felt cold inside; was this Pete's way of telling me things were over?

'Go on Kate, you do your thing for another couple of years, get it out of your system, and I'll still be here waiting for you.'

'What are you talking about?' I demanded. 'I don't want to go off, I've got all of that out of my system. I want to be with you, I'm happy with you.'

But he kept on. 'I don't believe you have got it out of your system; maybe you should go out more with your friends.'

I was at a complete loss to know why he was saying these things to me. I hated him saying them and suddenly I felt angry and hurt; I wanted to shout out to stop the car and let me out. I wanted to go home. I wanted to cry and say, 'Why are you making me feel like shit on my birthday?' In the end I texted my friend Clare, saying I couldn't understand why Pete was ruining my birthday by asking me whether I wanted to be with him.

'Who are you texting?' Pete demanded, which was totally out of character for him as we never usually felt the need to ask each other this.

'Just Clare,' I muttered, and I had the right hump now. All the happiness I had felt at the theatre and over lunch had fizzled out of me.

Eventually we arrived at our hotel and we were running really late. Pete only had half an hour to get ready before he was due on stage at eleven-thirty. As we walked into our hotel suite I was still feeling in a bad mood, and on top of everything else I was now certain that I wasn't getting a present and my birthday was nearly over. But on the bed I noticed that there was a heart made out of pink roses and there was a bottle of pink champagne chilling by the bed. I couldn't help smiling and thinking that was sweet of Pete.

I turned round to look at Pete and thank him and once again he said, 'Happy birthday,' and apologised for having to drag me up here for his work. Then I noticed that one of his arms was behind his back, as if he was hiding something, and I thought, *What's going on?*

Then it all became wonderfully clear as Pete exclaimed, 'I can't hold it in any longer!' And to my total delight, he got down on one knee, held out a ring box and said, 'Kate, will you marry me?'

'Yes,' I cried, opening the box and letting out a gasp when I saw the stunning ring he had chosen for me. I threw my arms around him and kissed him. My dream had finally come true. Then he took my hand and slid the ring on to my finger. It was the most gorgeous ring – Pete knew I liked big rings and this one was massive! It was a large square baguette with a pink stone in the middle and edged with diamonds – totally blingtastic! Then Pete poured us each a glass of pink champagne to celebrate. He had just minutes to go before he was due on stage, but he said he wanted to ask me to marry him again! So we went into the bathroom, where he asked me there and we both admired my ring sparkling in the light; he then asked me in the lounge and then on the bed!

I was bubbling over with happiness but I was still puzzled by Pete's comments in the car. 'Why were you such a bastard to me earlier?' I demanded with typical frankness.

Pete replied, 'I was just testing you to see if you really wanted to be with me before I put this ring on your finger. I've had this ring for ages and I've been waiting to ask you, but I had to be sure that you really wanted to be with me.'

'How could you ever doubt it?' I said, putting my arms around him.

I wanted us to stay in the hotel room, and I wanted to keep my ring on, but we had run out of time. Reluctantly I returned my beautiful ring to its box and we raced to the club. I was so excited; I wanted to tell everyone that I was engaged to Peter Andre! But of course I couldn't. As Pete performed on stage he kept looking at me, and I couldn't stop smiling as I thought, *That's my fiancé!* But when Pete came off stage he accused me of eyeing up a bloke in the audience who had taken his shirt off!

'Of course I wasn't!' I told him, too loved up to care about anything so silly, especially when it wasn't true. As far as I was concerned I had everything I wanted: I'd wanted Pete and now I was with him; I'd wanted him to marry me and now he had finally asked me. I was over the moon.

Back at our hotel we were so exhausted after the day's events that we just curled up in bed together and held each other close. I had put my ring back on and I kept touching it in the dark, checking it was really there. As I drifted off to sleep I had a big grin on my face. I felt complete. Pete asking me to marry him had been the best birthday present ever and I had to admit that his making me wait three months made it even more special. This day that had started so badly had ended perfectly.

In the morning when we made love – making up for

our lack of performance the previous night – it was wonderful looking into Pete's eyes and thinking, *He's asked me to marry him! He's going to be my husband!* Afterwards as I lay in his arms, stroking his skin, I couldn't help comparing how deliriously happy I felt now, after Pete's proposal, with how I'd felt after one of the other proposals I'd received in the past. Scott Sullivan had proposed to me on Valentine's Day in 2003, and I remembered the sick feeling in the pit of my stomach when he'd handed me a Burberry teddy bear with a diamond ring on its paw. I had tried to make out that I hadn't seen the ring, knowing full well it was supposed to be an engagement one, but Scott got down on one knee and asked me, making his intentions crystal clear. All I could think of was that he looked like a little boy begging me – not exactly the right response. I knew with all my heart that he wasn't *the one*, and him asking me to marry him was the very last thing I wanted to hear. I said yes, which may surprise you, but saying no would have involved too much of an explanation. And even though I didn't want to marry him, I wasn't ready to leave him. Scott had become a little habit of mine, which I didn't break until I met Peter. I sighed, thinking, *Thank God all that's in the past*, once more touching my engagement ring to remind myself that Pete really had proposed and that I hadn't dreamt it all!

Overjoyed as I was by Pete's proposal, we both decided to keep our engagement secret from everyone – except our families. My mum and stepdad Paul had known about the proposal before I did, as Pete had asked their permission before asking me, which I thought was so sweet of him. And my mum bought us each a star as an engagement present – she always likes to think of something different to give me. We certainly didn't want the press finding out yet. They had already had a field day with us, claiming that our relationship was just a publicity stunt and wasn't genuine. I didn't want them saying that our engagement was just a publicity stunt too. Pete and I also agreed that we still needed time and space to let our relationship grow before we let the world in on our secret. Even though I had hated not being able to reveal the depth of our feelings for each other, I was beginning to accept our management's logic in wanting us to keep it a secret – Pete and I had built up a strong relationship, we were getting to know each other really well, and in the media spotlight that might have been more difficult. So just before we left our hotel, I very reluctantly took off my beautiful ring again and put it back in the box. There would be plenty of time to wear it in the future – the rest of my life, I hoped!

Now that Pete had proposed I let my imagination run wild thinking about our wedding day. I had long fantasised about having a big Disney wedding – I wanted something that would be totally over the top, and I mean everything. I wanted a fairy-tale day – nothing less would do. I wanted to be Cinderella after she'd got her prince. I had no intention of doing a Pamela Anderson and getting married on a beach in my bikini; I thought that would be a complete waste. For my wedding day I wanted to wear something amazing – a one-off, show-stopping creation. It would have to be pink, of course. I wanted a castle, a carriage, white horses, a day full of music and surprises. I knew exactly what I wanted in my head, it was just a question of matching my imagination to the reality. This was going to be the most important day of my life. But for the time being, until we had told everyone, I could only dream . . . but what a sweet dream that was . . .

CHAPTER NINE

DOSH AND PECS

It was a chilly June morning in 2004, the sun was nowhere to be seen, and I was freezing my tits off as I posed in a white bikini on Camber Sands. But for once I couldn't complain because I was being filmed for Pete's music video, 'The Right Way', and the show had to go on – I was doing this for my fiancé and love! I'd also agreed to do it because I didn't want him filming it with any other girl! I tried to keep warm by thinking about what Claire had told me just before we started filming. She said that later that day her partner Neville was coming down to see me because they had some good news to tell me about my music. Instantly I wanted to know what it was, but she told me I would have to wait as they wanted to get my reaction on film for the second series of documentaries about Pete and me. All day as I was being filmed I felt a buzz of excitement; perhaps, finally, they had got me a record deal!

When we finished filming the video I was ushered into a room with Claire, Neville and Shauna – who was filming us – and they asked everyone else to leave, including Pete.

Claire shut the door, turned round and said, 'Right Katie, we've got something to tell you, but it has to stay a secret and you can't tell anyone about it.'

'I'll have to tell Pete,' I exclaimed. I had no secrets from him and I had no intention of having any.

'Okay,' she replied, 'but no one else.'

'Come on, tell me then!' I said, desperate to find out what this big secret was.

'This is what you've been waiting for,' she replied. Immediately I thought to myself, *Don't get your hopes up.* I've been promised so many things in my time to do with my music that I've taught myself not to believe anything will actually happen until I've signed on the dotted line and my album is on sale.

'Oh,' I replied. 'What's that then?'

'We've got you an album deal with Sony!' she said, beaming at me.

'Wicked!' I said excitedly, but I was still thinking, *Don't get your hopes up, there's bound to be a catch.* 'So what's the deal?'

Then she told me that before I got the album deal I would have to take part in Eurovision. Straight away I thought, *Eurovision is tacky, I really don't want to do it.*

But, as if sensing my thoughts, Claire said, 'It's going to be great. It will work in your favour because it's a way of getting the British public behind you; once they've supported you in Eurovision they'll want to buy your album.' And she explained how there were going to be five different singers, including me, who would perform their song live on a BBC 1 show to be voted on by the public and the winner would go through to represent the UK.

On camera I said it sounded like a great idea, but inside I was full of doubts and I really didn't think

Eurovision was for me. When Shauna had stopped filming I had a sudden thought and said 'it all sounds like a good idea, but what if I don't get through on the show? Will I still get the album deal?'

'Trust me,' Claire assured me, 'you're bound to win, of course you are.' And that's what swung it for me – the way Claire sold it to me, I was convinced that I would win if I gave a good performance. When I confided in Pete he agreed with me that I should do Eurovision so long as I got an album deal out of it, and I allowed the tiniest flicker of hope to be born inside me. *This time next year*, I thought to myself, *I might be recording songs for my new album*, little knowing that I would have an entirely different event to celebrate in June 2005 . . .

I was very glad I had my potential album deal on the horizon because, apart from the amazing success of my first autobiography, I wasn't quite so happy with the direction the rest of my work was taking. When I joined Claire she said she didn't just want to take on another glamour girl, she was looking for a new challenge. She said she wanted to build on the Katie Price side of me people had seen in the jungle. Well that was fine by me; I knew that people had seen a different side to me both from the TV show and from my autobiography. The very reason I had wanted to write my book was to show that I wasn't just a glamour girl; I was Katie Price as well. And although Claire still insists that she changed my image, she didn't. My image was already changing when I met her – besides, I didn't join up with Claire to change my image, it was simply to do my music . . .

Throughout 2004 I hardly did any glamour shoots at all as Jordan, and when I did Claire banned me from doing any of my sexy poses – she didn't want me doing any saucy shots with my hands down my knickers or sitting in any suggestive positions. She put a stop to my cheeky trademark gestures, such as my wink and giving the middle finger. It was something we argued over a lot. She'd say, 'Don't be Jordan, be Katie. People want to see the nice Katie Price they saw in the jungle.'

And I'd say, 'Stop trying to get rid of Jordan! I've done nine years of modelling and I don't want to throw it away!' She'd reply that she wanted me to keep my options open and that I could get work as Katie Price *and* Jordan. And I have to admit she was right – bizarrely, she would get calls from people saying that they wanted to book Katie Price and *not* Jordan. They would say they hated Jordan and wanted to photograph and interview Katie. Or other people would phone up and book Jordan for a shoot. I'd think to myself, *Hello, I'm the same person!*

But I missed doing my glamour shoots as Jordan. From the moment I started modelling aged seventeen I loved it and I've never stopped getting a buzz from it. I love being provocative and sexy on camera. It's like anyone who has a talent for something: you love being able to use that talent and try and get better all the time. To me, being in the studio, getting my kit off and being photographed, is where I'm happiest; it's where I feel most confident and it's where I feel most at home. Usually I'm working with people who I know and who are my friends, and to me it doesn't feel like work, because I'm enjoying what I'm doing so much and because I know I'm good at it. I imagine it's like people who work in an office where they're happy because they know what they're doing, they're with people they like and they feel comfortable. Well that's how I feel, it's just that I wear fewer clothes to work!

It's ironic that I modelled less when I met Pete, because out of all the men I've been involved with he's the one who has absolutely no problem with my modelling career. Dane Bowers was the most unreasonable. He hated my work, hated me showing off my body, and would frequently go off on one about it, ranting and raving, saying how could I bear doing what I did, knowing that men would be wanking off with my picture in front of them? For Dwight I was the perfect trophy girlfriend and he wanted me to be Jordan the glamour model all the time, even though he showed no interest in my work. But there's no conflict whatsoever between Pete and me over my modelling. When I asked him if he minded my job, he said, 'No. Obviously I don't love you getting your kit off and knowing that men look at you, but I'd never stop you doing it because that's your job.' In fact he thinks it's great that I've been so successful, and he's always saying how proud he is of me. Of course he wouldn't like me to do porno mags, but what guy would put up with that? And I'm not likely to do that anyway. My shoot for *American Playboy* where I showed off my intimate love-heart tattoo for the first time is as revealing as I'll ever be, and Pete loves those pictures . . .

Suddenly it seemed that the only shoots I was doing were for *OK!*, with the odd tabloid one here and there, and while I earned a lot of money in 2004 and 2005 – hence one tabloid dubbing me and Pete 'Dosh and Pecs' – it wasn't from my glamour modelling. Claire argued that she got me shoots with different magazines and so increased my profile, but I told her that even before I was with her I was regularly in *OK!* I did appreciate the fact that Claire had put together a good team around me, and the way that she had editorial control over any interviews I did and she controlled the pictures, as this had never happened in the past. But I missed modelling for the red tops and for lads' mags; I missed doing all my cheeky interviews which accompanied the shoots. I thought I would go along with what Claire wanted and see what happened – as far as I was concerned, Jordan was just taking a bit of a break in 2004, but I had every intention of bringing her back . . .

I started doing more television work than I'd done before, though I had already filmed a three-part documentary series for the BBC, so I was no stranger to having my every move recorded, as it was for my series *When Jordan Met Peter*. But if I'm honest, I didn't really enjoy the TV work as much as modelling. Yes, I was getting more confident about appearing on TV and no longer needed my wine fix to get in front of the camera, but I still got nervous when I was interviewed.

In June I landed a job as one of the presenters on *Hell's Kitchen*. My role was to interview the celebrities on the red carpet as they came into the restaurant. I absolutely hated it! For a start I was miserable because it meant so much time away from Harvey and Pete – the production team wanted me there hours before we did any filming and I got sick of hanging around on set. It only gave me more time to get nervous for when we did start filming. I know people might not believe it if I say I'm a shy person, but in some situations I am and I absolutely hate going up to people who I don't know and asking them questions. I know what it's like being a celeb on the red carpet: sometimes you'll see someone with a mic and ignore them because you don't want the hassle of being interviewed yet again. As I was in the reverse position I'd think, 'Don't any of them dare walk past me!' But sometimes a celeb would do exactly that and the producer would order me to run after them and call them back for an interview, all of which I found extremely awkward and embarrassing. I wouldn't even have a drink before filming because I was trying to prove to myself that I didn't need wine to give me confidence, but a large glass of wine would certainly have taken the edge off my nerves! I hated feeling under pressure – something that I had never experienced when I was modelling. Looking back I think I'd have had more fun if I was presenting my own show, either with Pete or on my own – I'd feel more relaxed and more in control. I'm not cut out to do that confronting-people-with-a-microphone lark, but at least *Hell's Kitchen* proved I could do it, and it was good practice for if I ever got offered anything like it again.

My other TV work was fortunately less stressful than *Hell's Kitchen*. Later in the summer I filmed the ITV show *With A Little Help From My Friends*, which is one of the things I'm proudest of as it was for a very good cause. We were helping Activenture, a Sussex-based charity which gives children with disabilities or special needs the chance to experience things most of us take for granted. At the centre children can learn to rock climb, swim, canoe, even abseil. But due to lack of funds the centre was in urgent need of refurbishment and repair – in fact, if we hadn't come along when we did, the swimming pool would have been closed as it was in such a poor state. We helped renovate the swimming pool and create a sensory play area for visually impaired children – a room that would stimulate them and help them relax. And we built a wheelchair friendly obstacle course, all in five days! It was totally knackering but it was a challenge I was really glad to be given. Now I have Harvey I know how important such places are to children with special needs and their families. It was really important for me to get everything right, especially the sensory room, because I take Harvey to one every week and know how much he enjoys it.

Then there was *Jordan Gets Even*, where I had to try and deceive my mum, my old agent Sam Bond and Pete into believing that I wasn't Katie. The make-up was incredible: I wore a prosthetic mask, false teeth and a wig, and frankly I looked like a minging old bag! On looks alone I think I would have fooled anyone that knew me. I also had coaching to change my voice, and that's probably where I fell down – acting's never been my strong point. Still, it was a laugh and I'll never forget the look on Pete's face when he thought this raddled old woman was coming on to him!

In May 2004 the first part of my autobiography *Being Jordan* was published and it was an instant success, staying in the bestseller charts for weeks. I was thrilled that it was a bestseller. Not least because when I had tried to get a book deal no publisher would give me one. Eventually John Blake did, but it was only a ten-thousand-pound advance, which didn't seem that much when I knew people who'd been offered half a million pounds for their books. But I thought, *Go with it* – inside I knew that the book would sell, but even I had no idea just how well it would do. In fact a year later I found myself in the surreal situation of going to the prestigious British Book Awards – the Oscars of the book world – as my book had been nominated as biography of the year, along with Bill Clinton's and Sheila Hancock's – *Not bad for a glamour girl from Brighton*, I thought. In the end Bill Clinton won and I couldn't really complain about being beaten by someone who had been one of the most powerful men in the world, even if he wasn't British!

Looking back I'd had quite a life so far, with my rise to fame as a glamour model, my boob jobs and my string of disastrous relationships. So much had happened to me with Harvey being born blind, then my cancer scare, then falling in love on a reality TV show – honestly, you couldn't have made it up! I was proud that my book showed the real me – I was honest about everything that had happened in my life and I'd opened my heart and my feelings. I think people sympathised with me in a way they hadn't just from reading stories about me in the press. My fan base changed and I started to get letters from older women who told me how much they sympathised with all that I'd been through. Bizarrely, I'd also got people coming up to me at my book-signings and telling me that they hated Jordan but really liked Katie Price! *It's still me!* I'd think.

I had a hectic couple of weeks promoting my book, doing signings, chat shows and TV and radio interviews. I got my usual attack of nerves when it came to the signings. Every time I arrived at a venue I'd ask anxiously, 'Are there many people here?' I was paranoid that no one would turn up and I'd be left sitting on my own behind a desk, looking like a loser. Fortunately I always got the reassuring response that there were plenty of people waiting to see me. Unfortunately Pete couldn't come on my book tour with me because he was working. I totally understand why he couldn't come, but I would have liked him there beside me; it would have meant a lot to me. I had already decided to take a month off work and go with him when he went touring, the first time ever I had stopped working for a man in my life.

As soon as I found out in March that Pete had a tour coming up I knew I had to go with him. It wasn't just because I couldn't bear to be apart from him – it was more basic than that. I couldn't risk losing him to a dancer or any other girl who went after him. I knew all too well from my relationship with Dane Bowers what musicians are like when they're on tour and how they're surrounded by girls throwing themselves at them; even if they're not actually unfaithful to their girlfriends and wives back home, they still have girls all over them. There was no way I could stay at home and imagine that happening with Pete. So I told

Claire that I was going on tour with Pete and I wasn't going to work for a month – unless a really good job came in worth a lot, then I'd do it; otherwise my career could be put on hold for a month. I wanted to make our relationship work and I thought, *If we can survive a month on the road together, when we're in and out of hotels and living out of suitcases and with each other all the time – that will be a very good test of our love for each other.*

Pete's tour started in the middle of June. I was so glad I had made the decision to go with him, even if he did embarrass me at times by getting me up on stage with him! I felt we grew even closer, and even though we were spending all our time together we didn't argue once. We had Harvey with us of course. I knew that it must have been hard at times for Pete, knowing that Harvey wasn't his, but he'd always known that Harvey and me were a package. I loved Pete all the more seeing how he treated my son – the two of them had such a good relationship and I genuinely felt that Pete loved Harvey as if he was his own son. We were a family and it was a really good feeling, especially since we were now engaged.

Of course there were times when being away from

home for so long and not working did get boring, and sometimes I wished that Pete could have shown his appreciation that I'd sacrificed my work to be with him. I know he did appreciate it, but I've always been so strongly independent and it did feel strange not working. I didn't want anyone to think that I was like a groupie who just followed him everywhere. I could work if I wanted to; I had chosen not to.

After the tour we treated ourselves to our first holiday together in the Maldives. Our friends said, 'How can you go there for two weeks? You'll be so bored!' Because there really isn't anything to do except relax. But we had a brilliant time – the best holiday I've ever had. It was so wonderful being with Pete and Harvey – we hung out in our stunning water villa, which had a glass-floored living room through which you could see the Indian Ocean; we swam, lay on the beach, played scrabble and gin rummy, watched DVDs, had our beauty treatments together in the same room. And I actually read a book, on Pete's recommendation – A *Child Called It* – which was so unlike me. But for once when I was away with a man I felt I could let go; I didn't have to worry about entertaining him, I could just be me. In the past I

After the wonderful wedding, we jetted off on honeymoon to the Maldives.

Pete and Junior enjoy
some time out from
the photo shoots.

Bath time for Harvey!

Junior and I relaxed at our water bungalow in the Maldives.

Pete and I on a shoot on the
beach. I loved getting back into
my work after my pregnancy.

Sampling the local food!
I tried some lychees while we were away.

My beautiful boys, Junior, Harvey and Pete
all catch up on some rest.

I was really pleased with the *OK!* pictures.

Camera, set and action!
The documentary cameras
have followed our relationship
from the early days.

Pete makes a splash
at the resort.

A day of relaxation for me.

could never have imagined spending all that time together; I would have been itching to go out clubbing and party. But I didn't need to do that with Pete. Mind you, there really wasn't anywhere to go clubbing even if I'd wanted to!

The hotel and setting was so stunning – the best place I've ever stayed. And I was so in love with Pete, it really was like being in paradise. I've never had such a romantic and intimate holiday with a man before. One night Pete lit our balcony with tiny candles and we lay on the hammock and made love under the stars with the ocean beneath us, which was the most incredibly sensual and intense experience – though at one point we did hear some people walking nearby and Pete got a little shy!

Afterwards we fell asleep in each other's arms, and I thought I wouldn't want to be with anyone else, anywhere else, at this moment – this is my perfect moment, with my son sleeping safely inside, and me with Pete – my one and only love under the stars . . .

CHAPTER TEN

OUR BIG SECRET

'Oh my God, Pete!' I screamed in delight. 'Come and look at this, I'm pregnant!'

I ran out of the bathroom, waving the pregnancy test at him and pointing out the faint blue line in the window.

Pete stared at it and said, 'I can't see anything there, you can't be pregnant.'

'Pete!' I exclaimed, feeling a mixture of excitement and frustration, 'I am! It says in the instructions that however faint the line is, the fact that there is a line shows that you're pregnant!'

To try and convince him I did another test, and again a faint blue line appeared but again he wasn't certain. Looking back, I think he so wanted it to be true that he couldn't quite believe his eyes. I, however, knew that I was definitely pregnant. That night my mum was holding a murder mystery party and we all had to dress up as the different characters. We were also being filmed for our documentary *When Jordan Met Peter.* I might have seemed calm but inside I was feeling so many emotions.

'Shit!' I thought. 'I'm pregnant!' And even though it was something I had secretly longed for and even though I knew that I wanted to be with Pete and have a child with him, I still wondered if it was the right thing to happen to us at this time – we hadn't even been together a year. Then I thought, *Yes, there's no doubt in my mind, this is fantastic news and I'm having our baby.* Mind you, I didn't really have any choice if I wanted to stay with Pete: he is completely against abortion and when we'd talked about it in the past he had said that if I ever fell pregnant by him and had an abortion he would leave me. He was very shocked when I confessed that I'd had one in the past when I was with Dane Bowers. He found it very hard to understand how I could have had one, even when I explained that it was a decision I had agonised over but was definitely the right one for me at the time.

A few days later we did yet more tests and the blue line was much stronger, but Pete was still not sure.

'Pete,' I told him, 'these tests are 99.9 per cent accurate. Why won't you believe it?' Finally, after our ninth test, he decided to believe his own eyes and we could celebrate the fact that I was pregnant. We both decided not to tell anyone else yet. 'Let's just see how long we can keep it a secret,' I said to Pete. I didn't know how my mum would react and I didn't want people thinking it was too soon in our relationship for us to have a baby.

Within weeks of first meeting, Pete and I had talked about having children – to me, having a child together would complete us as a couple and as a family but we never actually said, 'Let's try and get pregnant now.' But neither were we exactly careful. Right from the beginning I had told Pete that I wasn't on the pill as I was so crap at remembering to take it, and in those early days we relied on the withdrawal method, which is hardly the safest form of contraception. But it was one that Pete was rather good at, having had years of practice from sleeping with girls and being so paranoid about getting them pregnant. After a while I started to feel quite hurt that Pete would never come inside me, as it made me feel that I wasn't any more special than all those other girls. When I told him he was shocked that I should feel like that and from then on he stopped being so careful. Every time I got my period we were both really disappointed, and by October our wish to have a baby was so strong that we bought a predictor kit that would tell me which were my most fertile days every month. We both knew that we shouldn't want a baby yet, but we couldn't help wanting one. By the beginning of November we had our wish and I was pregnant.

Even though I had wanted this to happen, I needed to get my head round the idea of having another baby. Unfortunately there was no chance for this as Pete and I had just announced our engagement to the world and were taking our family and close friends on a Caribbean cruise to celebrate. For eight days we were going to cruise to Puerto Rico, St Marten, St Thomas and the Bahamas – all stunning destinations.

As soon as we landed in Miami and before we set off on the cruise Pete and I wanted to have a scan to confirm that all was well with my pregnancy. We were reluctant to have one in England because we didn't want the news to leak out. So once we were in our hotel room and no one else was around we checked through the classified pages, found a clinic and made an appointment under a different name. Then we told everyone that we were going to get a new buggy for Harvey because the wheels on his were knackered, which was in fact true.

It was so amazing when we had the scan and the doctor confirmed that I was six weeks pregnant. Pete held my hand and we both had tears of joy as we looked at the tiny embryo – our baby. It was such a contrast with how I'd felt when I was pregnant with Harvey. Dwight had never been to any of the scans with me and I had felt so alone and unsure about what to do for the best. In fact my first pregnancy counts for some of the unhappiest times of my life. And now here I was with the man of my dreams, looking at the new life we had made together. We were given a picture which we carefully hid away, and then we had to dash to Toys R Us to pick up the buggy. When we arrived back at the hotel, hours later, we had to pretend that we had to go to several shops to find the right one.

We had so been looking forward to taking everyone on the cruise – we thought it would be the perfect way of sharing our happiness with our family and close friends. But from the start, what was supposed to be an idyllic holiday and a chance for our family and friends to get to know each other was a disaster. By now I was suffering from morning sickness – except it wasn't just in the mornings; I felt nauseous all the time and had to make frequent dashes to the bathroom to throw up. Poor Harvey suffered from seasickness, and every time he was sick and I had to clear up after him it made me feel even more sick. To be honest, all I wanted to do was curl up in my cabin with a bucket by the bed and go to sleep but of course I couldn't, I had to put on an act and pretend that I was feeling seasick.

Pete and I had imagined that the cruise would be a perfect opportunity for everyone we cared about to get to know each other. I always knew that Pete's family was very different from mine, but in the confined space of the boat those differences became even more noticeable. I adore Pete's family – they are all lovely – but the fact is they're completely different to my family – they really are chalk and cheese and Pete and I are the only thing they have in common.

We'd naively imagined that we'd all do activities together, like going on trips to the various places we stopped at or meeting on the boat to play golf, but people were reluctant to do everything as a group and preferred to split off and do their own thing. Whenever we tried to organise everyone to meet at the same place, at the same time, it felt like we were teachers running a school excursion. Some people turned up, some wouldn't, some would be late. It all seemed like very hard work and it was turning out to be stressful instead of relaxing.

And then there was the press. We had tried to keep the trip a secret, but somehow news had got out and a number of reporters had booked themselves on the cruise. Wherever I went journalists and photographers would be watching my every move and trying to get pictures, which put a real downer on the experience. When we had a private party to make our engagement official to all the family, we had to hire a private room and close all the curtains so no press could see. But somehow the press got hold of what went on – possibly from one of the waitresses – and when the story appeared in the papers they put such a negative slant on it, making out that there'd been arguments between our two families and that I'd fallen out with my mum. I admit that I had rowed with my mum, but it was nothing major. Because I'd been feeling so sick I was late getting to the party and my mum had been annoyed with me for keeping everyone waiting. If she'd known I was pregnant I'm sure she would have understood why I was late, but as it was I wanted to keep my pregnancy a secret. I think she'd sussed that there was something wrong with me on the cruise. She could tell that I wasn't being myself and that I seemed stressed. The press made a far bigger deal out of it than it actually was, which was upsetting because our engagement was so special and personal to us.

And the weather was shit. I had imagined sun-bathing by the pool but it was far too cold for that on board the ship, and as I'd only brought summer clothes with me I was cold all the time. So I felt sick, cold, miserable, claustrophobic, anxious that everyone would get on, worried about Harvey and worried that everything would be okay with my baby. All in all I couldn't wait to get off the boat and go home. As far as I was concerned the cruise had been a complete disappointment and I just wanted to forget all about it.

I felt a bit sad for Pete that the cruise hadn't lived up to his expectations. For him it is a really big deal when his family meet up – it doesn't happen that often because they are scattered across Australia and Cyprus – and I know he really misses them.

I said, 'I do feel for you that you don't see that much of your family, but it is your choice.' He's been apart from them since he was a teenager when he first went to Japan to start his music career. I am just as close to my family but they live up the road from me and we see each other all the time, so of course when we meet it isn't such a big deal. Pete reckons that we have completely different attitudes towards our families but I don't think we do, it's just that my family express themselves differently. I would do anything for my family and they would for me, but we don't go around hugging each other the whole time and telling each other how much we love each other. It goes without saying and we're English, for God's sake!

Pete also says that we respect our families differently. But just because my mum and I can argue and swear in front of each other, doesn't mean that I don't respect her – we just have a different kind of relationship. For a start, my parents are much younger than Pete's. And of course our parents were brought up in different eras and different cultures, so naturally our families are very different. He also says that his parents are more hospitable and more welcoming and that when you go to their house you'll immediately be offered food and drink. But I think that stems from their Mediterranean background. My mum and stepdad Paul are just as hospitable, but in a different way – it's more likely you'll be offered a cup of tea and a biscuit if you just drop by. But she pulls out the stops when she has people round for dinner. She's a busy woman and she and Paul are still working full-time. I think we just have to accept that our families are different, but it doesn't mean that I love mine any less than Pete's and vice versa. I just want everyone to live and let live. Fortunately the row was soon forgotten.

Back from the cruise I bought a baby book, showing all the different stages of how the baby developed, and Pete and I would look in it together every week to see what new features and skills our baby was getting. It was so lovely being able to share my pregnancy with him and he was as excited as me. But still, in those early weeks I had moments where I wondered if it really was the right time for us to have a baby. And in my heart of hearts I had really wanted to be married to Pete before we had a child. I would never want to be a single mother, again. Looking after Harvey on my own has been one of the hardest things I have done − of course I love being a mother, but because of his condition it has never got any easier. I have never had the experience of other parents when you can think, *Thank goodness that stage is over, I can relax a little bit now.* If, God forbid, things had gone wrong between Pete and me and I'd been left with two children to bring up on my own, I really don't think I could have coped. Because of Harvey's condition it would have been like having two babies to look after, except in many ways Harvey is harder to look after than a baby. But I tried to push those negative thoughts away. Pete and I were going to get married and there was no question of that – though now it would have to wait until after the baby was born as I had no intention of getting married when I was pregnant. It was my big day and I didn't want it ruined by being too large to wear the wedding dress of my dreams or by having morning sickness.

Wonderful as it was being pregnant by the man I loved, I also couldn't help feeling anxious. I was so scared that the baby might have Harvey's condition, and there was no scan that could detect it. No one had had any idea that there was anything wrong with Harvey when he was born; it wasn't until his six-week check that the midwife had noticed that there was something wrong with his eyes. All I could try and think about was that Harvey's condition was a one-in-a-million genetic defect. Just because I had one child with it, it didn't mean that I would have another one. I also thought, *Hard as it has been, I have coped with Harvey and I love him to bits and we are so close. If I have another child like him, painful as it would be, I would cope with them too and love them just the same.*

As soon as we got back from the cruise I had to get on with rehearsing the song I was going to perform on Westlife's Christmas show. I had been given a choice of two songs: one was completely unsuitable for my voice and the other was Nat King Cole's 'When I Fall In Love'. I felt it was a little unfair to expect me to pull off a ballad like that, and Nat King Cole's original is so fantastic that it's an almost impossibly good act to follow. *Still*, I thought, *I'll give it a go*. I'd been saying for so long that I wanted a singing career, and this would be a good opportunity to put my money where my mouth was and prove that I could sing. I'd been having regular singing lessons throughout the year and now I had two weeks of intensive lessons. I was still keeping my pregnancy a secret, so when people around me asked if I was okay I said it was just nerves. I was very nervous because it would be the first time I had sung live on stage in front of an audience. I was still suffering such bad morning sickness and frequently throwing up which didn't help.

On the day of the rehearsal I had a shock when I went into the studio. They were playing my song in the background but it didn't sound anything like me. *What the hell have they done to my voice?* I wondered, feeling horrified, *I sound like Minnie Mouse!* I felt like bursting into tears. The studio was packed with sound engineers, directors and producers, and in front of all of them I blurted out, 'That's not how I sing!' I told them that I would sing live at the rehearsal with the orchestra later that day to prove it. Even though it was just a rehearsal it was nerve-racking enough – I had a forty-one piece orchestra backing me, which was quite an experience seeing as I had never sung with one before. But I pulled it off with a performance I was proud of. Hearing what I really sounded like, the sound engineer realised that they must have recorded my voice at the wrong speed. *Great,* I thought to myself, *everyone must have been listening to me and taking the piss thinking what a weird voice I've got!* And when it came to the real thing, I felt I'd done well – I had positive press about my performance, no one slated me, people wrote that actually I could sing. *That seems like a good omen for Eurovision,*

I thought to myself, really pleased with how it had all gone.

* * *

2004 had been quite a year! I'd found the man of my dreams, we were having a baby together and he'd proposed. It looked like 2005 might be even more amazing with the arrival of our son and our wedding, and the icing on the very amazing cake was that it looked as if it might finally be the year that I realised my long-held dream of becoming a singer. I couldn't have been happier. I might have held back a little more had I known what the year would actually bring – a mixture of intense happiness, bitter disappointments and real lows – but as it was I threw myself into giving Pete the best family Christmas I could. It was his first, in fact, as he'd been brought up by Jehovah's Witnesses and they don't celebrate Christmas. I'd even got dressed up as Mother Christmas in a saucy little red and white number and hired a sledge and reindeer on a cold December night to surprise Pete. I think he appreciated the outfit – he wasn't so keen on the reindeer.

Luckily for me, Pete had got the hang of the present

part and showered me with gifts: a set of pink luggage, a pair of beautiful diamond earrings and a sewing machine. The last on the list might not sound like the typical present you'd give to a glamour model but I've always been into sewing and customising my own clothes and it was a very useful present as I needed to alter all Harvey's clothes to fit him. Pete did alright out of me too, and I gave him designer clothes, diamond earrings and treated him to a holiday in the new year. But it wouldn't have mattered what we bought each other – he was the only present I wanted . . .

CHAPTER ELEVEN

NOT JUST ANYBODY

When I got back from our Australian holiday in January 2005 the first thing on my mind was what was happening with my album deal. We were only three months away from the Eurovision TV show and I was starting to feel nervous. While I'd been away I'd been thinking about my career and all the managers I'd worked with. Claire is probably one of the first managers I've trusted and I think she's one of the best managers I've had so far. However, when I asked her to give me an update on the album deal she had some very bad news for me. She told me that Sony had just merged with another company and, because of restructuring, the people who had promised me the album deal were no longer in the position to make it happen.

'Don't worry Katie,' she tried to reassure me. 'You're still doing Eurovision and you're bound to get an album deal off the back of that.' I nodded, trying to contain my bitter disappointment, but inside I was fucking fuming. *Great*, I thought to myself, *here's me thinking for months that I've got this big Sony deal and, what a surprise, I've been let down again.*

I'm not saying it was my management's fault that this had happened, but they kept saying a million per cent that the deal was in the bag. The only reason I had agreed to do Eurovision in the first place was because they had told me I would get the album; I never would have agreed otherwise.

I only showed Pete how disappointed I was; to everyone else I put on a front and pretended I was fine. I was also still pretending not to be pregnant, something that was proving a real strain. Though finally my mum rumbled us as I had used her name to book my hospital appointments and she had opened a letter addressed to her that had arrived at my house when we were away. Although I felt a bit guilty that she had found out this way, it was actually a huge relief that I didn't have to keep up the pretence in front of her any more.

A few weeks after getting back from Australia I flew to LA to do a shoot for *Loaded* with one of my idols from the glamour world, the gorgeous Carmen Electra. I'd wanted to do a shoot with her for ages and I was so pleased with how it went. There I was dressed in nothing but a bra and thong and you've got to give me credit, I was nearly four months pregnant and nobody had a clue, in fact they kept saying how skinny I was. And I couldn't help noticing that my boobs were bigger than Carmen's and my waistline was smaller. But I can't say I felt my best during the shoot. I was conscious that my pregnancy might be starting to show and was having to breathe in all the time, which wasn't comfortable, and I was still suffering from morning sickness. But even with those problems it did feel good to be back doing the glamour – I had missed it and needed that boost you get when you know you've done something well. But when I returned home I had the opposite feeling . . .

* * *

'I've got a couple of great songs for you to choose from, Katie,' Nicky Graham, the music producer I was working with for the BBC show *Making Your Mind Up* said to me enthusiastically as we sat in the recording studio.

'Brilliant' I replied, praying that I would like them, remembering only too well from my experience of performing on the Westlife Christmas show what it was like to sing a song that I wasn't entirely happy with. Earlier I had asked him in my 'pretty please' voice to allow me to sing a ballad, but he had refused point blank, saying that ballads never did well at Eurovision – it had to be upbeat pop. The first track he played me was a shocker. To me it sounded like something the Cheeky Girls would perform, and alright, that kind of thing sells, but I didn't want to be seen dead performing a cheesy song. I wanted to make a career out of singing, not be seen as a one-hit-wonder novelty act.

As soon as the track finished I shook my head and said, 'No way am I singing that, it's just not me.'

'I'm sure you'll like this next one Katie,' Nicky and Deni told me.

He couldn't have been more wrong. I hated it. The only thing to be said in favour of 'Not Just Anybody' was that I hated it ever so slightly less than I had hated the first one.

'Yeah, that sounds fine,' I lied. I really didn't want to hurt his feelings or his wife Deni's, as she had written it. 'But it's way too high for me at the moment.'

'Not a problem,' Deni told me. 'We'll take it down for you.' Deni is very good with me in the studio and does get the best out of my voice.

I started to have a very bad feeling about Eurovision. This song was going to do me no favours at all. Why hadn't I gone with my gut instinct and said no to doing Eurovision? I had let my excitement at the prospect of getting an album deal override my better judgment and now it looked like I was going to pay for my mistake. I've heard some of Nicky and Deni's other songs which I love and only wish it could have been one of them.

As soon as I got out of the studio I was on the phone to Claire. 'Claire, I've got a problem: I hate the song, it's not me at all. It's not my kind of thing, there's no way I would ever go out and buy a song like that.'

She tried to calm me down by telling me that the song was 'very Eurovision'. 'Don't worry, it will be fine Kate.'

'Okay,' I replied, 'but this had better work out.'

I tried to stay calm and tell myself that it would turn out for the best. I thought *yes, the song did sound very 'Eurovision'* and that had to be a good thing didn't it? All I wanted to do was to get my record deal. I had been told that I would win the TV programme if I gave a good performance, *So*, I thought to myself, *it doesn't really matter what song I do* – but I had a horrible feeling that it would matter.

It was a month till the TV show and I had a lot of work to do. First I had to get my head round the song, but even though they took it lower for me, I still hated it. I just wasn't comfortable performing it and I couldn't put my emotions and feelings into it. People will say that there are many singers who have to sing songs they don't like but they do it because they know it sells. But that argument doesn't work for me. I'm already successful, I've already made it as a model, and I want to sing what I like. I don't want a music career to make money, I want one because I love singing and I want to sing something that I can have fun with and enjoy, although it's still nice to earn as you can never have enough money! But when it came to performing 'Not Just Anybody' fun was the furthest thing from my mind. It was made harder because I was being filmed for my next series of documentaries and I hated rehearsing my song with the camera rolling as it was all new to me. If I felt like this with one camera on me, how the hell was I going to feel singing live in front of seven million people? Scared shitless, no doubt. I couldn't bear to think about it.

Along with learning the song I also had a dance routine to remember. Now, I can't dance to save my life. There's a bit of rhythm there, and obviously when I've had a few drinks, like anybody, I think I'm the best dancer going, but the reality is I'm crap. And I was feeling extra crap as I was pregnant and didn't want anyone to know. On top of my morning sickness, which seemed was never going to go, I was now also feeling sick with nerves. The only thing I seemed to be able to keep down was soup. I started to fantasise about running away. Then I'd try to be strong and pull myself together; I had said I would do Eurovision and do it I would. But I was having a miserable time. I hated going to the dance studio and being surrounded by so many skinny dancers when I felt so fat and frumpy. I'd wear baggy sweatshirts to hide my bump and tight leggings to distract attention away from my belly – luckily my legs still looked slim as I hadn't put any weight on them. I even felt awkward singing the song in front of my dancers, as I hated the way I sounded.

By now news of the TV show and the line-up was in the press and the papers were hot with speculation about who would win. The contestants had been announced: up against me – as Katie Price, not Jordan – there would be Javine, Andy Scott Lee, Gina G and Tricolore. There was much talk about Javine and Gina G and how seriously they took the programme and how much they wanted to win. And I got a gut feeling – what if I don't win? Obviously there were no guarantees. So long as I gave a good performance I could be the UK's Eurovision singer. Though of course if I ballsed the song up I wouldn't.

I was starting to feel more and more anxious – I had only sung live once before and the thought of it was terrifying. I tried to focus on getting the song right and learning the dance routine but I kept forgetting the moves as my nerves were so bad. When the BBC said they wanted to come and film me rehearsing the song I panicked, but I managed to pull off a good performance and the producers seemed really impressed, telling me that I was going to be excellent on the night. That made me feel a little more optimistic.

But the stress of keeping my pregnancy under wraps was really getting to me. I thought, *I've got to tell Claire the truth*; keeping it a secret from her was making me feel ill. I wasn't brave enough to tell her face to face so I took the cowardly route and texted her. 'I'm really sorry,' I told her, 'and I don't know how you're going to take this, but I'm five months pregnant.'

Phew, I'd done it. Immediately she called me back and told me everything would be alright, and that she had suspected for some time that I was pregnant. The thing that shocked her was how far gone I was.

And I said, 'Admit it, Claire, if you'd known that I was going to get pregnant would you have put me forward for Eurovision?'

And she said no, exactly as I knew she would.

'You think like everyone else,' I said. 'Just because I'm pregnant, you think I can't do anything. But I can, and I'm going to prove it. I am going to do Eurovision and being pregnant isn't going to stop me.'

I told her that if anything my being pregnant would be to my advantage, as when I got through to the final I would be the one they'd all remember as the singer who was so heavily pregnant on stage! And people would admire me for doing it. When you're singing in Eurovision you're representing your country and it doesn't matter what you look like – skinny, fat, pregnant or not. Unfortunately I was about to find out that when it came to Eurovision pregnancy was a big no-no . . .

'Are you sure you still want to wear the pink catsuit?' Claire asked me as we ended our conversation.

'Yes,' I said confidently, 'I know I can hide my bump.'

We'd already had a bit of a tussle over the outfit. My management had wanted me to enter the contest as Katie Price and wanted me to dress as people would expect Katie to dress. *Bollocks to that*, I thought; I wanted to be outrageous and glamorous, to make an impact. They could call me Katie Price but I was going to be Jordan. And to do that I needed my all-time favourite outfit – a rubber catsuit. I had one made for me in shocking pink and decided to wear a diamanté belt which I hoped would disguise my bump.

Time seemed to be on fast forward, and before I knew it there was just a week before the live show and I had to promote the song in the press, on TV and on radio. It was a hectic schedule and I felt really under pressure. My nerves were so bad: from the moment I woke up all I could think about was Eurovision – how was I going to sing on stage, live, in front of seven million people? And the fact it was for a contest and I've never taken part in one of these before, made it even more stressful. I've never felt so stressed and nervous in my life, not ever. And it was incredibly stressful keeping my pregnancy a secret.

So far I had managed to get away with it, but I knew it wouldn't be long before my secret was out. No one sussed me for one of my TV appearances on Channel 4's *The Friday Night Project*. Luckily for me the boho look was in and I wore a loose dress. But I felt uncomfortable and I'm sure people watching the show thought, God, she's put on weight! I also had to do a photo shoot for *OK!* with the other contestants and all I wanted to do was be sexy and flirty, the way I liked to be in front of the camera, but because of my condition I couldn't so I had to wear a poncho. As we all sat together for a picture I said jokingly, 'This shoot feels really weird for me as I'm actually covered up for once!' And Javine made a really snide comment along the lines of how usually I used my body to sell myself. I was so tempted to say, 'Fuck off, I'm pregnant!' But I bit my lip and bided my time.

On Friday 25 February I had to perform my song on GMTV. Yet again I had to wear a baggy top, but I teamed it up with a little skirt and leg warmers and I tried to breathe in as best I could because I knew my belly was starting to show. I felt very nervous as it was live TV, but luckily I didn't have to sing live, so that was a relief. Pete had told me that if I thought I was in danger of forgetting the words I should hold the mic really close to my mouth. Fortunately I remembered them that time and I even managed my dance routine. It was on the sofa that things got difficult. Before the live interview Claire had gone through the questions I was going to be asked, which was good because my other managers hadn't done this for me. One of them leapt out at her – was I going to have more children? Immediately Claire told the production team that there was no way they could ask me that. So when I sat down for my interview with Ben Shepherd and Jenni Falconer I was expecting a nice little chat about my singing. But just as I was getting into the swing of the interview Jenni said, 'We've had a lot of calls today, Katie, from people wanting to know if you're pregnant. Are you?' It felt like the world flashed past me and straight away I said indignantly, 'No I'm not! Thanks a lot everyone, do I look fat then?'

Shit, I thought, *how am I going to get out of this one?* As soon as I was back in the dressing room I said to Claire, 'You're going to have to write a press release now, we can't wait any longer. I've just lied on national TV and I don't want to be known as a liar. And you're going to have to let the BBC know.' Claire really didn't want to reveal that I was pregnant but I insisted. In the car, as we drove to the *Top of the Pops* studio, we agonised over what to say.

'Look,' I told her, 'I've been working my arse off, rehearsing this song and promoting it and surely you can see now that just because I'm pregnant it doesn't mean I can't do things. I'm not letting it stop me.' And even though Claire was obviously worried that people would be negative about my pregnancy, she gave in and issued the press release.

But as I sat back in the car and tried to breathe deeply and relax, I thought, *I bet now that everyone knows I'm pregnant, I won't win.* But then I thought, *No, I'm not going to pull out, I'm still going to do it. I'm going to be strong.* So when we arrived at the studio Claire told the BBC producers my news, though she didn't mention quite how far gone I was.

'Congratulations!' they said.

I told them, 'Look, I don't want my being pregnant to make a difference.' But I had a nagging feeling that it would.

Sure enough, a few days before the show the BBC

producers were on the phone to Claire, worrying that me being pregnant would be a problem. They wanted to know if I would be alright to fly to Kiev in May and whether I would need special hotel accommodation.

'For God's sake,' I told Claire, frustrated, 'I'm only pregnant, I'm not ill!'

The odds at the bookies' were in my favour, which didn't please everyone. Javine kept having a pop at me in the press, who loved to build the pair of us up as rivals even though there were three other contestants. Then I found out what Gina G thought of me when she performed at GAY. According to a member of the production team from the BBC show who was there, Gina G brought a drag queen on stage with her, wearing balloons for breasts. Gina G said something along the lines of, 'We won't be having Jordan here tonight, will we?' and then proceeded to pop the balloons, taking the piss out of me in a very public way.

Well no one does that and gets away with it! I had my revenge on *Blue Peter*, where all the contestants were appearing in a game show. I had made sure I was sitting on the level above Javine and Gina G. I

After a few cocktails, Pete and I headed back to the hammock to sit under the stars.

Relaxing between filming
and the pictures.

My stylist, Kerri-Ann and Gary put the finishing touches to another outfit.

Enjoying a kiss with my lovely new husband.

Setting sail on a day trip. I wanted to protect my hair so I chose a glamorous swimming cap!

My team of stylists, make-up artists and hairdressers know how to create the perfect Jordan look, time and time again.

Letting my hair down with Pete and Harvey at our water bungalow.

Getting ready
for a night out
in the Maldives.

Feeling all relaxed –
mum and I went for
some lovely spa
treatments while
we were away.

Raising a glass
to married life.

Relaxing in the
sun and topping
up that tan.

Pete and I at the end of our blissful honeymoon.

didn't want to sit next to them because I knew I'd end up having a go at them for what they'd been saying about me. But as we sat there waiting for the programme to go on air I was feeling more and more wound up and I wanted to say to Gina G, 'Why the hell are you taking the piss out of me?'

We were at the rehearsal stage, but we were all miked up so whatever we said could be heard by everyone. *Keep calm*, I told myself, but before I knew it the angry gremlin in my head took control and I blurted out, 'Gina, I've got something to ask you. Why were you taking the piss out of me at GAY? If you've got something to say to me then say it to my face. I've never taken the piss out of you.'

'Look,' she hissed, clearly uncomfortable with the fact that everyone could hear our conversation, 'can we talk about this later?'

'No,' I replied. 'We'll do it now, in front of everyone. You probably thought your little stunt slating me would get you some publicity – well you didn't get very far, did you, because it didn't even make the papers. So why don't you just get a life and grow up.'

It felt so good to get that off my chest. I was all fired

up and ready to start on Javine for all her snide comments about why was I entering Eurovision when I wasn't even a singer. She didn't even dare look at me. Then I said to everyone sitting there, 'I won't have anyone taking the piss out of me.' From that moment all the other contestants must have thought, 'Shit, she's feisty, don't say anything to upset her!' A minute later the *Blue Peter* signature tune started up and we were live on air. I had cut it fine to have my say!

When I came off the show and walked into my dressing room Claire said, 'Oh my God, how embarrassing, but good on you, you showed her.' And I was glad I had, but I could have done without the added tension of Javine and Gina G criticising me. Then I thought, *Bollocks to you, I'm more successful than the pair of you anyway. At the end of the day you need Eurovision and I don't.* As for the other contestants, they were lovely – I'm very good friends with Andy Scott Lee and his girlfriend, Michelle Heaton. I think he's a really good singer and I loved his ballad. And Tricolore were nice guys too. It's always the girls who have a problem with me . . .

I might have come across as feisty, but inside I felt

sick in the gut with nerves. And while I was relieved that people knew I was pregnant and so I didn't have to keep up the pretence any longer, I also felt disappointed because I knew that I wouldn't win the show now. And I knew I would end up getting slated in the press. I could just imagine what they'd write – look, she couldn't even get Eurovision . . . Pete was a great source of comfort and reassurance to me during this time, and every time I told him how I felt he did his best to cheer me up and kept saying, 'Just go out there and enjoy it. Own that stage and go for it.'

'It's easy for you to say, Pete,' I told him gloomily. 'You're used to being on stage but I'm not, and I've got the added pressure of being pregnant, plus knowing that however well I do I'm not going to get through.'

Finally the much-anticipated and dreaded day arrived – Saturday 5 March. I was scared shitless. Usually I'll have a bowl of Weetabix for breakfast, but that day I couldn't manage a thing. Half of me wanted to get the whole thing over and done with as soon as possible, and the other half didn't want eight o'clock at night ever to arrive. By the afternoon I was at the

TV studios for rehearsals. It felt so strange singing live on stage and I thought my voice sounded really loud on the mic, but actually I did okay. *See*, I told myself, *you can do this.*

But as I got ready for the show, having my hair blow-dried and styled and make-up put on, I kept thinking I was going to have a panic attack. I'd first had one when I was a teenager. I was swimming and suddenly I felt as if I was dreaming; I tried to lift my head out of the water and call for help but I felt as if my body had been turned to jelly. It was as if I was being dragged under the water and I was powerless to do anything about it. I felt as if I was drowning – I think I might even have blacked out – and had to be rescued by the life-guard. I've no idea why I had a panic attack in the water, because up till then I'd always been a strong swimmer – after that I really lost my confidence and I don't like to be out of my depth in water. Since then I've had more panic attacks – usually I get them when I'm in crowds. It's a feeling you never forget because once you've had one it always feels like another is just around the corner, and every now and then they tap you on the shoulder just to remind you what they're like . . . *Don't have one now*, I told myself, *you've got to go on stage and sing live.* But I was really feeling the pressure. Just before I'd had my first panic attack all those years ago I'd had the most horrible sensation that my tongue had disappeared, and I was getting that feeling now. I thought, *If I eat or drink anything now I'll get that sensation and it will bring on a full attack.* I tried as hard as I could to block out the feeling and concentrate on going through the song with Deni. We went over it again and again; even when the show had started and the other acts were on I kept going through it. She must never have met someone who was so nervous before, and I kept saying, 'I can't do this!'

'Yes you can,' she replied repeatedly.

I have never been so nervous in my life. The whole experience of waiting to go on stage was like a form of torture. I didn't want to go ahead with my performance; I wanted to pull out. But I forced myself not to give in, determined to prove that I could do it. Even in the seconds before I went on stage I had the song playing in my earpiece – I didn't want to hear the audience clapping, fearing it would put me off. I was humming along to the track and shaking with nerves. Then came the announcement I'd been dreading: 'Here's Katie Price singing "Not Just Anybody"!'

I took a deep breath, walked on stage and got into position on the couch, surrounded by my dancers. Then I gasped in horror as I saw the sea of faces confronting me in the audience. I looked for Pete and my family, knowing that my mum had made a banner to show their support, but even when I saw them it didn't make me feel any better. As I lay down I said to myself, *This is live on TV; don't balls it up.* Then the first notes of my song started. This was it, the moment of truth. I was so nervous that my voice had tightened up and at first I thought I wasn't even going to be able to get a note out. *Oh my God*, I thought, *I can't do this, I'm really out of tune.* But after the first chorus I recovered and got into my stride. I have never watched my performance played back so I'm only going on what I can remember, but I think after that first hiccup where I was slightly out of tune I actually did okay, though I know I forgot the dance routine, but it didn't seem to matter. And then it was over. My first time ever singing live and what a baptism by fire it had been – in front of an audience, being filmed on TV in front of seven million viewers. Sometimes I don't take the easy route . . .

Thank Christ for that! I thought as I walked off stage. I felt as if I had run a marathon, and was physically shaking, but my ordeal wasn't over – I still had an hour to wait for the results. Back in my dressing room I was met by Pete, my mum, Paul, my sister Sophie, Claire and Nicola – they cheered as I walked in, and everyone rushed over to give me a hug and congratulate me, telling me how well I'd done.

'Tell the truth,' I said. 'How did I do?'

'You did great,' Pete replied. 'You were a bit off key at the beginning of the song but then you got better and you did a really good performance.'

'I'm so proud of you,' my mum said as she hugged me, with tears in her eyes.

I was feeling so physically and emotionally exhausted that all I wanted to do was take off the catsuit, pull on a tracksuit and curl up in a ball. But I couldn't. I was certain that I hadn't won, but even so I put on the long pink dress I'd had made, just in case I did.

'Why didn't you wear that?' Pete asked me. 'You

look so much more classy. I don't know what you were thinking wearing the catsuit.'

'Thanks a lot for that vote of confidence!' I replied.

I really don't think my choice of outfit would have made any difference to how I did, and even with Pete's comment I was still glad I wore my catsuit. It was my little rebellion. I had wanted to show that even though I was pregnant I could still look good and it was my way of saying, *Yes, you can call me Katie Price, but I want to look like Jordan.*

That hour before the results came out must have been the longest hour of my life. It was an agonising wait, and after I was changed I had to go into the green room with everyone else. As soon as they started getting the results in and announcing them it was obvious that the contest was between Javine and me. She was sitting opposite me, and every time she won an area she was openly chuffed and I thought, *Get over yourself, I bet it's fixed anyway!* I hated sitting there with the cameras catching my every expression and with Javine's gleeful face in front of me. *Why am I letting myself be tortured like this?* I thought bitterly. *And why on earth am I letting people do this to me?* I wanted to leave but I knew that would look like I was a bad loser, so I thought, *No, just sit here, smile, get it over with; at least you're not last.*

Finally Javine was announced as the winner, by the smallest of margins – half a per cent. She came marching over to me and shook my hand – I thought, *You bitch, why shake my hand and no one else's?* – as if the whole thing had been a contest between just the two of us.

Inside I was burning with anger and humiliation. Claire obviously felt bad because she cried after the programme, but I was too angry to cry. I think she was so upset because she had convinced me that I was going to win and have a record deal and none of it came off. I had nothing. In fact, I felt as if I was in a worse position than before regarding my music. I felt that my credibility had been damaged. I told Claire that even if I had won the competition I would have pulled out of the final because I wouldn't have wanted the stress of performing when I would have been eight months pregnant. But I only said that because I was so angry. I would have gone to Kiev.

With a voice shaking with anger and unshed tears I asked her what would happen now with my record deal. Yet again she brought up Sony's restructuring situation. 'But you will get a deal, Katie,' she said. I shrugged, not trusting myself to say anything more.

To this day, if I have any regrets in my life it's that I took part in Eurovision. It even beats any regrets I have about some of the men I've got involved with, because at least you can learn from your mistakes with them. But there was nothing to learn from my Eurovision experience. I felt I had made a total tit of myself, singing a song that I hated and which didn't showcase my singing ability at all. I had been thrown in at the deep end – this was only the second time I had sung live on stage, my hormones were all over the place and I felt ill because of my pregnancy. It was the worst thing I had ever done.

Of course the following day, as I predicted they would, the press slated me for my performance and said that Javine had beaten Jordan. Javine was quoted as saying that she was really pleased because she thought I was going to win, and I thought, *Why doesn't it say that she beat everyone? Why do they have to single me out?* I thought, *I'm not going to stick around any more to read this.* I had to get away. That day I told Pete I was going to book us a flight to Australia and I went ahead and did it. That was the first time I have ever walked away from anything. Usually I can face the music – when horrible stories appear about me in the press it doesn't bother me because I know the truth and usually what's been written is all bullshit. But this time I knew I was in a no-win situation. I felt such bitter disappointment. It felt like a real set-back to my dreams of becoming a singer and I prayed that in the future I would be able to do a ballad and showcase my voice.

We were only supposed to stay in Australia for a couple of weeks, but we ended up staying nearly four. I tried my hardest to relax in the Australian sunshine with Pete and Harvey and to forget that I had ever taken part in Eurovision. I needed the time to clear my head and think about what I wanted to do. I even thought about leaving my management. They had stopped me doing my glamour modelling and promised me the record deal but I had nothing to show for their promises. I thought if I stayed away for a while that would give Claire a chance to sort out a record deal. But when I came back she hadn't made any progress on advancing my singing career. I knew that it wasn't a good idea to make big decisions when pregnant, so I decided to bide my time. When we returned and I met up with Claire I said, 'Never, ever promise me anything again a million per cent unless you can definitely back it up.'

After much agonising I signed a new contract with Claire, giving her until February 2006 to get me a record deal. But she put in a clause saying that I had to have forty singing lessons by that time, and if I didn't she wouldn't have to get the deal by then. It made me so cross. It was as if they were saying I had to show my commitment to singing by having these lessons. But I don't need lessons to prove my commitment. I can throw money at having them but that's not going to get me a deal. It's not like I'm an unknown. All I want to do is get a single out with me singing a song that I love – to prove to people that I can sing, that I just need to do it my way . . .

CHAPTER TWELVE

GREAT
EXPECTATIONS

As soon as I found out I was pregnant I had just assumed I would have the baby at the same Brighton NHS hospital I'd had Harvey. I'd never been into the idea of having the baby at a private hospital. *What's the point?* I thought, *Harvey and I were looked after really well by the midwives and doctors at my local hospital.* If I went private I'd just be spending loads of cash on a posh room. But then Pete and I were told about these amazing 3-D scans you can have of your baby and they're only available if you go private. The Portland in London is one of the few places that does them – however, you can't just book in for scans; we would have to have the baby there too. 'Perhaps we could be sneaky,' I said to Pete. 'You know, pretend we're going to have the baby there, but just have the scans and have the baby in Brighton.'

But as soon as I had the scan and met the obstetrician, Dr Gibb, and he explained the set-up at the Portland and the kind of care I'd receive, I thought, *Hang on, I really like it here and I really like the doctor.* I looked at Pete and could tell he was thinking along the same lines as me. When Dr Gibb left the room to get something, I said to Pete, 'I want to have our baby here,' and he agreed. Yes, it would be expensive, but we could afford it.

At eighteen weeks pregnant I was able to have the first 3-D scan, but if we were expecting to see our baby's face we were in for disappointment, as he kept his hand firmly clamped over his face or turned away shyly. I don't quite know what I'd been expecting from the 3-D scan but to me the colourful image of the baby moving around looked a bit like a lava lamp! I was still glad we'd made the decision to have the baby at the Portland, though – whenever I felt like seeing the baby I could just phone up and pop in for a scan, something that would have been impossible on the NHS. Mind you, I wasn't always that pleased with what I saw – on one scan I finally got to see the baby's face and I thought his nose looked really big!

At my twenty-week scan the doctor asked if we wanted to know whether we were having a boy or a girl. I had always said that I wanted a boy who didn't have Harvey's condition – even though I knew I would have coped if he had – because I liked the idea of Harvey having a brother to look out for him. I know all my family and friends thought I wanted a girl I could dress up in pink to my heart's content, and maybe I was just the tiniest bit disappointed when I said that I did want to know the sex and I found out I was having a boy. But it was a feeling that didn't last more than a few minutes. All I wanted was for my baby to be healthy and happy; it didn't matter if I was having a boy or girl. But afterwards I thought *Oh, why did I find out and not keep it as a surprise?* Next time I'm not going to find out what I'm having . . . and then at least Pete and I might avoid having some of the terrible arguments we went on to have about the baby's name . . .

Before we knew whether we were having a boy or a girl, we both decided that if we had a boy we would call him Daniel, which is a name I've always liked, and of course it's my brother's name and one of Pete's brothers is called Daniel. We hadn't thought of any girls' names. But then Pete went over to Cyprus for a weekend without me to visit his parents, and when he returned he delivered this bombshell: 'If the baby's a boy we must call him Savva and if it's a girl we must call her Thea.'

It was a shock to hear Pete talking like this, and when I challenged him he replied that he'd forgotten that it's a Greek tradition that you call your firstborn son after your father and your firstborn daughter after your mother.

'Hang on a minute,' I replied. 'It's my child as well, and I've got a say in the naming. It might be your tradition but it's not mine, and you know I really like your dad and respect him, but I just don't like the name Savva. It's not right for our son.' I felt very upset and emotional – I would have felt upset even if I hadn't been pregnant to hear Pete talking like this, but as I was it made it even worse.

'I'm sorry Kate, we're going to have to call him Savva for my parents; it will break their hearts if we don't,' Pete replied.

I couldn't believe that the man I loved was being so unreasonable. We had both agreed on the name Daniel – he couldn't just change his mind like that, it wasn't fair and I wasn't going to sit back and let my son be called something I didn't like. I quite liked the name Thea and I agreed that if we had a daughter we should call her Thea Sofia – the Sofia after my sister Sophie – even though I thought it a little strange as one of Pete's brothers already had a daughter called Thea. *Surely Pete's parents can't expect all their children to use their names?* I thought to myself.

But I had a real problem with the name Savva.

'Pete, I really don't want to call our son Savva,' I said again.

By now we were both getting angry and upset and Pete wouldn't budge an inch. 'Why can't we call him Daniel and have Savva as his middle name?' I demanded.

'No!' he shouted. 'He's our first son, he has to be called Savva.'

'Look!' I screamed back, having lost my rag. 'I don't fucking like the name Savva!'

Pete was furious and thought that I was being disrespectful towards his dad and that I had a problem with him.

'I've got nothing against your dad. I just don't want to call my son Savva!'

It was an argument that wouldn't go away and Pete seemed unable to compromise. Even when I suggested we forget the names Daniel and Savva and come up with another one, Pete stuck to his guns. It had to be Savva.

'It's Greek for the name Stephen,' he told me, as if that would make me feel better about it.

'Well, I don't like Stephen either!' I replied.

I even offered to phone up his dad and explain that Pete and I had already agreed to call our son Daniel, but no, Pete said he couldn't go against tradition and he couldn't upset his parents. I couldn't imagine feeling like this about my parents; they would never expect me to give my son a particular name. And I'm also sure that if I had been able to explain my feelings to Pete's parents they would have understood my point of view.

So when we found out our child's sex at the twenty-week scan, as well as being happy that I was having a boy, straight away I also thought, *Well, I'm not calling him Savva!* Pete was over the moon at the news he was having a son. But I couldn't help feeling angry that he thought he could call his son what he wanted and disregard my feelings. As my mum and sister were at the scan with us, I thought I'd better not bring up the name thing.

But as we all drove home my mum asked if we'd thought about names. Pete told her how he wanted to call our son Savva and the reasons why, and I knew my mum would understand exactly how I felt. She obviously didn't want to get involved and I really didn't want to have an argument in front of her and my sister, but before I could stop myself I had burst out, 'I don't want that name!' and Pete and me were back rowing. I really could have done without the stress. It took another two months for us to finally agree that we would have Savva as a middle name.

'Couldn't we choose a name which shows our son is a mini-you?' I suggested to Pete. And we came up with PJ – Peter and Jordan – but our family and friends were negative about it. And then we thought of Junior. At last, a name we both liked. To me it was also special because Junior had been the name of my grandad's brother and Harvey is named after my grandad. I named my new horse Thea, after his mum.

By the end of May, at seven months pregnant, I was feeling enormous and, highly unusual for me, my sex drive was at an all-time low. I felt so unattractive and uncomfortable that I really didn't want to make love. I looked at Pete and still found him incredibly sexy, but looking was as far as it went – any bedroom action would have to wait until I was back to my old shape. Feeling slightly anxious, because I'd never lost my libido before, I talked to two of my close friends who were also pregnant and to my relief I found I wasn't the only one – they felt exactly the same. In fact one of them hadn't had sex from the moment she discovered she was pregnant, so Pete should count himself lucky, because it was only in the latter part of my pregnancy that my libido went on strike and even then he still got regular BJs . . .

But the fact that we weren't making love did upset Pete, and he confessed that he was worried that I was going off him. 'Don't be daft!' I told him, keen to reassure him. 'It's not you, it's me! I feel really fat and ugly. I still fancy you like mad!' It took a while to convince him. He even brought up the ill-fated affair I'd had with Gareth Gates when I was five months pregnant with Harvey. And my desperate attempts to get affection from Dane Bowers by having sex with him, also when I was pregnant.

'That was different,' I told him. 'I was single at the time, and I was desperate for reassurance and love.' Sex was the only way I could get any affection from Dane. At the time I had still been emotionally attached to him, even though he had left me, and I felt very vulnerable when I was pregnant. I could see that Pete was beginning to understand where I was coming from and I added, 'Also, I didn't have sex with them when I was heavily pregnant; it was really early on when I hardly showed.' What I didn't say was that I had a strong sex drive throughout my first pregnancy, as I knew that being a man he'd find it hard to understand why I didn't have one now. But I knew that all pregnancies are different.

Possibly if I had been less sure of Pete I might have forced myself to make love with him, terrified that he would be unfaithful if I didn't. But I totally trust him (well 99.9 per cent!) and I'm so comfortable with him that I knew he wasn't going to leave me if I didn't have sex with him. I was so confident that my sex drive would return after I'd had the baby that I told him, 'If you're still not getting any sex from me after I've had the baby, then I give you my permission to go off and find sex from someone else.' But even as I said it I thought, *It had better bloody come back, because if Pete ever was unfaithful it would break my heart!*

For my twenty-seventh birthday in May, Pete planned a wonderful surprise trip. Unfortunately our romantic weekend didn't get off to the greatest start. We asked my mum if she would have Harvey for the weekend, as it was our last chance to be on our own before we had the baby. She's the only person we can leave Harvey with because she's the only one apart from me who can give him his medication and knows how to look after him. But she was annoyed because she felt we were taking her for granted and thought we'd just assumed that she would have him, so we ended up having a row. In the end she agreed, but she arrived late at our house (when it comes to punctuality she's even worse than me!) and it was touch and go whether we would make our flight. The row continued, with her saying it was irresponsible for me to fly in this stage of my pregnancy, even though I had a doctor's letter saying it was safe. Pete was so stressed out by the arguments that at one point he said perhaps we shouldn't go because he didn't want to cause trouble between my mum and me. But in the end we all calmed down and Pete and I made our flight. I was over the moon when we arrived at the airport and discovered that we were going to Venice.

I could hardly believe my eyes when we arrived and took a water taxi to the hotel. Geography was never my strongest point, and I hadn't realised that Venice is surrounded by water and has canals instead of roads! Pete had booked a wonderful hotel overlooking one of the canals and it was beautiful, very luxurious and very old-fashioned. I felt a bit like I was in a movie. We had the most romantic time together – we were rowed round the city in gondolas, taking in the sights; we chilled out, shopped, chatted, cuddled, played Scrabble. Some people may call us sad, but how else do you pass the time when you're heavily pregnant? It was lovely spending this time together but it was also strange, and each morning I'd wake up with a start, thinking that I had to give Harvey his medicine – happy as I was, I really missed my son. We knew the Eurovision Song Contest was on, but we deliberately didn't watch it and went out for dinner instead. By then I'd managed to let go of some of the anger and humiliation I'd felt over what had happened, but I still bitterly regretted taking part and think I always will. When I found that Javine had come third from bottom I felt embarrassed for her. She had been so cocky and obviously expected to do well.

Earlier that month I'd finally got what I thought of Javine off my chest. Pete and I had presented one of the prizes at the Soap Awards – it was the night when I wore my outrageously revealing little black dress. *Just because I'm pregnant*, I thought to myself, *it doesn't mean I have to dress in a boring way*. I felt like being Jordan again and was tired of my manager Claire trying to keep Katie Price so nice and goodie-two-shoes, and I wanted to prove to her what made the papers. That dress did it, of course. I was enjoying being out and socialising with my friends, but suddenly I caught sight of Javine and my hackles were raised. I hadn't forgiven her for her comments about me in the press. She then walked up to me and said, 'Hiya Jordan, how are you?' nice as pie, as if she'd never had a bad word to say about me. That did it!

'I'm fine thanks,' I replied. 'But don't come up to me being two-faced, just fuck off!' Everyone around us stopped talking and turned to look at us, but I didn't care.

Pete tried to calm me down, saying, 'Forget it, Kate,' but I couldn't let it go.

'If you think you can come up and pretend to be nice when you've been slating me, well you can fuck off!'

'What do you mean?' she demanded. 'I haven't been slating you.'

'Yes you have,' I shouted back. 'I'm not stupid! But just remember one thing: yes, we both entered Eurovision, but you're the singer, I'm not, and I still came second. I'm successful without Eurovision and at the end of the day all you'll ever be is a one-hit wonder.'

'You've got a classy bird there!' she exclaimed to Pete.

'Yes, I am classy, just like you, you one-hit wonder!' And for good measure I added, 'Fuck off slag!'

I was so angry. I was holding a glass of water in my hand and I was so tempted to throw it at her, I was just waiting for her to give me a reason to. I know I must have sounded like a common slut, but do you know what? It felt so good to have told her what I thought of her. How dare she be so smug and come up and act as if she had never criticised me? I tried to calm down and decided the best plan would be to leave the party and go on to a club. I knew that my exchange had been witnessed by quite a few of the people there, including my ex-manager. *It isn't just my dress that it is going to make the papers*, I thought to myself, *I bet what I said to Javine does as well . . .* which of course it did.

My group went on to the Embassy, and as we chatted in the VIP area I tried to forget about what had happened earlier. Then I realised that my ex-manager was sitting at a table opposite us, with all his friends who I used to hang out with, which made me feel awkward, and then to cap it all Javine joined them. Later on I had to go to the ladies', which isn't in the

VIP area. The girls in there were really sweet and all wanted to take pictures of me with their phones, but just as I was chatting to them Javine came in and said, 'Jordan, can I talk to you?' I had nothing more to say to her, and I totally ignored her. I thought, *Say what you like about me, I'll be around a lot longer than you will.* And, surprise, surprise, after Eurovision did she have a single out? No. Did she get an album deal? No.

But back to Venice. Instead of brooding on the past Pete and I talked endlessly about the future. We kept discussing our wedding plans then we'd laugh and I'd say, 'Hang on, aren't we forgetting something? We're having a baby first!' Who would have thought that less than two years after we met we'd be having a baby and getting married? It seemed incredible. I told Pete about my experience with a clairvoyant some six years earlier, who, bizarrely, seemed to have predicted some of what was about to happen in my life. I used to go to a hairdresser's in London and they told me they knew someone who predicted futures. All I would have to do is send her a snippet of my hair, along with a list of questions. Thinking it would be a laugh, I did just that. Her reply made fascinating reading – apparently by 2005 I would have two boys, and after a whirlwind romance I would be having a wedding in September. I would be marrying a man who came from abroad and he would have a house on the beach, and when I first met him he'd be wearing cufflinks. When I first received her answers I thought she could be referring to Ralf Schumacher, the German Formula One racing driver I'd had a brief but unconsummated relationship with, because he was foreign, wore cufflinks and probably had several houses on several beaches! But when I met Pete for the first time in Australia he was wearing cufflinks. And at the moment he is building a beach house in Cyprus. So it's all a bit spooky how her prediction came true, because of course I did go on to have a son and we were getting married in September . . .

We both talked about how we wanted to get back into shape after the baby was born. Pete said that he couldn't wait to get fit again; he felt that he was fat. And even though his famous six-pack was now more like a two-pack, as far as I was concerned he was still perfect. I, of course, couldn't wait to have the baby and get my figure back. I was more anxious about how my body would look after I'd had this baby.

When I had Harvey my body snapped back into shape without me having to work out at all or go on any special diets – I'm very lucky, I know! But I had a feeling I might not be so lucky this time round, and I told Pete that I was determined to go to the gym to shift the weight, which would be a first for me. In the meantime we both stuffed our faces on the gorgeous Italian food – the diet could wait.

I also told him how determined I was to get back into modelling once the baby was born. I'd read in a magazine that some glamour girls had written me off, saying that once I'd had two kids I'd be off the scene for good. Well I had news for them – I was coming back! As far as I was concerned I'd done the Katie Price thing for a year – it had worked, I'd been successful – but now I was itching to be Jordan again. I told Claire that I wanted to get back to the glamour modelling and to do it my way and that it would be back to my cheeky middle-finger gestures and hands-down-the-crotch shots. I know what works, I know what sells.

I'd talked about this with Pete over the previous months and he completely supported my decision to return to glamour modelling. In 2004 I was voted cover girl of the decade for *Loaded,* and while I might not win that again I was going to give it my best shot. I also received an award from *FHM* for being in the hundred sexiest girls, but for the first time ever I wasn't in the top ten or even the top twenty – I was forty-one. I know it was just a poll but it did needle me. I was also pissed off because my website had received twenty per cent fewer hits in the last year as I wasn't doing any of my glamour modelling. *Bollocks to that*, I thought, *I'm going to make a comeback. If it works, fantastic, and if it doesn't, so be it. But there's life in the old girl yet and I refuse to give in to the idea that just because you've had children you can't be seen as sexy.* It was great being able to confide in Pete. He seemed to totally understand where I was coming from.

The only downside to an otherwise perfect trip were some of the English tourists we encountered when we were strolling through the narrow streets or taking a gondola ride. They tried to take pictures of us, which enraged me. I'd call out, 'Why are you taking pictures? We're away on holiday just as much as you are. You're rude and you've got no manners!' They hadn't even asked if it was okay; they just went ahead and snapped. But then their rudeness was cancelled out by a charming couple who approached me and congratulated me on my makeover show, *Jordan Gets Even.* They asked me if I was interested in acting and I said, 'No way! It's Pete who wants to act.' The husband turned out to be an extremely successful producer/manager who has worked with stars such as Orlando Bloom and he gave us his card. Something might come of it or nothing, but it's always good to have contacts . . .

Back home I was still doing shoots and interviews and we were still trying to find the perfect venue for our wedding, which was starting to stress me out as it was only five months away! We saw a number of places but none of them were quite right. Finally we found one that looked as if it fitted the bill – a huge stately home in Windsor. I loved it as soon as I set eyes on it; it had the definite wow factor, which was what I wanted. However, it was a National Trust property – we could hire the rooms and they would be closed off to the public, but the grounds would have to be kept open, so there would be nothing to stop people looking in through the windows and taking photographs. I hardly wanted a great load of strangers gawping at me while I made my wedding vows! So that venue was out and the search for somewhere else was on again.

It was stressful and also, when I should have been putting my feet up and taking it easy, I also had to deal with a problem involving one of my employees. Shelly had worked as my stable-girl for the last two years and she'd also done some cleaning for me, but increasingly I wasn't happy with her and decided that I didn't want her in my house again or doing any work for me. Through my solicitors I wrote her a letter informing her that she must never come on to my property again. I knew as soon as she realised she wouldn't be working for me any more that she would go to the papers, and sure enough she did. Luckily my solicitor managed to stop the story. I should be used to people selling stories on me by now, but it always shakes me up and it's not exactly what you want to be dealing with when you're about to have a baby.

I was feeling increasingly anxious about the birth. Some people say that you forget the pain of childbirth once your child is born, but believe me, I had not – the excruciating agony as Harvey came down the birth canal and the hideous ripping sound of my flesh as his head emerged is something that will stay with me for the rest of my life. I was still planning to have a natural delivery again, though this time I was going to have an epidural. However, that also made me feel stressed as I have a complete phobia of needles – yes, yes, I know I've had surgery and should be used to them by now, but I'm not. And I have to inject Harvey with his medication once a day, but just because I can do it doesn't mean I want to. I've had to get used to using needles because I know the medication Harvey is on keeps him alive. I also made the mistake of watching a programme about giving birth and was totally freaked out by the size of the needle they use to administer the epidural. The thought of that going into my spine made me feel sick.

But above all I was anxious to know that my baby was going to be healthy. By now I'd had a number of scans to check on the baby's well-being and we'd been told he looked completely normal, but the anxiety was always with me in the back of my mind. There is no scan that would have picked up Harvey's condition. Until my son was born and was at least six weeks old we wouldn't know if he suffered from the same rare genetic condition as his brother. And yes, I know I would have coped if he had, but I longed for everything to be alright.

The doctors were very reassuring but they can't guarantee that your baby will be okay. Pete also reassured me but he was also feeling the strain too. Like all new fathers, he was worried that he wouldn't be able to cope with the baby. I tried to support him, saying, 'If you can handle Harvey – which you can – you'll cope with our baby.' It was all new territory for him, whereas I already knew what to expect. He was planning to be with me at the birth and I gave him strict instructions to stay by my head. 'Don't go down *there!*' I warned him, concerned that it would put him off me for life! Much as I wanted him in the room with me, I was also worried about him seeing me in that much pain.

Pete is incredibly close to his family, so it was no surprise he wanted his parents to be among the first to see his son. He asked me if his parents could come and stay with us a week before the baby was due. 'Of course they can,' I told him, 'and they must come to the hospital too. My family are all going to be there and once the baby's born you're going to want to show him off to them.' And then I launched into a full-on Katie Price lecture . . .

'But I'm warning you now that after I've had the baby I'll be exhausted, my hormones will be all over the place and I really won't want to be sociable. Your parents are still welcome to stay, I just want to tell you what to expect.'

Pete seemed to take it all on board and promised that his folks wouldn't get in the way – all they wanted to do was help in any way they could. But I knew he wouldn't really get what I meant until after the birth. Inside I was also dealing with some feelings of insecurity. I couldn't help feeling worried that his family might try and take over and I felt intensely possessive of my baby. I suppose when I had Harvey I was on my own – I had to be independent, there was nobody to tell me what to do – and even though my mum and family were very supportive, it was just me and Harvey and the bond between us was incredibly strong right from the start. I wanted to feel that close-ness again. I didn't want anyone to come between me and my newborn son.

'Pete,' I said, 'I'll also tell you what I told my mum. When the baby is born I don't want anyone interfering and telling me what to do. I don't want anyone saying you should do this or you should do that.'

'Understood,' Pete replied.

There ended the lesson. Having got all that off my chest I just needed to have the baby!

Pete and I had decided to hire a maternity nurse to help us take care of our son for the first six weeks. Mainly we took the decision because we still had the wedding to plan and I knew we would be knackered if we didn't get our sleep. I also know that sleep deprivation leads to arguments and I didn't want to be rowing with Pete in the run-up to our wedding! I reasoned that I could afford the extra help. I wanted the nurse to help us get our son into a routine and I hoped that she would be able to take care of the night feeds. During the day I wanted to feed the baby, be close to him and bond with him. And because of Harvey's special needs I wanted to have plenty of energy left to look after him as well so he didn't feel left out.

By the beginning of June I was feeling calmer and the

house was finally ready – the nursery was almost finished, we had bought all the baby equipment we needed and we'd hired a maternity nurse. I was feeling excited about seeing our new son. There was still over a month before the baby was due, and I was looking forward to resting at home for a few weeks. But at one of my check-ups and scans Dr Gibb expressed concern. The familiar and awful feeling of panic gripped me when he told me there was a problem. Immediately I thought there was something wrong with the baby.

'No, no,' he reassured me, seeing the stricken look on my face, 'the baby is fine.' He went on to explain that he was worried about the unusual membrane they had noticed in one of my earlier scans, two centimetres above my cervix. At the time he had just said that it seemed unusual but he hadn't seemed worried. To me the membrane looked like a piece of seaweed attached to the seabed and I thought, *Trust me to have something unusual!* I hadn't worried about it because the doctor hadn't. But now it seemed the membrane was something to worry about.

Dr Gibb went on to say that by now the baby should have turned and his head should have been engaged.

He said that he hadn't wanted to worry me about the membrane, but he had been keeping a close eye on it and it was now a matter of concern to him.

'I don't like it,' he said. 'Watch this.' He turned the baby round, which was quite uncomfortable, and gently pushed the baby's head against the membrane. I could see that the baby couldn't get through it. 'That's why the baby's not turning.' He went on to say that if things didn't change I wouldn't be able to have a natural delivery; I would have to have a Caesarean – and an early one at that.

Even though I had been dreading giving birth naturally again, I had been prepared to go through it – I knew it would be better for my son and for me. I definitely wasn't one of those mothers who was too posh to push and I wouldn't have chosen to have a Caesarean. Now it looked as if I had no choice. The operation itself didn't frighten me as much as the epidural. If I were going to have a natural birth I just might have coped without having one; now I would have to.

Back home in Sussex I tried to get my head round the prospect of having a Caesarean. Secretly I was relieved that the doctor had made the decision for me to have a C-section, so sparing me all those hours of agonising labour. I was sure I'd be able to cope afterwards because I'd had surgery before and thought I knew what it was like to recover from an operation. The one thing I wasn't happy about was the scar. I didn't want it to show but I suspected it would. Still, I reasoned, it would be a small price to pay for having a safe delivery.

Then I started getting very powerful Braxton Hicks contractions, which were quite alarming, as Dr Gibb had said I wouldn't be able to have a natural birth. I called him and he said he was rather worried and that I should come up to London every day to be assessed. He said if the contractions carried on as they were he might well have to do an emergency Caesarean very soon. Well, I really didn't fancy driving up to London every day so I called the local midwife and asked her to come over and check me out. She also thought my Braxton Hicks contractions were very strong and advised me to go and see my doctor. But I still didn't fancy traipsing up to London if Dr Gibb was just going to monitor me and make me go full-term anyway.

'What would you do?' I asked the midwife.

'I would definitely go up to London and see your doctor,' she replied. I realised I ought to go up to London, if the two of them thought so. But typically I left it that night and the following night. By now even I was becoming anxious. I called Dr Gibb and he told me to come up and be prepared to have a Caesarean the following Wednesday. Things were obviously serious. So on Friday 10 June Pete, Harvey and me drove up to London. Thinking I was going into hospital imminently, I had packed my suitcase and Harvey's, with enough clothes and toys to last well over a week. By now Pete's parents had flown over from Cyprus to be with us and they joined us at the Portland for the scan and consultation.

As Dr Gibb scanned me he said, 'That's quite good news. The baby's turned round and his head's engaged.'

'What does that mean?' I asked.

'Well, we don't have to do an emergency Caesarean after all.'

It was not what I wanted to hear. By now I was all geared up mentally to have a Caesarean. I no longer wanted to have a natural birth. After the scan Pete and I sat round the table with Dr Gibb and Pete's parents.

'It seems as if you might be able to go full-term, Katie,' said Dr Gibb, obviously expecting me to be pleased.

'So you can't do the Caesarean on Wednesday then?' I asked.

'Well, there's no need to now and I'm reluctant to perform one this early on. I think we should leave it a few more weeks.'

Well I want him out now! I thought. I felt fat, extremely uncomfortable and I was sick of waddling along and not being able to do anything. Worst of all, I couldn't pick up Harvey any more and it was even hard giving him a cuddle because of my enormous bump. And the thought of four more weeks of feeling like this was almost unbearable.

'I'm telling you now, Donald, the baby always moves around,' I said.

'His head's engaged now, Katie,' he replied.

Then Pete's dad chipped in. 'You should listen to the doctor. It would be better to go full-term, let him grow inside you a little bit longer.'

I know Pete's dad meant well and he was only thinking of the baby, but I really didn't need anyone putting their oar in. I was feeling very strung out emotionally, my hormones were making me feel all over the place and I was physically exhausted as I hadn't been sleeping properly. *It's my body and it's my child*, I felt like shouting, *I'll decide what I want to do!* I wanted Pete's parents to leave the room so I could talk to the doctor on my own with Pete and explain how I felt. But I couldn't say anything because he was Pete's dad and I didn't want to upset him. I was very pissed off and upset, which Pete instantly sensed because he kept asking me if I was alright.

'I'm fine,' I replied, knowing that I wasn't at all. I knew his dad meant well but it really wasn't his place to say anything. Yes, it was Pete's baby as well, but it was my body; I was the one who was carrying the baby. I knew his parents weren't in favour of Caesareans, and would want me to have the baby naturally, but I wanted to say to Pete, *I know they're your parents, but this is my choice, and I'm not going to have a natural birth just to please other people.*

As we left the hospital I was in a foul mood. I called my mum to update her on what the doctor had said and I wanted to burst out crying because I felt so angry and frustrated. I was driving us all back to the hotel, where we were going to spend the weekend because Dr Gibb wanted to keep an eye on me, and I wanted to tell everyone to get out of my car and leave me alone. I needed some time to clear my head and calm down.

That night we were all in the hotel suite and I felt the baby move and my belly change shape. I was certain his head wasn't engaged any more. I grabbed Pete's hand and put it on my bump. 'I'm telling you now, Pete, he's moved again,' and inside I was thinking, *I really hope he has.* The following day as I drove back on my own to see Dr Gibb, I was thinking, *Please have turned round because I can't take another four weeks of feeling so uncomfortable and huge.* I know a lot of people might read this and think how selfish, you should only be thinking of the baby, but I wouldn't have wanted him to come out early if I knew there would be any risk to his health.

Surprise, surprise, when Dr Gibb examined me he discovered that the baby had indeed turned. He told me that he would now definitely have to do a Caesarean because of the membrane. There was no way the baby could get past it. I wouldn't go into labour naturally and even if they induced me they wouldn't be able to break the membrane. It was potentially dangerous for the baby and me for the pregnancy to continue any further. Dr Gibb didn't want to wait until Wednesday to perform the Caesarean; he wanted to do it as soon as possible. So his secretary checked his diary and I was thinking, make it today! But the earliest he could perform it was on Monday. When she asked me if I would like morning or afternoon, I had no hesitation in replying, 'Morning please!' *Yes!* I thought, *my baby's going to be out soon; don't let anyone come into this room and change the doctor's mind.* Then I suddenly felt anxious again for my son's health, thinking, *this is serious, my baby is going to be four weeks premature.* I asked Dr Gibb if he was sure it would be safe for my son to be born this soon. He assured me that it was – obviously the longer a baby is inside you the better, but the only risk in my baby's case was of having fluid on his lungs. Dr Gibb also measured the baby and he estimated that he was about six pounds. So

God knows what he would have been had I gone full-term; I'd have had another whopper!

I left the hospital with a big grin on my face; my foul mood of yesterday had given way to happiness and I couldn't wait to give Pete the good news that I'd be having our baby on Monday! He was shocked but delighted when I told him, throwing his arms around me and kissing me, but his parents were very concerned.

'What's wrong?' they wanted to know.

'Nothing's wrong,' I assured them, explaining that it was just as I predicted, the baby had turned and a natural birth wasn't possible.

'Are you sure?' they asked, still looking worried.

I wanted to say, *I'm having the baby on Monday morning whatever you think!* I didn't get angry but I didn't want anyone trying to persuade Dr Gibb not to perform the operation – not that he would have been persuaded, I'm sure.

Once I explained to Pete's parents what Dr Gibb had said then of course they understood. I know that their only concern was for the baby and me.

On Sunday night Pete and I drove to the Portland. We

were told to get there for seven, but typically we were late, as we'd had dinner with his family and my mum and Paul, and I'd wanted to settle Harvey, so we didn't arrive there until nine o'clock at night. I was pleased that no one saw us enter the building. I didn't want the press to know I'd gone in; I didn't want them to get that final picture of me about to have my baby. As soon as I had revealed that I was pregnant I had never said what my due date was because I didn't want the press to know. In recent weeks I had played games with them, saying the baby was due any day because I wanted to keep them guessing and stop them from bothering me when the time came for me to go into hospital. Pete held my hand as we were shown to our suite. I looked at my watch: this time tomorrow night I'd be here with our new baby . . .

CHAPTER THIRTEEN

HELLO JUNIOR!

As we unpacked in our suite I thought to myself, *This is where so many celebrities have had their babies – Victoria Beckham and Claudia Schiffer – is it really that posh?* At first glance I really didn't think our suite was *that* amazing. It wasn't how I had imagined it – I'd been prepared for wall-to-wall luxury, imagining the kind of decor and extras you'd get in a top-class hotel. After all, it was costing us twelve hundred pounds a night to stay here! Don't get me wrong, my suite was very pleasant – there were two rooms, my bedroom and a lounge area for visitors, and each room had its own bathroom. But the double bed Pete and I had been promised was actually a sofa bed in the lounge. I had a tiny TV in my bedroom and it didn't even have Sky. But of course it was quite a lot more luxurious than the old NHS . . .

Pete took a picture of me as I sat on the bed, and I pointed at my belly saying, 'Look, this bump is going to be gone tomorrow!' And I thought, *This is my last night of being so enormous – thank God!* But like all expectant mothers I was feeling nervous, anxious that the baby would be okay, and I was also feeling very uptight about having the epidural. Pete and I watched a bit of TV together, just to take my mind off the morning, and then he got the sofa bed ready for us. I was so huge that I couldn't cuddle him properly and my sciatica was killing me – I had suffered from it throughout my pregnancy. But eventually I managed to go to sleep.

At seven we woke up. I had two hours before the Caesarean and the time passed really slowly. I had a shower, using my strawberry bodywash from the

Body Shop – even now I can't bear to wash myself with it because it reminds me of being in hospital. The nurse had told me not to put any moisturiser on my body, but I decided to put on make-up – foundation, blusher, mascara and lip-gloss. *Well*, I reasoned, *I haven't got to do the labour bit. I'm not going to get hot and sweaty so I may as well try and look halfway decent this time*. My hands and feet were all nicely French-manicured, I'd St Tropezed myself, so I was a lovely golden colour, my eyebrows had been done and my hair had been blow-dried straight. The nurse had told me I might need to shave *down there* and I replied, 'Don't worry, it's bald as a badger!' I always keep it hair-free because of my pink love-heart tattoo. So I was basically ready to go! Pete and I had arranged for Shauna, who films us for our documentary series, to film the birth. It would be a film just for Pete and me, it was never going to be made public – I'd never want anyone else to see such personal footage.

Around eight o'clock our families arrived and the suite suddenly seemed crowded – there was my mum, my stepdad Paul, my brother Danny and his wife, Louise, Pete's parents, Pete's brother Mike,

Claire and Shauna. I was really starting to panic about the epidural. I wasn't worried about the operation or about being cut open or feeling anything during the surgery – it was just that bloody needle! I tried to put on my usual brave face, saying, 'Look, everybody, my belly's going to be gone in a minute and I'll have a baby!' Around half past eight the nurse came in and said, 'Okay Katie, we're going to take you down now.' Pete and Shauna had to put on green gowns, hats and shoe covers and my heart was racing. My mum took a picture of the three of us just before we left the room and I just about managed a smile. But as we went down in the lift and my mum came down with us to say goodbye, my eyes started filling up as I thought about the needle. Mum was watching me closely, and when she saw me welling up her eyes started filling up too, then Pete's did! *Please don't cry*, I was thinking, knowing it would make me feel worse. I tried to hold back the tears but when I came to say goodbye to my mum I really started sobbing. 'I can't bear the thought of the needle,' I cried, shaking as she tried to give me a hug. Seeing me in such a state made my mum cry as well. I tried to calm down but it was no good; I had well and truly lost it. My poor mum had to go back in the lift, knowing I was in such a state. As Pete and I walked into the pre-theatre room I could see that Shauna was looking at me in complete amazement, because she had never seen me cry before and I know she thinks that I'm this really hard character. Even Pete has never really seen me cry before.

I had to lie down on the hard, narrow, operating couch. The nurses spoke reassuringly about how everything was going to be alright, but I was panicking, even though they hadn't even done anything to me yet! I was surrounded by surgical equipment and the antiseptic smell of the room was making me feel nauseous.

'We need you to lie really still now Katie,' the nurse told me.

But I cried out, 'No! Don't do it, I know it's really going to hurt.'

'No it won't,' he replied. 'It will just be a little scratch.'

But by now I was sobbing hysterically, physically shaking and shouting, 'You liars! It's going to hurt, I know, I've seen that needle on TV!' When I lose it, I lose it big time.

Pete was desperately trying to calm me down, saying, 'Come on, it's alright. You're going to be fine, I promise.'

'What are you doing?' I called out, thinking that they had started putting the needle in.

'Kate,' Pete said soothingly, 'they haven't done anything yet.'

I tried to take deep breaths and calm down. I looked at the clock; it was five past nine. The nurse told me it would all be over by ten to ten and I would have my baby. *Just think of that*, I told myself, *in less than an hour it will all be over, I'll have my son*. But it was no good; I couldn't calm down. I couldn't stop crying and shaking. The next thing I knew I had a mask over my face and was being given gas and air to calm me down. I started to feel light-headed, to have that dreamy, mellow feeling, like the one you have when you're starting to get drunk. By now it was twenty to ten. I was aware of the nurse putting what felt like stickers on my back.

'Pete, have they done it yet?' I asked. But they hadn't.

Then I felt something on my back and Pete told me that the epidural had gone in. I felt this extreme pressure on my back. It didn't hurt but it felt extremely strange. *I can cope with that*, I thought, but I was still crying. The anaesthetist told me that the needle was now in, that everything was fine but I had to keep still. But I kept imagining the needle in my back. I knew they put a tube in as well and the thought of it was making me feel sick. I looked once more at the clock and it was now ten to ten. It should all have been over by now, but it had taken me so long to calm down. And then the epidural took a good twenty minutes to take effect – for the first ten minutes I could feel my belly and my left leg, and then I started worrying that I would feel them cutting into me. But they kept monitoring me, spraying ice-cold liquid on me to check that I was feeling numb. Pete was fantastic – he kept hold of my hand and kept reassuring me that everything was going to be alright and that soon we'd have our baby. By this point I had finally calmed down, mainly because I'd had so much gas and air. I felt as if I was on a different planet. *Just get him out!* I thought.

Then the nurses opened the doors to the theatre and wheeled me in and I started crying again, panicking that it would hurt. There was music playing in the background and I tried to focus on that. The room felt quiet and relaxed and I felt as if I was in a dream, hearing the doctors busy around but feeling out of it. They put a screen up across my belly so I wouldn't be able to see them operate. The doctor brushed iodine across my skin where he was going to make the incision, and it was such a strange sensation because you sense something on your skin but you can't actually feel it. Pete was by my side, holding my hand and every now and then peeping over the screen and watching the doctors. Suddenly he winced and said, 'They've cut you!' Of course I couldn't feel it, but as they performed the Caesarean I had the weirdest feeling – as if someone was washing up in my tummy – and I could feel all this tugging and pulling.

'The baby's going to be here any second,' the doctor said. By now Pete was crying, and suddenly a song came on the radio that I absolutely love and I said, 'Can you turn the radio up please.' It was 'A Whole New World', sung by Vanessa Williams, from the Disney film *Aladdin*. It's such a beautiful song with wonderful lyrics that really sum up how Pete and I feel about each other. It was a real coincidence, as the

day before Pete and I had gone shopping for CDs. I
had wanted to get the instrumental version of the
song because I was thinking of performing it as a duet
with Pete at our wedding. And now this song was
playing as our son Junior was born, someone who we
wanted to show the world to. As soon as Pete saw his
son he started bawling. I've never seen a man cry so
much – these weren't just a few tears; he was sobbing
his heart out! Then I heard our baby cry. I'd like to
say that I too was overwhelmed with emotion but
actually I felt sick. I told the anaesthetist and he
assured me that I wouldn't be, then he gave me some
more drugs to stop the nausea. I was thinking, *If I am
going to be sick, then I don't want to be sick on my
hair!* Meanwhile Pete had cut the cord and the
paediatric nurses checked Junior then handed him
back to Pete. I chose this magical moment to be sick.
Bollocks, I thought, *I've been sick on my hair. Now
it's going to stink and go curly.* I know that seems like
such a trivial thing to be worried about when your
son has just been born, but in fairness I wasn't myself.

Pete was holding Junior and saying how beautiful
he was, but I felt totally out of it. When Pete came
over and showed me our son, I turned and looked at

him and said, 'Oh he's gorgeous, so cute.' But inside I didn't really want to know; I felt so ill, I just wanted everyone to go away and leave me alone. The whole experience wasn't at all like I had imagined. I had watched Caesareans on TV and the mothers were always smiling and laughing when they saw their new baby, but I felt awful, spaced out and sick. All I wanted to do was turn over on my side and curl up but I couldn't move; I had to lie there on my back, numb and helpless. It was so different from my experience with Harvey – even though I had been in agony I still remember holding Harvey for the first time and feeling such a surge of love running through me.

It felt like I was in theatre for ages as they sewed me up. Then I was wheeled into recovery and they laid Junior next to me. He was wrapped in a blanket and still covered in vernix. Pete was still being incredibly emotional and kept saying, 'Look at my son!' I was beginning to feel a little more with it, but was still spaced out. After half an hour I was wheeled back upstairs, holding Junior. At some point Shauna had nipped back to the suite to reassure our families that everything was alright and to explain why we'd been so long. They were expecting us back after an hour and we'd been gone for two and a half – I knew they'd be frantic with worry, especially my mum.

As soon as the lift doors opened everyone was waiting for us, with big smiles on their faces. Once Pete saw his mum and dad he started bawling his eyes out again! Then it seemed like everyone was crying, and I was crying too, but I was also thinking, *Please everyone, just leave me alone with my baby.* I'd had so many drugs I really wasn't thinking straight. I remember everyone being in the room and looking at the baby and saying how gorgeous he was, and I felt very protective towards my son. But I felt overwhelmingly weak and drained of energy and I couldn't move my lower body because I was still numb from the epidural. After a couple of hours my mum left with Paul, my brother and Louise, saying that she'd be up in a few days but she really wanted me to rest. And shortly after them Pete's parents also left. Then it was just Pete, our new son Junior Savva Andrea – all 5 lbs 13 oz of him – and me alone together at last. I could see how perfect he was, how tiny, how helpless, how beautiful and I felt so protective towards him, but I also felt so helpless myself and I missed having Harvey with me; it felt like my family wasn't complete.

I hoped that I would feel stronger the next day, but if anything I felt worse and the doctors told me that they had some serious news for me. Instantly I thought it was to do with Junior and I panicked, but they told me it was about me and they wanted to speak to me on my own, so Pete's parents left the room. The doctors then informed me that I was very anaemic and that my red blood-count was extremely low. Apparently I had lost far more blood than was normal during the operation and they were very concerned. I had already been told before I had the baby that I was a little anaemic, but I hadn't been unduly worried as a lot of pregnant women are. But the doctors were now taking my condition extremely seriously. They strongly advised me to have a blood transfusion. I really wasn't keen on having one, thinking, *Knowing my luck I'll have one and then six months later I'll end up with some fatal disease!* The only alternative was to eat a lot of food that was rich in iron and take iron tablets. I would also have to have complete rest for at least the next three weeks, put my feet up and not do anything to exert myself. I definitely preferred the second option.

When I told my mum of my decision she was instantly concerned and said, 'I hope none of Pete's family are influencing you not to have the transfusion. You're my daughter, and if you really need this you're going to have it.' She knew that Pete's parents are Jehovah's Witnesses and they don't believe in blood transfusions. I tried to reassure my mum. 'No one's told me what to do and Pete has said that if I really need a transfusion I should definitely have one.' *Here we go*, I thought wearily. I really didn't want to row with my mum, or to have bad feeling between our two families. All I kept thinking was, *Please everyone, leave me alone with my baby*. I felt so weak, I just wanted to sleep and sleep.

I stayed at the Portland for a week, and looking back it feels like a bit of a blank, with all the days blurring into one. On the plus side, the staff looked after me and Junior so well that I would definitely have another baby there. The food was some of the best I've ever eaten and I could cheerfully eat there any day of the week – it was fantastic. But I don't think I allowed myself to rest enough. We had visitors every single day – my friends came to see us, including Michelle Heaton and her boyfriend Andy, Michelle Clack, Sally Cairns and Sam Howard. My sister Sophie came up and so did Lynne and Louise, two close friends of my mum. My room rapidly filled up with flowers and cards that I so appreciated. Even though I knew my mum would love to see the baby she gave us a few days' space to bond as a family, but Pete's parents came every day, which I didn't mind because they are lovely, but I felt so drained. When you have visitors, however nice and well-meaning they are, you still try and entertain them and you don't rest.

We had arranged for Junior to go to the night nursery where the nurses would feed him so that we could sleep, as we knew when we got home it would be full-on with Harvey and the baby. For the first few nights I was so weak I couldn't even push his crib along the corridor and Pete took him. When finally I was up to the walk and could take Junior, I felt guilty about leaving him but I tried to tell myself it would give me the chance to rest. We had just found out that the maternity nurse we had booked had cancelled because she'd injured her knee, and we didn't know how quickly we could get a replacement. But ironically, even with putting Junior in the night nursery, I didn't feel rested. I was still exhausted and weaker than I have ever been in my life. By Thursday the doctors strongly recommended that I had a day on my own with Pete and without any visitors. I was secretly relieved, as I was feeling almost at the end of my tether with exhaustion and I thought a day on our own was exactly what I needed. But late that morning there was a knock at the door.

'Yes?' Pete and I both said wearily, thinking it surely couldn't be a visitor as the hospital always called us first to check it was okay. The door opened and it was Pete's big brother, Danny, who had flown over specially from Australia to see the baby. I was really happy to see him and it was really sweet that he'd made the trip just for us – that's what you call a good brother – but at the same time all I wanted to do was rest. And I started to panic about where everyone was going to stay. All I wanted to do was be at home with Pete, Junior and Harvey and shut out the world till I felt strong again, until I felt as close to

Junior as I did to Harvey. But now I was confronted with the prospect of a house full of visitors. I felt upset and emotionally fragile. I really didn't think I could cope.

CHAPTER FOURTEEN

THE BLUES

I was longing to be home and to be reunited with Harvey. Mum had brought him into hospital to see me, but it wasn't the same as being at home with him. I had missed him so much and didn't want him to feel left out because of the baby. But during our first weekend back home Pete and I had some of the worst arguments of our relationship, which left me feeling even more drained. All along I had said to Pete that I wanted his family to be able to see Junior whenever they wanted – I knew how important it was to them, especially as most of them lived abroad and wouldn't be able to see as much of him as my family, who only lived a few miles away. But there really was no room in my house for everyone to stay, as the maternity nurse – we had managed to find another one – would be having the guest bedroom. I told Pete that his family were welcome to spend the day with us, but at night I really wanted to rest. I told him that I needed my own space and I needed space to be with him. I begged him not to take it the wrong way – it wasn't that I had anything against his family, because I didn't, they're lovely people – but I'd just had a baby and I desperately needed to rest. I had just had major surgery, and even though I'd been discharged from hospital I felt more exhausted than I ever have in my life. Pete seemed to have got the message and booked his family into a hotel which was literally down the road. It was a relief knowing that I would be able to have time alone with Pete, Harvey and Junior. But then it all went wrong when he called his sister Debbie, who was due to fly over from Cyprus to see us. She told him not to waste his money on a hotel and that she'd sleep on the sofa. I was very upset when Pete told me and I said I couldn't have everyone staying in the house, that I would find it too stressful.

'You don't normally mind people sleeping on the sofas,' Pete said crossly, and I knew he was offended.

'I don't usually mind,' I replied, and he was absolutely right – usually I don't mind people staying over, especially his family, who are always welcome. 'But I've just had a baby, I need some space!' In the end he agreed that his family, including his sister, would stay at the hotel, but it was horrible arguing and not what I needed and it was absolutely nothing against his family.

With that row out of the way, I was looking forward to us spending the weekend together, but on Saturday his parents called from north London, where they were staying, asking if Pete could come and pick them up as they didn't know how to get to us. I really felt that they could have found a way – I was feeling so weak and didn't want to be left on my own with two children. My feelings must have shown because we ended up having another row. This time Pete said that he'd told his family not to come and see us, that I wasn't well enough and that I wasn't up to having visitors.

'Pete,' I said wearily, 'phone them back. Tell them of course they can come.' But it didn't end there. Pete told me that his family values were obviously different to mine, in a way which clearly showed he thought his values were better. I thought, *I don't need this agro*. I felt so emotional, I was a physical wreck, I could hardly walk anywhere and I hardly had the strength to pick up Junior.

'Pete, please understand, I feel so weak and you want me to have a houseful of people – it's too much for me. I told you, your family are welcome, I just need to have some space at night.'

'Oh, so shall I tell them to go at six every evening then?!' he said crossly. He just didn't get how I felt. We had never argued like this before and I hated it. And it was the last thing I needed.

'I meant around nine or ten, just so I can have some time with you and the baby. I really don't mind your family being with us.' But because I felt so emotional all I wanted to do was be alone with Pete, Harvey and Junior – my new family.

Eventually Pete called his parents back and arranged to pick them up on Sunday. But I was starting to dread everyone coming to the house because I didn't feel in the right frame of mind to cope with visitors, even if those visitors were Pete's family, who I felt close to. I felt the same about my family coming round, and even the smallest things were being blown out of all proportion in my mind. Pete was going to drive up to London in my new car – a Range Rover Sport that I had only just taken delivery of. In fact it had been dropped off the night before I went into hospital and I had been so excited with my new toy that I instantly took it for a spin round the block. After my Caesarean I wouldn't be able to drive for six weeks, and I was really looking forward to driving my new car, as I've got a thing about motors. I really resented the fact that Pete was going to be driving my new car that had no mileage on it before I was, and that it was going to be full of people. It sounds mad and unreasonable, I know, but it's a sign of how stressed I was – usually I wouldn't have minded Pete driving my car at all. And I didn't like him leaving me alone with two children, in the state I was in, while he went to pick them up. I spent the rest of that Sunday worrying about how I was going to cope being surrounded by so many people.

*

On Monday morning Pete's parents and sister arrived at our front door at eight o'clock. Immediately I got out of bed and got dressed, even though I knew I should be resting – the doctors had been really insistent, but I didn't want to be parted from Junior and I knew I wouldn't be able to have him in his crib next to me with his family downstairs, all desperate to see him. But all I wanted to do was bond with my baby. I was very aware that after a week I still didn't feel that I had bonded with him, in the way I had with Harvey. I don't know whether it was because I had a Caesarean and felt so ill during the operation that it created a barrier between us, and because I felt so physically weak and helpless afterwards, but something wasn't right. All I knew was that I needed time to get close to my newborn son.

I tried to be rational, thinking that of course Pete's family wanted to see the baby because they lived abroad and of course I wanted them to see their grandson, but I found it hard being surrounded by people all the time. My mum came to the house every day to take Harvey to nursery and to check up on me – she wanted to make sure that I was taking my iron tablets, eating properly and getting plenty of rest.

And I even dreaded her coming to the house because I knew she'd be nagging me about what I'd been eating and I really couldn't handle it.

When Mum saw how many people were in the house she had a face like thunder – I knew that she wanted me to rest. But that stressed me out even more. 'Please don't say anything, Mum,' I begged her. 'I've said it's okay for them to be here.' Pete's dad cooked dinner every night and I really wanted my mum and Paul to come over, as I thought it would look strange if they didn't. In the end they did come over and everyone got on. From the outside it must have looked like I was fine, but inside I was struggling to cope.

I wasn't getting enough rest. I felt I had to be entertaining my guests and I didn't want to sleep in my room, knowing that the baby was downstairs with Pete's family. It's a mother's instinct to want to be near her baby. But it was more than that – I didn't want anyone else near my baby, I didn't want anyone else picking him up and holding him except me. Even though it was hard – I was so weak I could hardly lift him – I still wanted to feed him and hold him. It wasn't that I was jealous that they wanted to hold him, but every time they went near him I had a knot in my stomach and I wanted to cry. *Please, just leave me alone with my baby*, I wanted to say so many times. *Let me bond with him.* I was so used to how it had been with Harvey and me, when it was just the two of us, and I didn't have to worry about anyone else . . .

Peter's parents and his brother Danny and sister Debbie are lovely, lovely people but I was feeling overwhelmed. I wanted to spend every minute of the day with Junior when he wasn't sleeping. We had a maternity nurse to look after him at night, so those daytimes were precious to me. But even though I was thinking about how much I wanted to be close to my son, something inside me was stopping me from going near him. I wanted to pick him up and cuddle him, but I couldn't. Even though I felt like this I still didn't want anyone else holding him – that's why I knew I had a problem. No one else knew; even to Pete I was covering it up.

One of the reasons for getting a maternity nurse was not only to help me have a good night's sleep and get over the operation, but also so she could help us get Junior into a routine. It was only in the last few months that I'd started having a full night's sleep again, as Harvey would wake up, needing to have milk or a cuddle, and I know only too well how lack of sleep takes its toll on you emotionally and physically. Pete and I had lots of work on and we had the wedding coming up, and the last thing I wanted was for us to be arguing because we were knackered. I had already established a feeding routine with Junior that he would wake every three to four hours for a feed, and that when he was sleeping in his room he wasn't to be disturbed. So I really didn't want anyone going into his room to disturb him. However, Pete's sister Debbie couldn't resist going in and kissing him. I knew all she was doing was showing her love for him, but it made me feel incredibly tense. I wished she wouldn't; I felt that any moment I was going to lose it and shout, 'Look, will you stop going into the fucking room?' I know that it will surprise everyone close to me that I felt like this – and it surprised me – but I felt out of control, not so much yummy mummy as psycho mummy . . .

I also found it hard explaining to Pete's family how to deal with Harvey. I do have a particular routine and I do have a certain way of dealing with him that

I have worked out over the years and which Harvey seems to respond to best. He really isn't the easiest of children to deal with and I don't like anything to upset him. Debbie was very good with Harvey on the whole, but she wanted to cuddle him *a lot* and I'm afraid that sometimes Harvey gets really wound up and he's best left on his own. Of course, when he got wound up I was the one who had to sort him out, and it wasn't easy dealing with Harvey just after I'd had my operation. I couldn't pick him up and it was even more difficult than usual trying to calm him down. Probably if I hadn't been feeling so emotional none of this would have mattered, but as it was everything felt too much.

I had a problem with everyone around me. When my mum's sister, two of her grown-up daughters, their children and my nan turned up at the house a few days after I came out of hospital I nearly lost it. Although of course I knew they wanted to see the baby, I ended up having a go at my mum, saying, 'Why are they here? I can't cope with all these visitors, you didn't tell me they were coming.' I remember I was upstairs in Junior's room and watching them from the window like a possessed

woman, thinking, *Fuck off – just go home and leave
me alone.* When all they wanted to do was to show
they cared . . . Pete was lovely, offering them food
and drink and being so welcoming like he always is.

I hoped that as the week went on I would start to feel
stronger and more laid back about having Pete's
family around, but if anything it got worse. I wanted
to cry all the time – which is unheard of for me. I kept
trying to put on a brave face and pretend everything
was fine, but I know I came across as being moody
and Pete was wondering what on earth was wrong
with me. I felt as if I had so much anger building up
inside of me – it was like a gremlin of rage – that I was
going to explode and tell everyone to fuck off, and yet
they hadn't done anything!

Of course Pete's family wanted to hold the baby, it
was only natural that they did, but I really didn't
want anyone to hold Junior except me. I made Pete
tell everyone that they had to wash their hands if they
wanted to hold him – he was so tiny because he was
four weeks premature and I really didn't want him
picking up any infections. Pete was strict on this too
– he was wary about people picking him up, telling

them to support his head; such a proud dad. Two days into their stay, when I was sitting on the sofa cradling Junior in my arms, Pete's brother Danny said, 'Here, let me have a hold of him.'

I wanted to scream *No*; I was just about to feed him. But then I thought, *I can't be selfish. His mum, dad and sister have come all the way from Cyprus and Danny has flown over from Australia – I can't deprive them of their chance to hold Junior.* So I handed him over and Danny, seeing that I was about to feed him, took the bottle from my hand and tried unsuccessfully to put it in Junior's mouth. It was bad enough watching anyone else hold my baby, but watching someone try to feed him was torture and I wanted to cry and scream, *Just give me my baby back!* I felt on the verge of losing control but instead I said, 'It's okay, I'll do it,' as if it was no big deal. Even when I changed Junior I would have an audience and it made me feel awkward, as if I didn't know what I was doing. Of course I did, because I'd brought up Harvey on my own, but the fact that Junior was so tiny and fragile made me feel that I didn't.

Over and over in my head, all I kept thinking was, *Please leave me alone and let me bond with my baby,* over and over. If only I could have expressed what I felt, but I was so scared and confused about why I was feeling like this. And even though I was desperate to bond with him, the more we were surrounded by other people the more I felt as if I was putting a barrier up between Junior and me. I felt like saying, *Okay, you lot all hold him, you lot change him and I won't even try and bond with him*, which was unfair on Junior and totally irrational. But I felt irrational. And the more time Pete's family and the maternity nurse spent with the baby, the stronger the barrier became. I wanted to cry and shout and let it all out, but I kept pretending everything was fine when it so clearly wasn't.

I was even feeling intensely jealous of how much love Pete was showering on our son – a feeling that had started in the hospital. I had said jokingly, 'I've lost Pete; he's giving the baby more attention than me!' Everyone laughed, but I meant it seriously. I felt that now he had his son he didn't want to know me. I did feel jealous of the love he was giving Junior – I was usually the one who got all his attention and now I felt rejected. I felt like a machine that had produced his son and now he had what he wanted he had gone off me. I couldn't believe I was feeling like this. Deep down I knew Pete still loved me – he didn't leave my side in the hospital and he couldn't have been more loving. I should have been celebrating the fact that Pete was such a wonderful father and so open about expressing his love for his son. It was such a contrast to the way Harvey's father was with him. I'm sure Dwight loved Harvey but he never expressed his love for his son, in front of me, in the way Pete does. I should have been happy but I wasn't, and I couldn't help how I felt. And it seemed that every time I managed to have a cuddle with Junior, Pete would say, 'Let me hold him,' and instead of saying no, I would hand him over because I wanted Pete to bond with his son, leaving me feeling left out yet again.

I did feel sorry for Pete. He could tell something was wrong and it must have been hard for him having me being so moody while his family was here. Pete was a new father and he was so proud, wanting to share his happiness about being a father with everyone, especially his family. But men don't really understand how women feel, especially when you've just had a baby and feel so vulnerable. All I wanted to do was sleep in my room with Junior beside me, but I couldn't. I was up and on guard from the moment Pete's family arrived to the moment they left, because I didn't want anyone else near my son. I just wanted to be alone with Junior. I felt like saying, *You're all making me want to reject going near the baby*; I felt as if they were somehow stopping me from loving my son, when really it was down to me – I was the only one stopping me . . .

Part of the problem was that I didn't know how to explain how I felt to Pete, because I didn't understand why I was feeling this way. I had expected to know how I would feel after the baby was born, and nothing had prepared me for this. Maybe if I could have told someone how I was feeling it would have helped. I half-thought of confiding in the midwife who came to see Junior and me. But the one I saw immediately after I came out of hospital made me feel even worse. She was a real old-fashioned matron figure. It was a boiling hot day and I was feeling very weak. We sat in the garden next to one of the bushes and there was a foul smell. I thought there was probably a dead animal there, but I was too weak to move our chairs away and she didn't offer. She wasn't at all friendly to me and immediately it put my back up. Junior was asleep in his room and she asked about him. I told her he was fine, but that I didn't want to wake him up. I didn't even want her to see my baby. I thought, *Why should you be privileged to see him?* My attitude was vile, but at least I admit it. She asked if he'd had his pin-prick test (the Guthrie Test) in hospital – where the baby's blood is tested to check they haven't got a rare condition which causes brain damage if it isn't treated; it also checks the baby's thyroid function. I replied that I thought so, but unfortunately I couldn't find any of his medical records. I'd only just got home and everything was in a state of chaos. She said she would have to do the test again if I couldn't find the paperwork. I dragged myself up and had another look in the kitchen, but I still couldn't find the paperwork. I had no intention of letting her do the test on Junior again.

'I really can't find his records and I really don't think much of that test anyway,' I said, coming back into the garden. 'It never picked up on Harvey's thyroid problem, so I don't have any confidence in it.' She was none too happy, but she couldn't force me to make my baby have the test again.

'So where did you have him? The Portland, wasn't it?' And the way she said it sounded like she was looking down on me, trying to make me feel like I was some stuck-up snob who'd gone private. I'm not like that at all. I wanted to say, *Why don't you get your stuff and fuck off out of my house!*

When she asked me how I was feeling, I just replied, 'Great, thanks.' There was no way I was going to confide in her.

After she left I called up the number I had for the local midwives and said I didn't want to see that woman ever again. I asked to see the one I had seen before I went into hospital, who was lovely, and luckily she was able to come and see me. But even with her I still made out I was fine, even though I was desperate to ask, *Is it normal to feel this angry and this jealous? Is it normal to feel that I haven't bonded with my son?*

Nothing seemed to be going the way I thought it would. Pete and I even argued about the maternity nurse – she was very expensive and was supposed to be on duty twenty-four seven but I only wanted her at night. It caused friction between Pete and me, as he said, 'You should have her in the day as well to help you, that's what we're paying her for.' But I insisted I wanted time with the baby. Even though I had said I needed a maternity nurse to do nights, I'm not sure if it was the right thing for me. I thought that when Pete's family left I could establish that bond with my son, but even by the time Junior was eight weeks old I simply didn't feel that I had bonded with him as much as I did with Harvey. And I didn't understand why – I couldn't have been happier when I found out I was pregnant, and all through my pregnancy I was so excited that I was having a baby with Pete. Maybe by having so many people around us I couldn't have that closeness that I had with Harvey – I was with him all the time, after all, and even when I went back to work I'd take him with me wherever possible. Maybe it was because of feeling so weak and drained after the Caesarean, but then again I felt exhausted after my labour with Harvey and I was so sore I could hardly walk or sit down for two weeks. Part of me felt, *Give up, just accept that you can't bond with Junior in the same way because your circumstances are different.* But I knew it wasn't normal to feel like this; it was like part of me had shut down. Gradually, instead of wanting to do everything for Junior myself, I started thinking, *Let Pete or the maternity nurse do it – let them feed him or change him or bathe him – I'll just pick and choose when I want to see him.* Whenever the maternity nurse tried to tell me that Junior does this or that I wanted to say, *Don't tell me what my own baby does, I know.*

What added to the problem was that just after I had Junior it was the summer holidays, which meant Harvey wasn't at nursery and so I really did need the maternity nurse to help me. My mum was taking some well-earned holiday and I found it very hard coping with the two of them. Harvey needs so much attention that it's almost like having another baby in the house. He can't be involved in the same way that other three-year-olds can – I couldn't say, 'Harvey, go and get the baby's nappy,' or, 'Pass him that toy.' And I can't leave him in the room with the baby in case he hurts him by mistake. And it was very hard going out with both of them – Harvey has a disabled buggy now and I can't push that on my own and carry the baby; nor can I rely on Harvey walking, because if he doesn't want to he won't. But I've always been fiercely independent and hate not being able to do things on my own when I want to. I used to enjoy going out when Harvey was a baby – it was really easy doing the odd bit of shopping and he would always be contented; even if it was coming up to one of his feed times he'd still sleep in the car – but Junior is a very different baby and when he's due a feed and we're out in the car, he'll scream. It will play on my nerves and I'll end up thinking, *Well, I may as well go home then and not bother to go out at all.* When Harvey was Junior's age I knew every trick in the book to calm him down and stop him crying. But Junior just seems to cry whatever I do. I never had to give Harvey a dummy but Junior has one – it's as if I haven't got the patience or energy to try and calm him myself, and I don't know why.

Then our first maternity nurse left and we had to get another one. She was extremely well-qualified and experienced but I didn't feel relaxed with her, and that added to my feelings of depression that I hadn't bonded with Junior. One day when I was feeling particularly low I ended up confiding in her – she was very sympathetic and went away and printed off some information from the Internet on postnatal depression. But then I was paranoid that she would go to the papers and sell a story about how I was suffering from depression, which made me feel worse.

I also had the pressure of losing my baby weight because I had committed myself to filming an exercise DVD at the end of August, and I wanted to be in top shape for our wedding in September – just three months after I'd given birth. Immediately after I'd had Junior I weighed ten stone and two pounds. My usual weight was eight stone and two pounds, so I had two stone to shift. I waited six weeks before I started exercising, as you should when you've had a Caesarean, and I had a personal trainer working with me every day, but even though we began by taking it gently I felt very weak and I was still bleeding when we started the programme. It was such hard work – after a few minutes I'd be thinking, *Why am I putting myself through this? It's agony!* And I found it frustrating because I'm the kind of person who likes to see instant results. Before I started exercising I'd said cockily that I would train twice a day. Let me tell you: that didn't last longer than the first day . . .

I had listened to the doctors and I'd spent the six weeks after Junior's birth making sure I ate a lot of food that was rich in iron and taking iron tablets, and by the end of the six weeks my red blood-count was completely normal. The exercise programme alone was not going to be enough to shift my baby weight because I had such a tight deadline, so I also had to go on a diet, which probably didn't help my mood swings. During the day I would drink juices made from apples, celery, spinach, avocado, pineapple and a bit of ginger, whizzed together in a blender, which sounds absolutely revolting, but was actually delicious, and in the evening I would eat steamed chicken or fish with vegetables or salad, no carbs. That diet definitely worked, though it took a couple of weeks to kick in. I liked the juices, but after a while I started to miss proper food – I really missed my pasta and jacket potatoes, and every now and then I'd have the odd sneaky curry.

As well as my DVD to prepare for, I was also back doing photo shoots, showing off my post-baby weight loss and telling everyone that Jordan was coming back. For the first time in over a year Claire, my manager, wanted me to pose in front of the cameras as Jordan. She wanted to sell the pictures as 'The Return of Jordan' – in some of the shots I was wearing a crown to show the Queen of Glamour was back. But much as I wanted to get back to glamour modelling, I was pissed off and said, 'For a start, Jordan hasn't been away, because whenever I go out I look like Jordan! She's always been part of me.' But I went ahead and did the shoot, doing all my saucy, sexy poses again. However, it didn't feel right having Claire watching me, as she had spent the last year drumming it into me that it was wrong to do my wink, or wrong to do the middle finger – that I had to be nice Katie Price. Claire and the photographer kept calling out, 'That's it, be Jordan!' And when I winked, Claire called out, 'Great! Jordan's back!'

Yeah, I thought, *and I wish you hadn't stopped me being her for so long.* Claire had obviously realised that being sexy sold – something that I had told her all along. She even wanted me to present a sexy image when I was singing – I wasn't to be Katie Price, I was to be Jordan, and that was who she was going to try and sell to the record companies. I felt like saying, *Hang on! One minute you're telling me not to be sexy, the next minute you're saying I've got to be! Make up your mind!*

*

By the beginning of August I felt a little stronger physically – though not my usual self by any means – but emotionally I was still all over the place. Maybe I had taken on too much, I don't know. When I had Harvey I was straight back to modelling and I loved it. In the past I'd always been able to cope with whatever life had thrown at me. When I'd discovered Harvey was blind I was devastated, but I got on with things and tried to give my son the best possible life. When I had my cancer scare, I didn't fall apart; I dealt with it and moved on. I'd always been the strong one but I really didn't feel like that now. I felt emotionally fragile and vulnerable, for the first time in my life . . .

Ten days after Junior was born Pete, Harvey, the baby and I did a shoot for *OK!* magazine. I must have looked like the perfect mother who had it all – beautiful new baby, loving fiancé and a fabulous wedding to look forward to. But as I smiled away I felt this searing pain inside me – it wasn't all perfect. Yes, I had the beautiful baby, but I felt so distant from him, even as I cradled him in my arms. In between shots Pete called me over: 'Come and look at our son – he's so gorgeous!'

'I can't Pete,' I replied. 'I'm just sorting out my

outfit for the next picture.' But the truth was I didn't want to look at him; I didn't want to be reminded that we hadn't bonded in the way I longed to. I felt like an outsider in my own family and, for the first time in my life, I felt a sense of failure and I wasn't sure how to put things right.

And if that wasn't enough to deal with, at the beginning of August Harvey was admitted to Great Ormond Street Hospital for tests. Me being me, I felt the only thing I could do was to put on a brave face and pretend everything was fine – I had to be strong for my little boy. For some time we had been very concerned about how much weight Harvey was putting on. He barely ate anything and yet he weighed five and half stone – far too much for a child of his age. As well as putting a dangerous strain on his heart and lungs, it was stopping him from being active because every time he tried to do anything he would quickly get out of breath. And at night he would sometimes stop breathing, alarmingly, because of his weight.

I was glad that the doctors were taking our concerns seriously because I had been so worried about Harvey. When we met the doctors we asked how dangerous his condition was. They replied that it was extremely dangerous for him to be so big, and if he didn't lose weight it could be fatal as he could have a heart attack. I had suspected as much, but it was still devastating to hear the doctors put my fears into words.

'Thank God he's in hospital now,' I said to Pete afterwards. 'They'll sort it out, won't they? They'll find out what's wrong with him and put it right, won't they?'

Pete put his arms round me and held me tight. 'Of course they will. He's in the best possible place.'

For the first few days that Harvey was in hospital I admit I did breathe a bit of a sigh of relief – I trusted the doctors to look after him and I needed a bit of a break because he can be such a handful. I also thought it would give me more time to spend with Junior. But after three days I really started missing him. The house suddenly seemed so quiet, as I was so used to him trundling around and playing with his toys. I'd go into his bedroom and sit on his bed and press his duvet to my face, breathing in his special Harvey smell. We booked into a London hotel so we could spend as much time with Harvey as possible, but it wasn't the same as having him home with us. He was so excited every time he saw me, and I knew that even though he couldn't express it he missed me as much as I missed him. The nurses told me that if one of the hospital staff came into his room who had big boobs, Harvey would always go over to them and want a cuddle. The nurses told me that one night he was really crying because he missed me and, unable to calm him any other way, one of the nurses lay beside him and cuddled him and he finally fell asleep, which is what he was used to doing with me every night. I was comforted that Harvey had such lovely people looking after him, but I longed to have my son back.

Before he was admitted into hospital I had to keep a diary of what he ate for four weeks, and I couldn't help feeling that the doctors might think that I was somehow responsible for Harvey's weight gain because of what I fed him. I wrote down what he had for breakfast, lunch and dinner, which should have been proof enough that his weight was not down to what he was eating, because he hardly eats anything.

He doesn't always eat his breakfast and, because I'm so anxious that he should eat something at the beginning of the day, like any mother, if he rejects his Weetabix I will give him toast. The nutritionist said that I shouldn't be giving him the option, that if he doesn't eat the cereal I should take it away and not give him anything else. It seemed a bit harsh to me, especially since Harvey can't tell me whether he wants Weetabix or toast and I have to guess what he wants. I know that often he won't eat for the rest of the day, and knowing that he's on so much medication, I like him to eat something for breakfast. But the nutritionist said they would do this with every single meal, and if he rejected the food it would be taken away and then he wouldn't be given anything to eat until the next meal.

Part of the problem of getting Harvey to eat three meals a day is to do with his sleeping pattern, which is all over the place. He will often sleep for hours during the day and be awake during the night, and even on more 'normal' days he always has a sleep during the day, which lasts several hours, and he is very hard to wake up. When you try and wake him up he is nearly always in a bad mood, and if you put his dinner in front of him he'll simply push the plate away and lash out. When I explained this to the doctors they said they would try and get him into a routine with his nap time and his meals.

The hospital drew up a plan of giving him three meals a day and said that we weren't to give him any snacks in between, not even the raisins that Mum and I would give him. They also wanted to change his diet and get him to eat vegetables. It had taken Harvey a long time to eat solid food and I did my best to introduce him to a healthy diet with plenty of fruit and vegetables, but from the start I was fighting a losing battle – and with the exception of raisins and roast potatoes he wouldn't touch them. So when they told me they were going to give him these I said, 'Good luck!'

It didn't take the hospital long to realise just how difficult Harvey could be. After his nap they would try and wake him for lunch, and they had exactly the same problem that I had. They admitted he was a nightmare to wake up – it took three of them to do it and it took them an hour. When they finally managed to wake him he was in such a foul mood that he didn't want his food. Well, I'm a working mum and

I've got another child now to look after; I don't always have a whole hour every day to try and wake Harvey up.

Because of his weight the nurses had to use a hoist to get him out of bed and to pick him up, and they said to Pete and me, 'How on earth do you deal with him at home without one?' We replied that it was normal for us and we were used to it. But I was glad that they admitted what hard work it could be looking after him, because now people can appreciate what I have to go through. They also said that he could be very difficult to deal with when he had a tantrum and threw himself around – *Welcome to my world*, I thought. But of course when he's in a good mood, which they saw as well, he's the best child ever.

The hospital quickly realised that his weight gain had nothing to do with what he was eating. They stuck to their plan of trying to give him three meals a day and trying to give him vegetables with no success. When he pushed his food away they didn't give him anything else and he went for several days without eating anything at all, except a bottle of milk. Initially they thought his weight might be to do with his medication, but they checked it out and it wasn't that either. I had hoped that Harvey would be back home after two weeks but the doctors said they wanted to keep him in for at least another four weeks, to find out what the problem was and to try and sort out his eating and sleeping. He would only be out of hospital a few days before our wedding. I hated being separated from my son. I felt very low anyway and this was making me feel even worse.

Harvey wasn't the only one who was undergoing tests. In August 2001 I was diagnosed as having an extremely rare type of cancer called leiomyosarcoma, or LMS. I had discovered a lump in my finger when I was four months pregnant with Harvey, but it wasn't until I had him that I had surgery to remove it. In its advanced state there is a very poor survival rate for this disease. Fortunately I was operated on early enough and the surgeon removed all the cancerous tissue. However, I have to have regular MRI body scans to ensure it hasn't returned. I'd had one just before I became pregnant with Junior and everything was fine. But I couldn't have an MRI scan while I was pregnant because they can potentially harm the baby.

I was a little anxious after I had Junior because I knew that pregnancy can accelerate the rate at which the cancer spreads. That anxiety became greater when I discovered several lumps under my arm. My first instinct was to ignore them because I didn't think I could cope with anything else. But my mum immediately got on my case and insisted that I go back to see my consultant. He didn't think that the lumps were cancerous, but thought I should have a scan just to be on the safe side. I had the scan and then I received a letter from the hospital asking me to go for another test. *Have they found something?* I wondered fearfully. But then I did what I've always done: I tried to block out the worry as I've always tried to block out the fact that I've had cancer, reasoning that if you have it, you have it, and it's best to get on with life. And as Harvey was still in hospital I really didn't have the time to worry about myself. Plus I had a wedding in four weeks' time . . .

CHAPTER FIFTEEN

WEDDING FEVER

Pete and I realised very early on that we wouldn't be able to plan the whole wedding ourselves, even with the help of our management – we needed a wedding planner. For a start I didn't want us to argue about what we wanted. I had seen the video of his brother's wedding, which seemed to me to be a full-on Greek affair – complete with Greek dancing, balalaika-playing and pinning money to the wedding dress – and wonderful as it looked I really didn't think a wedding like that would reflect my background. Pete said that he wanted half our wedding to have Greek influences and I agreed to have some bits, though when it came to the tradition of pinning money to my dress I thought, *No way, I'm going to be spending a fortune on it, I don't want it to be ruined!* Luckily Claire found a fantastic wedding planner called Emma. As soon as I saw her portfolio I thought she would be ideal – she'd done some amazing events, like the after-party for the *Phantom of the Opera* and a stack of other film premiere after-parties. It looked like she would be the perfect person to give us the fairy-tale wedding I had dreamt of.

We didn't manage to find the venue for our wedding until mid-July, and by then time was ticking away as we had set the date for Saturday 10 September. I was getting so worried that I even considered having a marquee in my garden, but that didn't exactly match my dreams! Emma would go and look at a venue, then Claire would check it out and then Pete and I would go, but nowhere seemed right; nowhere had the wow factor I so wanted. But as soon as I saw Highclere Castle in Berkshire I knew it was the one. It had all the ingredients: a long drive

After a wonderful honeymoon, it was time to head home again.

Relaxing in our garden with the family.

I'm really close to my younger sister, Sophie.

The adorable pony we bought Harvey for his third birthday.

As *A Whole New World* topped the bestseller lists it was time for some signings!

I had my fourth (extremely painful) tattoo done in Las Vegas.

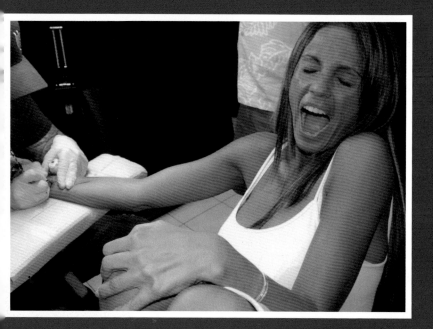

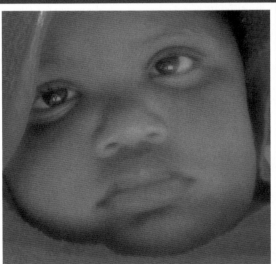

My beautiful boys.
Junior looking cool and
Harvey all wrapped up
after a swim.

Harvey giving his little brother a hug.

Strike a pose!

through stunning grounds, leading up to the beautiful Victorian building where I imagined myself making an entrance in my carriage; a grand, elegant room with high ceilings, where we could have the wedding ceremony; and plenty of space in the grounds for our marquee. And it could be completely closed off from the public and the press. Pete wasn't with me but I went with my instincts and said that it was the one and I knew he would trust me.

We had decided to do a deal with *OK!* magazine for exclusive pictures of our wedding and honeymoon, and that meant the press couldn't be allowed to get a picture of us – security would have to be very tight. We also decided to have the wedding filmed as part of our documentary series – I don't think there's ever been a film of a celebrity wedding before, except of course for royalty! And I thought that as we were going to be photographed for a magazine we may as well go the whole hog and be filmed as well. I'm so used to cameras now that I don't really notice them – at least that's what I thought until my wedding day, when I changed my mind, but that comes later . . .

Thank God for *OK!* is all I can say, because although I knew our wedding would be on the expensive side, when we started to get quotes in I couldn't believe what people were charging. Before we found Highclere some of the other venues were quoting us £100,000 just to hire them – and that didn't even include the cost of the marquee, which we would have to have as none of the castles had rooms big enough to hold the reception. Everything seemed to come at such a high price. We received catering quotes of £70,000; flowers were quoted at £20,000. I soon found out that the fantastic wedding planner expected to receive a fee of twenty per cent of whatever the wedding cost, though in the end we managed to come to an agreement which was less.

I know people think that we must have made a fortune out of our wedding, but the truth is we didn't make as much as everyone thinks we did as the wedding cost so much. We always wanted a fairy-tale wedding, so it was always going to be a big affair, but in order to get the deal with the magazine and ITV we really had to pull out the stops. We weren't just going to have a ceremony followed by a few speeches and a sit-down meal and disco – we were planning a series of spectacular entertainments. It would be more like watching a show, packed with surprises and wows. I told the wedding planner that I wanted our wedding to be like opening a fairy-tale book – I wanted it to look like the Cinderella story from the moment the guests arrived at the castle. And I wanted a lot of pink!

But while Pete and I weren't going to be making that much money, Claire, our manager, was going to be taking her usual percentage of the money we received from *OK!*, which really pissed us off. I knew that she had worked very hard to get the *OK!* deal and of course we appreciated that, but we couldn't help saying to each other in frustration, 'It's our wedding day and she seems to be treating it like any other job!'

'Please Claire,' Pete said to her on the phone. 'Won't you consider halving your percentage as it is our wedding day.' But she wasn't having any of it. In contrast, my make-up artist Gary Cockerill and hairdressers Nick Malenko and Royston Blythe said that they would do my make-up and hair and Pete's hair for free, as well as my mum and sister's hair and make-up as part of their wedding present to us which Pete and I so appreciated. And my friends Danielle

Charman and Melodie Pope who I'd known for years also did the bridesmaids' hair for free – also much appreciated.

In fact Pete and I got so fed up about how much money the wedding was costing us that we even considered having a beach wedding. But then we thought that, knowing our luck, someone would get pictures of it and make a killing out of selling them, and if anyone benefited from our wedding we really thought it should be us. And in my heart I knew I would be bitterly disappointed if I didn't have my fairy-tale wedding and get to wear my dream dress.

Ah yes, the dress! I decided to have it designed by the haute couture designer Isabell Kristensen. I love her glamorous and dazzling outfits. She's designed dresses for stars such as Shirley Bassey, Nicole Kidman, Jerry Hall and Helena Christensen. She had designed the gorgeous pink dress I'd worn in 2004 to present a prize at the British Book Awards – little knowing that the following year I'd be back as one of the nominees! We had planned a cheeky little twist on my evening dress: because I was going on to the *Loaded* awards, later that night, she had also made me a pair of tiny pink hot-pants – a much more appropriate outfit for a lad's mag bash – which I revealed when I took off my full-length skirt.

I told Isabell that I wanted a fairy-tale dress, that I wanted to look like a princess – it had to be big, sparkling, show-stopping and, of course, pink – and she took all my ideas on board. Every time I had a fitting I'd say that I wanted it bigger, that I wanted more glitz on it, more sparkle, and she'd say, 'Are you sure?'

Yes I was! The dress ended up being three metres wide, with a seven-metre long train. Isabell used thousands of Swarovski crystals to give the dress the sparkle I wanted – apparently it took twelve people over three weeks to hand-stitch them all on. The skirt was pale pink satin with pink tulle on top, covered with rose-pink crystals, as was my pink satin train; the top was a skin-tight bodice made entirely from rose-pink crystals, which showed off plenty of cleavage. Some people say that you shouldn't show cleavage on your wedding day, but I was going to show mine! That's what I'm about, and as it was my wedding day I thought I would do exactly what I wanted. As for the dress, it was perfect and it completely matched my imagination. Isabell said that making my wedding dress had been her dream job because no one had ever been as over the top as me! It was the biggest dress she'd ever created and has more crystals on it than any other. I had definitely picked a designer after my own heart because she told me, 'Too much for me is never enough!' I loved the dress – maybe not the price – I could have bought a house for what it cost me!

Because my dress was so huge I decided that I would have to have big hair and a crown, otherwise I would end up looking like a pin-head. So I had a beautiful crown designed, with rose and clear-coloured Swarovski crystals in the shape of inter-locking love-hearts, which I was going to wear with a waist-length tulle veil encrusted with diamanté. I had also decided to go brunette again – I'd loved being platinum blonde but it was such a high maintenance look to keep and I had ended up knackering my poor hair, which kept breaking. I also had a hairpiece made to give me extra-big hair.

As I was going to look like a princess, it was only fitting that I should arrive at my wedding in style. I was going to be in a carriage pulled by six white horses (or 'greys' in horsey speak) with pink plumes, each horse with a footman to lead him, dressed in silver top hats and tails. And not just any old carriage – this was a glass-domed Cinderella carriage. The inside had been customised for me with baby-pink satin-lined seats and a pink fur carpet. Outside was decorated with roses, lilies, feathers and, yes, Swarovski crystals again! Unfortunately, because of our magazine deal the glass had to be covered by pink satin curtains so I wouldn't get papped by any photographers flying overhead. 'Great,' I said to Claire. 'So while everyone is enjoying themselves, drinking champagne, I'll be cooped up in a bloody round ball. What fun is that?!' I threatened to sneak a peep through the curtains but Claire said there was no way I could because of the strict terms of the *OK!* deal. And because my skirt was so enormous I couldn't actually fit it in the carriage and so I had to wear the little pink tutu Isabell had made for me – also in pink tulle and encrusted with crystals. I planned to wear the tutu later on in the evening so I could do some serious dancing.

And after the dress, what does every girl want? A ring, of course! Typically I said that I wanted the biggest ring ever, so Pete and I went to our jeweller with our ideas. Bling doesn't even begin to describe the rings he came up with: Pete's is a whopper – handmade with twenty princess-cut diamonds mounted in platinum – and mine is so big I can hardly bend my finger! It's handmade, mounted in platinum, with thirty-five princess-cut diamonds, elevated on a bridge of pink gold (which is really rare) and encrusted with pink diamonds – it is just stunning. Both rings cost a fortune – mine more than Pete's naturally, but that's a bride's prerogative.

Then we had the thorny issue of who to invite. I was determined that none of Pete's many exes would be at the wedding – I knew it would completely spoil my day if they were. Earlier in the year, before I had Junior, I had flown to LA to meet Pete. He was recording some tracks there and I saw Lisa, the air hostess he had slept with years before we met. Immediately my back was up and I said to Claire, 'I'm going to get my revenge, just you watch this.' So when we left the Virgin first-class lounge for the plane and were escorted by another air hostess, I made a point of saying, 'Thank God, we're out of there!'

Immediately she asked me if everything was alright.

'Not really,' I replied. 'I've just seen Lisa, who Pete slept with years ago, and to be honest it makes me feel sick. And if she thinks she's coming to our wedding, she's got another thing coming!'

Just to make sure the message got back to Lisa, when I was on the plane and another stewardess was giving me a shoulder massage and commented how tense I was, I replied that yes I was tense, because I had seen Lisa, and I told her the same thing I'd said to the other girl.

When I arrived at LA Pete told me he'd just received a text from Lisa out of the blue, asking him to help her with her tai-chi moves.

'What a cheeky bitch!' I exclaimed. 'She's definitely not coming to our wedding!'

'Kate,' Pete sighed, 'I've got to ask her. She's such a good friend of the family, and what happened is in the past; I don't think of her like that any more.'

'She's not coming, Pete! And that's final.'

'Please, Kate, it's going to be really hard explaining her absence to my family,' Pete pleaded with me.

'I don't give a shit, Pete. You should have thought

about that before you shagged her. I bet you wouldn't like it if I invited any of my exes to the wedding, would you?'

He admitted that of course he wouldn't.

'Well then,' I said, 'you're not doing it to me!'

I returned home on a separate flight, and when he arrived home Pete told me that as soon as he got off the plane Lisa was there to meet him. Immediately he told her that he couldn't be seen walking with her because if they were photographed together I wouldn't be very happy. She then asked if she was still invited to the wedding. Pete replied, 'It's not just down to me. It's Katie's day as well and I know you won't be getting an invite from her.'

She persisted, 'But you'll invite me, won't you Pete?'

'No,' he replied. 'You're not coming.'

I was hugely relieved when Pete told me – I didn't want to see her face when I was marrying the man of my dreams. Katie Price 1, Pete's exes 0 – and that's just the way I wanted it to stay.

But it wasn't just over Pete's exes that I had a problem – I discovered that my manager also intended to ask someone who I really didn't appreciate being invited: her sister Vicky. She was the one who had stopped me from seeing Pete in Australia, and even though Pete told me she was only doing what Claire had told her, I still didn't want to see her at my wedding. Eventually, when Pete explained that he'd known her for years, I realised I would have to ask her, but I insisted I only wanted her to come to the reception – I didn't want her at the ceremony. She wouldn't realise that there was a problem between us as I'm always nice to her but I've never forgotten what she put me through.

We could only invite 150 people to the ceremony as the room couldn't fit any more – my dress and train were so huge that I needed an extra-wide aisle to walk down! So I really wanted the people at the ceremony to be the ones who mattered most to us both. I was furious when I looked down the wedding list and saw that Vicky and her other half had been invited to the ceremony. I quickly put a stop to that but was annoyed when I saw she was sitting at the central table at the reception with Richard Desmond and his wife. The press tried to make out that we'd asked people we'd never even met and printed snide little comments alleged to have been made by those celebs about how they weren't coming. Well, the truth is that some of the people the press mentioned hadn't even been invited – we didn't ask Myleene Klass, Shane Richie or Patsy Kensit. We had invited Frank Skinner because I've done so many interviews with him and he was quoted in the press as saying he would rather go to the football than come to our wedding. He then wrote to us apologising for that comment. To be honest it was no skin off my nose. Quite often when you do a deal with *OK!* you have to invite a certain number of celebrities just to get the deal, but our deal wasn't like that – it wouldn't have made any difference if we hadn't asked any at all.

Stressful as some of it was, I loved planning my wedding. It was so exciting seeing all the ideas coming together – though typically we left registering our marriage right until the last minute and did it just within the six-week deadline! But as our wedding day got closer Pete and I had some of the worst arguments of our relationship – so bad that at one point I even wondered whether I should be marrying him. I was still feeling low, not myself at all – I felt vulnerable, all my emotions felt raw and at the surface. Pete had just finished writing his auto-biography and I didn't want to read it, as I knew that reading about his exes would do nothing to improve my mood, but a friend told me about some of the things he'd written – in particular his description of his sexual exploits with Mel B really upset me. I know I have been frank about my lovers in the past, but this was so graphic. Perhaps if I had been feeling stronger I might have been able to laugh it off – as it was I felt incredibly hurt by it. I was already pissed off about the whole Mel B affair because when I had been at the jeweller's earlier in the year and was flicking through the catalogue I came across a picture of Mel B wearing a ring exactly like my engagement ring, except it had a green stone in the middle.

'It's not nice, Pete, knowing that she's got the same ring as me!' I had said. Pete replied that he hadn't known that she had that ring and so it wasn't his fault. Which was true, and I did love my engagement ring. I just wished she didn't have the same one . . .

Then I started to feel anxious about whether I could trust Pete. I found myself thinking, *Does he really love me? Does he really want to marry me?* He had planned to marry the woman he went out with before he met me and he wasn't faithful to her – could I really trust him to be faithful to me? I think every bride-to-be has cold feet at some point. And it wasn't just me – Pete kept having nightmares that I was leaving him. He'd wake up in the night saying, 'Please don't cheat on me Kate.' Probably because he's been so bad in the past it's coming back to haunt him. But he has no need to worry – I'm not going to be unfaithful. At least I had finally got rid of his mobile phone with all his exes' numbers on it, a month before the wedding, which reassured me.

Bizarrely, just before I went into the jungle my mum and I discovered a mobile phone had been left on Harvey's buggy. When we checked it over we realised that it was Pete's and he must have left it there by mistake. I meant to tell him but it slipped my mind once we started filming and my mum took it home with her. When we arrived back in England I remembered the phone, but I decided I didn't want him to have it back in case it had numbers of other girls on it. Some months later I mentioned to Pete that we'd found his phone, but he didn't believe me, and finally Mum brought it round to our house in August 2005. While Pete was downstairs in the kitchen, cooking, I sat in my dressing room and read through all the texts, getting more and more wound up. Many of the texts were from some of the exes I'd already met, and some of them were very saucy and intimate, saying things like, 'I'm thinking about what I'd like you to do to me' and, 'It was horrible leaving you in bed asleep this morning' and 'I love you too', obviously in reply to him saying he loved them. I looked in the outbox but couldn't find any of his replies. That did it! I went downstairs and found Pete and started quoting some of the texts to him.

'What are you on about?' Pete demanded.

'Nothing,' I replied sulkily, then blurted out that I'd found his phone and read his texts, and I pretended I'd read his replies.

'Give it to me then,' Pete said, holding out his hand.

'No way!' I shouted. 'I'm going to delete all the numbers and all the texts.'

And then Pete started getting really aggressive, shouting back, 'Give me my phone! Don't think that you can control me!'

So I stormed upstairs, grabbed the phone, raced downstairs and threw it at him, saying, 'Go on then, have your fucking girls' numbers!' And I ran back upstairs, locked myself in my bedroom and threw myself on the bed, shaking with anger and hurt. He followed me and stood outside laughing, saying, 'Are you really that jealous? That's so sweet!'

'Fuck off, Pete,' I shouted back. 'Don't wind me up!' I hated the feeling that he was patronising me.

'Please open the door. I promise I won't say anything else.'

Reluctantly I got up and opened the door.

Pete smiled at me. 'Come and sit on the bed with me. I've got something to show you.'

We sat down together and Pete held out the phone. 'I'm going to delete all the numbers now – I always would have done, I just don't want you to think that you're in control of me.'

So he went through all the numbers and deleted them, and read all the texts and deleted them. Finally he took out the SIM card and destroyed it. *Yippee!* I thought. And my bad mood instantly lifted. If only everything could have been resolved that easily . . .

* * *

The weekend before our wedding was Pete's parents' fiftieth wedding anniversary. Pete wanted to spend

the week before in Cyprus seeing his family and
friends, but I couldn't go because I had to film my
fitness video and I also had to fly to Monaco for a
final dress-fitting. Pete asked if he could take Junior
with him and, even though I wanted to say no
because I knew I would miss him and I knew I still
hadn't bonded with him in the way I wanted to, I
found myself agreeing that he could. It was a mistake.
Although I was working and wouldn't have seen as
much of him as I would have liked, I still needed to
be close to my baby. I could at least have spent time
with him in the mornings and evenings, on my own.
As it was, I was trying to be fair to too many people –
letting Pete's family have time with Junior and
thinking that as Pete was the father he was entitled to
do things with his son – and not thinking enough of
my own needs. Inside, all I could think was, *Please
don't take my baby away from me.* Not only did I not
want to be separated from him, but also I hated the
thought of so many different people picking him up
and holding him. I felt that ever since Junior was born
I'd had no time with him to bond because we'd been
surrounded by so many people and because I'd been
working and planning the wedding. Sometimes I felt

that Junior didn't really know that I was his mum – a feeling I never had with Harvey.

I hated Pete being away with the baby. Harvey was still in hospital and I felt stressed out and lonely and missed everyone. My hen party happened that week but it was a disaster. With Harvey still in hospital I really didn't want to do anything too wild. It ended up being planned at the last minute, and as a result hardly any of my friends could come. I had especially wanted my friend Clare to be there. She's one of my closest friends and I've known her since I was eleven. I was upset because I knew she probably wouldn't be able to make the wedding either, as she was pregnant and her baby was due just a few days before then. I had hardly seen her during my own pregnancy and I really missed her friendship. She hadn't wanted to come on the cruise as she had just fallen in love and hadn't wanted to be parted from her new boyfriend – I completely understood because that's exactly how I felt about Pete.

I had met her boyfriend when I asked Clare and him round for dinner along with some other friends, the day before Christmas Eve. Usually Clare would have been in the kitchen with all of us, having a laugh, but this time she stayed in the lounge with Darren and both of them were very quiet during dinner, which wasn't like Clare at all. When we spoke afterwards I managed to get it out of her that Darren thought I was arrogant.

'Clare,' I said, 'you've known me all these years; you know I'm not like that!' I felt really hurt that her boyfriend was coming between us. I asked her if she still wanted to be one of my bridesmaids and she replied that she didn't because she was pregnant and didn't want people staring at her. I asked if Ella, her daughter, could be one and she agreed, so I had a dress made for her. After I'd had Junior, and a few weeks before the wedding, I went round to see Clare. It was so good to catch up with her but neither of us mentioned the wedding, which was a bit strange, then as I was leaving her boyfriend appeared. He simply said, 'Hi,' to me and then walked into the kitchen; he didn't even come into the living room and have a proper chat or see Junior, and I sensed that he really didn't like me. I wanted to challenge Clare and say, 'Do you really want to let a guy like this ruin our friendship?' but I knew her hormones were all over the place and I kept my mouth shut.

Still, I was very upset when she didn't make my hen party.

My hen party was a shambles. I was two hours late getting to Champneys Forest Mere – a health farm in Hampshire – because my navigator wrongly directed me and I ended up in the middle of a wood, thinking it was a wind-up! But I didn't feel like laughing. From the moment I arrived the day just felt like work – it was all about getting enough pictures for the magazine. I had been promised lots of relaxing treatments, which I really could have done with as I felt so stressed, but I only had my toes painted. I had just got into the flotation tank – which is supposed to make you feel like you've had eight hours' sleep after just twenty minutes – when Claire, my manager, opened up the lid, switched the lights on and said I had to pose for a picture.

'Thanks a lot, Claire,' I exclaimed. 'I'm naked under here!' And that was the end of my flotation-tank experience. Yes it was good to be with my friends and family, and yes the setting was lovely, but it wasn't a laugh and everyone got fed up with having to pose for pictures the whole time. I just wanted to get the day over and done with and go home. I left at half past seven and the final straw was being pulled over by the police for speeding and getting fined. When the pictures were published I thought it was obvious that I hadn't been enjoying myself. To add insult to injury Pete had been having a great time out in Cyprus – going out with his mates every day, sunbathing, swimming and generally having a laugh and enjoying the build-up to the wedding – whereas I couldn't have felt more stressed and unhappy.

Given my bad week I was really looking forward to being reunited with Pete and Junior, but things didn't get off to a great start. From the moment I arrived in Cyprus I felt that Pete was watching how I was with the baby and comparing how close I was with Harvey. I know he didn't mean to make me feel bad, but because I felt so vulnerable I couldn't help feeling that he was criticising me. Whenever I walked into the room where Junior was Pete said, 'Aren't you going to say hello to your son?' before I'd even had the chance to go over and pick him up.

I felt like saying, *Shut up! I know he's there; you don't have to tell me what to do*, but instead I'd reply, 'I have said hello to him.'

'Well you don't look very happy to see him,' was

his answer. Which really wasn't helping me. I felt Junior had been taken away from me. On one of the days Pete's mum had him lying on her bed in his nappy because it was so hot, which was totally the right thing to do, but it upset me because I hadn't been the one looking after him; I hadn't been the one in control. I felt like saying, *Please don't do this to my son, ask me first.* And it seemed like every time I got a few minutes to hold my son, Pete's mum or sister would say, 'Oh, let me have the baby.' And because I didn't want his family to feel like they were missing out I handed him over, even though it hurt. I knew they just wanted to show love to Junior and I also knew they had no idea how I was feeling – why would they? I hadn't even been able to show Pete the full extent of my sadness because I felt so overwhelmed – I'd never felt like this before.

I also discovered that when Pete had gone out every day with his mates, his mum had looked after Junior. When I challenged him about this he said that his mum had six kids so she knew what to do. Of course that was true, but I still felt like saying, 'Thanks a lot, Pete. I've been working my arse off while you've been out here having fun, leaving your mum to look after the baby.' Everything was winding me up and stressing me. He told me his mum had said that I was really good to let him bring Junior with him, because if it had been her she never would have allowed that to happen. There I was trying to do the right thing, and it turned out that she would have understood if I had said no. But I knew Pete would have argued with me if I had said he couldn't take Junior, because he was often saying, 'He's my son as well; I've got a say.'

A few weeks prior to our Cyprus visit we'd had another argument. We had been trying to sort out our pre-nuptial agreement and Pete had happened to ask his solicitor who would get custody of Junior if we split up. I'd told him that I thought the mother always got custody, saying you couldn't separate Harvey and Junior as they're brothers. Suddenly the idea of us splitting up really upset me and I turned round to Pete and said, 'I bet you're only with me because you think you would lose out on Junior if we broke up.'

'Yes,' he replied. 'That's one of the reasons.'

'Well, I don't want to be with someone who's only marrying me for that!' I shouted.

'Kate, I love you, but I don't love you that much to put up with all your shit,' he replied.

I know that we were arguing when he said what he did about Junior, and I know that you often say things you don't mean when you argue, but I knew he meant this and it stuck in my head. And as if him criticising me about Junior while we were in Cyprus wasn't bad enough, I also had to deal with one of his exes – Lisa, the air hostess – who his parents had invited to their fiftieth anniversary party. Before I flew out I told him straight that I didn't want to see her, that I didn't care if she was a friend of the family; it was disrespectful to me to have to sit in the same room as her. I even texted Pete's sister, because Lisa is such a good friend of hers, saying I really didn't want her there. His sister replied that she didn't really know about the situation, but that Lisa had already flown out. I felt like saying, *Who is more important – her or me? Who is about to be part of the family?* Once I arrived I discovered that she was coming and I was distraught. Pete came up with the usual arguments – how their affair had happened years ago and there was nothing in it, and how he couldn't say anything to his parents because she was a family friend and it was their party

– when really he didn't want to admit that he'd shagged the girl. And I know for a fact that if his mum and dad had known how upset I was about Lisa coming they wouldn't have invited her.

Earlier Pete had said that he wanted to add 'respect' to the list of our wedding vows and now I threw it back in his face, saying it hardly showed respect for me having his ex put in my face. We argued over it so badly that I ended up shouting, 'Why don't you get your stuff and fuck off out of my house then?!'

Pete still didn't seem to get why it upset me so much and replied, 'Why are you stressing so much? It's making me hate you and I can't get close to you. What's going on?'

I think it was perfectly reasonable for me to be upset about having to see one of his exes, but it's true that I was stressing about everything – I think my deep unhappiness over feeling that I hadn't bonded with Junior was spilling out into all areas of my life. Pete and I had never argued like this before, and when I was pregnant we had both been so happy and excited. But when Junior was born everything changed. I phoned my mum up in tears, saying that we weren't getting married and that it was all over, and she was in the hairdresser's having a dress rehearsal for her hair. As I sobbed down the phone I knew inside that I was being angry and stressed, but I couldn't stop myself feeling like this. For a few horrible moments I thought I hated him.

In the end I put on a brave face and went to the party, but the atmosphere between Pete and me was shit and we were barely speaking. I was seriously wondering whether I should marry him and we were only a week away from the wedding. But he was cool about Lisa, and when he went round saying hello to all the guests he made a point of not saying anything to her as he knew I was watching. But the final icing on the cake was that another of his exes turned up – the daughter of the restaurant owners. Pete told me he couldn't help that either. *Well*, I thought to myself bitterly, *I suppose I've just got to accept that wherever I go with him there's going to be girls he's shagged*. But I hated it.

I flew back to England on my own because I had publicity photos to do for my fitness video, and Pete and Junior flew back a few days later. It was good to be reunited with them and I tried to put the events of

Cyprus out of my mind. I loved Pete and I wanted to marry him, I just hated feeling so angry and so out of control. I had told Pete a little of my anxieties about how I felt I hadn't bonded with Junior, but typically I had underplayed just how bad I felt. But on the Wednesday before our wedding we saw the doctor and for once I didn't put on a brave face and Pete saw the depth of my sadness. We had taken Junior to the Portland to have his injections. When the doctor asked us how things were Pete immediately said, 'Well I hope she changes after we get married because she's seriously stressing me out.'

Well fuck off then! I wanted to say.

'It's normal to be stressed with the wedding coming up, especially when you've just had a baby,' the doctor put in.

Now was my chance to say how I felt. 'To be honest, I don't think I'm bonding with the baby.'

He asked me why, and suddenly I found myself in tears as I tried to explain what had happened with us having Pete's family to stay, having a maternity nurse and me working.

'You've had no time with the baby and you need quality time – forget the work, forget the cameras. It's not good for you or the baby that you've gone straight back to work; you need time,' the doctor said calmly, and I knew he was right.

He went on to say that he didn't want to put me on medication, even though he thought I might be suffering slightly from depression. He wanted us to try and work through it. 'But please,' he said, 'stop the cameras.'

'I can't,' I sobbed. 'They're going to be at the wedding and even the first few days of our honeymoon.' But even as I cried, I felt slightly better for having told someone at last. The doctor helped explain to Pete how I felt. I didn't feel quite so alone any more as I knew that Pete understood. I was also feeling happier because we had rehired the first maternity nurse who had worked for us and I felt much more relaxed with her.

I still didn't have any time though – Pete and I had spent the day recording our duet, 'A Whole New World', which was going to be played at the wedding. We recorded it with the same music producers who I'd recorded my Eurovision song with and they couldn't believe how different my voice sounded now I wasn't pregnant. They said my voice was much more powerful and it was obvious that the baby had been restricting me before. They also confirmed what I'd known all along – ballads suit my voice best. But I felt a rush of happiness that Wednesday – Pete now knew how I felt and that had to be a good thing. Best of all after nearly six weeks we could pick up Harvey from hospital.

The doctors had finally come to the conclusion that Harvey's weight gain was caused by his septo-optic dysplasia. Usually a child with Harvey's condition wants to eat constantly and that's why they can get so big. But in Harvey's case he has all the symptoms – i.e. he is larger than he should be, as if he does eat a lot – but in fact he can survive on very little food and still have energy. He doesn't become lethargic or moody when he doesn't eat, like the rest of us would; he can still carry on. They said that they had never seen a child like him before. They measured his metabolic rate and found out how many calories he needs and how much exercise he needs to do to burn them up. They admitted that I was right about his eating – i.e. his refusal to eat vegetables and needing to eat food with a hard texture and they ended up having to give him what I did, except in smaller portions. They discovered that he can exist on two Weetabix or two slices of toast for breakfast, a lunch of no more than five chicken nuggets and no more than ten chips or where possible a healthy alternative, to be supplemented with two vitamin drinks. If he has any more than that he will put on weight unless he has more exercise to burn off the extra calories.

I was told I must stick to the same routine with his eating and not offer him snacks between meals if he has rejected his food. They had also tried to get him into a routine with his nap so he would have a two-hour sleep in the afternoon. The hospital had also devised an exercise plan that we would have to do with him every day. They planned to take out his tonsils and adenoids later in the year and he needed to lose weight to minimise the risk of having a general anaesthetic. They hoped that by removing his adenoids he would stop getting earaches, and that might stop him being so upset by loud noises and would help with his breathing at night. *At last*, I thought, *they're going to do something about his sensitive ears – that should make all our lives so much easier.*

To try and get Harvey's sleep pattern into a normal routine the doctors were considering giving him melatonin – a drug given to people to help them overcome jet lag. They hoped this would stop Harvey having such long sleeps and being so difficult to wake. While I was glad that this might help, I thought, *Poor Harvey, he's going to have even more drugs pumped into him.* But I was so happy to have my little boy back home. We could be a family again and I could look forward to my wedding day.

CHAPTER SIXTEEN

A WHOLE NEW WORLD

On the day before our wedding I had arranged to do a photo shoot in my wedding dress – without Pete, obviously! I thought it would mean that I would have to do fewer photos on the big day itself and so would have more time to enjoy myself. But I hated doing it – after all, what woman wants to put on her wedding dress the day before and have her hair and make-up done exactly as she will on her wedding day? Which is what I had to do so no one would know that these pictures had been taken at a different time. I couldn't help feeling that it had taken some of the shine off my big day.

Pete and I were also pissed off because one of the papers had run a story about our wedding, and because some of their details were so accurate it was obvious that there had been a leak from someone involved in our wedding. Up until Thursday the only people who knew exactly what was happening on our wedding day were Pete, my mum, the wedding planner, Claire and me, and up till then practically everything the press had printed had been wrong – apparently the wedding cake was in the shape of my boobs – I mean, please! Thursday was the day when everyone involved in the wedding – from the caterers to the performers – was given the itinerary, and someone must have got straight on the phone to the tabloid. But I tried not to let it get to me – it was the day before my wedding and I really didn't want to be stressed.

Later our families and some of the groomsmen and bridesmaids arrived at the castle and we all had dinner together. Finally I started to relax, enjoy myself and feel excited about the next day. But I was still absolutely knackered – I probably needed a really early night but I didn't get to bed until 2 a.m. I was sharing a room with some of my bridesmaids – Sarah Harding, Michelle Heaton, Sally Cairns and my sister Sophie. Sarah, Michelle and my sister got peckish in the night and nipped downstairs to raid the kitchen, where they met up with Pete and his groomsmen, and they didn't go to bed until 4 a.m. – cheeky devils!

My other bridesmaids were Pete's sister Debbie, Michelle Clack and Kerry Katona. I knew all along who I wanted as my bridesmaids – they were all people I felt close to. My only regret was that my friend Clare's daughter, Ella, wasn't going to be one of my bridesmaids after all. Clare had her baby, a girl called Carys, on the Wednesday before my wedding and so wasn't up to coming – I had also invited her mum and dad hoping that they might bring Ella, but they didn't. Claire texted me in the morning saying, 'Have a great day, and so sorry I can't be there.' And I was sorry too. I had always imagined that Clare would be there to share my big day with me. I decided that I would send Clare Ella's bridesmaid dress and the diamond bracelet

I'd had made for her, as I was giving to all my bridesmaids.

On Saturday 10 September I woke up at seven, with butterflies of excitement. I was getting married today! After checking that it wasn't raining I went straight into Harvey and Junior's room, wanting to spend time with them as I knew it would be hard later on. I fed Junior and played with Harvey, then Pete knocked on the door.

'You can't come in!' I shouted to him. 'I'm in here and it's bad luck to see me before the wedding!' So off Pete went. *Still*, I thought to myself, *he's got a nice surprise coming to him*, as I'd had a pair of cufflinks made for him – with a 'J' on one and an 'H' on the other in diamonds – as a wedding gift, which he was going to be given in a couple of hours.

We weren't getting married until four in the after-noon and the day really seemed to drag – I wanted to get down that aisle and marry Pete! Gary, my make-up artist, and Nick and Royston, the guys who do my hair, started working on me at ten. I'd had all these visions that I'd be sipping champagne, but when someone offered me a glass later on I found I couldn't drink. I took a few sips and really didn't enjoy it – I certainly didn't get that nice warm, fuzzy feeling I'd been hoping for. Instead I felt very emotional and kept crying. And my family and friends didn't help, as they kept bursting into tears as well! We were listening to 'A Whole New World', the duet Pete and I had recorded for our wedding, and that kept setting us all off!

'Please will everyone stop crying!' I begged them all. 'And don't look at me, because you're making me start!' In fact my right eye got so sore from all the tears that Gary, my fantastic make-up artist, had real difficulty getting my false eyelashes to stick on!

For once in my life it looked as if I was going to be on time, and as it got nearer to the ceremony everyone around me was stressing and running round like headless chickens whereas I felt incredibly calm. *Wow*, I thought to myself, *I thought I'd be the one who was stressed out*, but I wasn't. Because of the exclusive *OK!* deal it was crucial that no one else got a picture of the wedding and security around the castle was incredibly tight. It was like a scene from *Mission Impossible*, getting to my carriage without giving the paparazzi a chance to snap me. I had to be smuggled out of the castle, under a number of umbrellas, and into the Range Rover with blacked-out windows in order to be driven to my carriage. I had put on my tutu skirt as there was no way my three metre wide dress would fit in the carriage. Outside I could hear the helicopters buzzing overhead – no doubt full of paparazzi dying to get a shot of me, but I was not going to let that happen! As we moved along the drive Vanessa Feltz came in the opposite direction, preventing us from getting to the carriage. Everyone panicked and Nicola, who was driving, said, 'What shall I do?!'

I said, 'You're driving a 4×4, just go on the grass. What's the big deal?!' *Honestly*, I thought to myself, *I should have driven.*

Then as Nicola reversed into the marquee she nearly hit one of the posts holding up the marquee. It was not *Mission Impossible* anymore but more like a *Carry On* film! And then I discovered that they hadn't attached the horses to the carriage and we had to sit in the car for half an hour while they attached them. I knew that all my guests were having a lovely time outside the castle, drinking champagne and chatting, and I wished I was with them. But finally we could get into the carriage.

'Right then,' my stepdad Paul said, 'this is your last chance – is this definitely what you want to do?'

'Yes!' I exclaimed.

'So long as you're sure, because you can still pull out if you want to.'

'I'm getting married!' was my reply.

Then the horses set off – I was on my way! But suddenly we turned a corner and the carriage got caught on a bush. *Shit!* I thought, *this really could only happen to me.* As the horses carried on the carriage started tipping. 'Stop!' we called out in a panic. The driver managed to halt the horses but the carriage was still tipping over and we couldn't get out because the bush was blocking the door and the helicopters were flying above us. Somehow the footmen managed to right the carriage and we were off again. *I bet the press got a picture of that*, I thought and they'd call it 'Jordan's wedding day bush!', but luckily they didn't, as it turned out. As we approached the castle and our guests, a fanfare struck up and I couldn't resist opening the curtains and shouting out 'Wayhey!' to everyone, even though I'd been given strict instructions not to.

When we pulled up round the other side of the castle the security guards had put umbrellas up again to shield me from the paps, but I could still see the helicopters through the gaps and if I could see them they could certainly see me, so then we decided to go for a decoy. Claire, my manager, was draped in several white sheets and got out of the carriage. All that you could see of her were her pink-ribboned shoes. Well it worked: she was photographed and the next day her shoes appeared in the press and everyone thought they were mine! The press obviously thought they had their shot and backed off slightly, and that's when I nipped out of the carriage and into the castle.

I then had to get into my skirt and have the train attached. By now I was feeling nervous and it seemed to be taking for ever to get my guests through security and into the ceremony room. *Hurry up!* I wanted to say, *I'm ready now and this dress is bloody heavy, let's get on with it!* Suddenly the gospel choir started singing and I knew that my sister Sophie and friend Sally would be walking with Harvey up the aisle. We had rehearsed this the day before and I just prayed nothing would upset him and he would have his big moment – it meant so much to me and Pete that he was out of hospital and with us for our wedding. Then it was my turn, as the choir sang Whitney Houston's 'I Have Nothing'. Paul held my hand and I could see that he was crying. I thought, *Please don't look at me or you'll start me off again.* I kept having to wave my hand in front of my face to stop the tears. As I walked up the aisle everyone applauded and I could see Pete standing at the top with his back to me. This was it, the moment I had been waiting for.

But I suddenly had a horrible thought that I might have a panic attack – I guess I was feeling so over-whelmed by emotion. I was also extremely hot. *Don't have a panic attack!* I told myself. I was also thinking of how I had to read out my vows with everyone watching me, plus I was being filmed. *Oh no!* I thought, *I'm not going to be able to cope.* But as soon as Pete saw me he said, 'You look so beautiful!' and he cried, so the tears streamed down his face. I knew what he was going to be wearing because we had decided on it together with Isabell Kristensen, but even so he took my breath away because he looked so handsome.

We had chosen our vows and I had been rehearsing them in the run-up to the wedding, but, typically, on the day I couldn't get some of my words out properly, and matrimony didn't come out quite right – it sounded like I'd had one too many glasses of champagne, when I'd barely touched a drop! In the vow, 'I promise to respect, love and be faithful always,' I did a bit of cheeky ad-libbing and my version went: 'I promise to respect, love and be absolutely faithful always.' I wasn't sure if you could add words, but I did it anyway. At one point my nerves got the better of me, and I went blank and forgot that I was supposed to be repeating what the registrar said, so there was a rather awkward pause in the proceedings.

Then my brother Daniel read the poem 'Love Is'.

> More beautiful than roses
> Much deeper than the seas
> Stronger than a hurricane
> But timid like a breeze

Real as in a picture
But yet it can't be seen
More beautiful than anything
As vivid as a dream

Precious as rare jewels
A bond between two hearts
A symphony of feelings
When time is spent apart

Sharing common interests
Working through all fears
Looking at yourself
As if two were in the mirror

Finding common ground
On issues not agreed
Giving into arguments
Tending all your needs

Being there for always
Is all I want to do
Holding you forever
Because our love is true

He completely broke down in tears halfway through, which is totally unlike him – he's like me usually; he never cries. Even when our grandad died he wouldn't show how upset he was; he kept himself together. But he didn't now – the tears poured down his face and he could barely get the words out. As he read, I had to look away as I could feel my own eyes filling with tears; my nose started running and I was doing my best not to sniff. I didn't dare look at my family or the bridesmaids, as I knew that would make me cry more. It was the poem which had been read at his wedding and at the end he gave us a couple of lines of advice which his best man had given him at his own wedding – 'Live every day as if it's your last and live every night as if it's your first.'

I couldn't help thinking that there was so much emotion at my wedding – it was more like a bloody funeral at times! All I can say is thank God for Gary, my brilliant make-up artist, because my eye make-up didn't budge! Pete's brother Danny also read a poem, 'The Wedding Song', which we'd chosen for its beautiful lines such as 'I love you more than ever and I haven't even begun' and 'And if there is eternity, I'll love you there again; you're the other half of what I am.'

For one heart-stopping moment when Pete went to put the wedding ring on my finger I thought it wasn't going to fit, as it was slightly too tight, but he managed it and everyone gasped in amazement at the size of it! As he put it on my finger he was holding my hand tightly and we were really gazing into each other's eyes. In the days before the wedding we had been practising putting our rings on and had found it really hard to keep staring into each other's eyes – I'd have to blink or look away – but now we kept staring into each other's eyes. We held each other's gazes and it really was a magical moment. The registrar pronounced us man and wife and I got to kiss my husband for the first time . . .

The gospel choir burst into 'Signed, Sealed, Delivered I'm Yours' as we signed the register. I'd been filmed and photographed all day and it really hadn't bothered me, but suddenly the *OK!* photographer was calling out, 'Look at the camera Kate and Pete!' and I thought, *Can't I just enjoy this moment? I've only just got married – give me a minute!* Apparently not, because after signing the register for real we then had to stage signing it while he snapped away. Then I had the task of turning my dress round and walking back down the aisle – no small achievement I can tell you, moving that seven metres of train! It was so lovely seeing everyone smiling away at us as we walked past them. Inside I was bubbling over with happiness – we were married!

I wanted to see my family and friends right then, but as soon as I left the ceremony room we had to go into the room that had been set up for our photo shoot while all our guests made their way to the reception. I didn't have a problem with having photographs done and I'm eternally grateful for the *OK!* deal which enabled us to have our fairy-tale wedding, but I did have a problem with the photographer. I had already said before the wedding that I didn't want to be photographed by this particular man because while he might be a brilliant photographer, I don't get on with him and I don't like his way of working, but in the end I had no choice. I really wish it hadn't been him. As far as I was concerned he made no attempt to make the shoot fun and a laugh. From the moment he started taking pictures he was the one in control, shouting out 'Shuffle in!' and 'Look at the camera!' and 'Smile!' – suddenly my wedding day didn't feel like my wedding day any more, it felt like work. I had only just got married and I was on a high, but straight away it was ruined. The photographs burst that bubble of happiness I was in. He only seemed to be interested in photographing us with the celebrities. I had just seen Beverley Goodway – the photographer who took my pictures when I started out as a Page 3 girl, an absolutely lovely guy who I hadn't seen for years – and I really wanted to get a photograph with him, but the photographer just said, 'We'll do it later.' We didn't, of course. And I didn't even have a picture taken of my brother Daniel and me, only one in a group shot. *Fucking hell*, I thought, *This is really pissing me off!* He didn't even seem interested in arranging my dress so it was showed off to its best advantage.

'You know, you could say please and thank you!' Pete exclaimed after we had been bossed around for yet another picture. And I looked at Lisa Palta – the editor of *OK!* magazine – and raised my eyebrows as if to say, 'Help me, this is ruining my wedding day!'

'I can't bear it!' I finally said to Claire in frustration. 'How many more pictures have I got to do?!'

Dan, who is the other photographer I work with a lot, and who had been taking some of the wedding pictures earlier in the day as I was getting ready, always makes the shoots fun, and if he had been taking these posed pictures I would have enjoyed the experience. As it was, for two hours we were stuck in the room with the *OK!* photographer, and what should have been a pleasure was turning into a chore which I hated every single minute of – I just wanted to get it over and done with. I know all brides are photographed, but for most of them it's a novelty and they can get a buzz from it, whereas this was making it feel like work. Usually my *OK!* shoots are such fun, which is what this one should have been but it wasn't. My dress was really starting to hurt me as the corset top had been laced up too tightly, and the skirt was so heavy I was starting to feel tired and hot. I wanted to be celebrating with my guests. They were tucking into champagne and cocktails, nibbling on the delicious canapés and enjoying the string quartet while I was in a thoroughly bad mood.

Finally he was finished with us and we were free to join our guests in the marquee. Because we needed to be shielded from the press, there was a hundred-metre long canopied walkway with a fuchsia pink carpet leading into the marquee. As soon as I'd seen it I had thought it would make a great aisle. We had wanted our wedding to have three reveals, the first of which was the marquee where the guests had champagne and canapés. It was stunning, with white lining and pink carpeting, and the ceiling was draped with black fabric pin-pricked with tiny white lights, which made it look like the starlit sky. Hanging in the centre of the room was an impressive Swarovski crystal chandelier, and there were decorations round the room with shocking pink flowers, feathers and sequins. Unfortunately I didn't get much time to mingle with my guests before it was time to go through to dinner. And this was the second reveal: one of the walls of the marquee was lifted up to reveal the stunning dining area – the ceiling was filled with pink fairy lights and more chandeliers, and at the centre of each table was a bay tree decorated with crystals, and feathers and sequins. I had never simply wanted flowers – I wanted something more lasting

Pete and I on a fairytale photoshoot.

Taking some time out from the photoshoot to enjoy DisneyWorld.

Enjoying the magical Mickey Mouse trip.

Getting ready for another shoot.

Pete and I are happier than ever!

Earlier this year I went on a promotional trip to China.

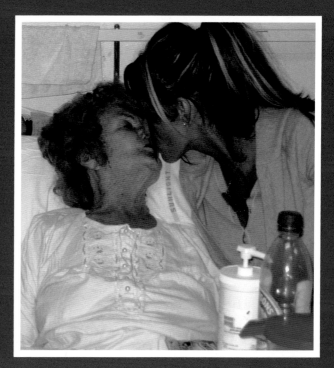

Sophie, Mum and I visiting my nan before she sadly passed away.

Enjoying a moment's rest on holiday.

and planned to have the trees planted in my garden. And Mum had arranged that after the wedding all the floral arrangements were going to be made into bouquets and sent to all the people who looked after Harvey in some way – from the nursing staff to the teachers from his special school. Because this was a fairy-tale wedding, like any princess should, I got to sit on a grand, pink, gilt throne – Posh and Becks, eat your hearts out! My mood brightened as we walked in with all our guests and saw how amazed they were by the room; it really did look incredible. The lighting had been set up to get pinker and pinker as the night progressed to give the room an even more magical feel. After all our guests had taken their seats, Pete and I then walked along the walkway which led from the top table to cut our fabulous cake – all five feet of it made of rich, dark chocolate, covered in white chocolate roses and love hearts and thank you choccywoccydoodah for giving it to us as a wedding present. Everyone was cheering and clapping. At that moment the new Mrs Andre felt very happy and very blessed.

But then the photographer was at it again. 'Kate, Pete, look this way,' do this, do that! After he'd been clicking away and ordering us about for a few minutes I said, 'I think you've got the picture now, haven't you?' God, he was annoying me! I didn't mind being photographed but I wanted natural ones of my friends and family – I didn't just want all these posed shots. And he kept telling me to smile.

'I never smile in pictures,' I replied crossly. 'I'll smile if I want to smile!'

Our wedding breakfast was delicious, but I couldn't really eat *anything*. I imagine that's how all brides feel – it's such an emotional day that your appetite goes, which is a pity because if it was in front of me now I could stuff my face on the lobster salad, the roast breast of Springfield chicken and the heart-shaped white chocolate and raspberry cake with our initials on it! My wedding day buzz returned as I chatted to Pete and our families and enjoyed the speeches. However, during my stepdad's speech, when he asked my real dad to stand up, I realised that there had been a cock-up with the table numbering and he had ended up on the wrong table at the far end of the room, along with my nan, and I was very upset about that. It looked as if I was pushing my family away, when really they were supposed to be next to the top table. But I loved Paul's speech – all about how he had always seen me as his daughter, and he's always been my dad as far as I was concerned.

Then came the third reveal of our big day – and the first part of the entertainment. Pete and I had seen the Tenors and Divas Incognito at a Vision charity ball and loved them, and we thought they would be perfect for our wedding. Basically, they start off pretending to be waiters and waitresses and then burst into song and it's a fab way of getting everyone's attention and getting them up and off their seats and dancing – which we all were when it came to their *Grease* medley! Though I couldn't really do that much in my dress.

My good friend Sally Cairns's speech was sweet and funny. She told the story of how we once ended up in the toilets of a nightclub drinking a bottle of champagne. We were so busy gossiping and getting drunk together that we forgot all about the time and before we knew it a cleaner walked in, in the early hours of the morning, because the club had closed!

Pete's speech was of course emotional, but I loved that too. He called me his 'absolute Princess of Princesses' and said, 'I love you sincerely, I gel with you in every way.' And he added, 'Although our personalities couldn't be more different, we complement each other in every way. I am well and truly over the party scene, whereas Katie reckons she'll be over it by this time next year!' Cheeky!

My speech was much quicker and more to the point. I just thanked as many people as I could – I hate speaking in public and I hate long speeches. *Best kept short and sweet*, I thought.

I can't really tell you too much about Pete's best man George's speech, as it was mostly in Greek!

Then it was time for the dancing. Pete and I were first on the dance floor – to dance to 'A Whole New World', the duet we had recorded. Before we started I joked, 'Don't worry, it won't be like Eurovision!' We both loved the song and when it had been played when Junior was born, by complete coincidence, we thought we would have to have it at the wedding. But even as I was dancing with Pete and enjoying our moment I could see the photographer out of the corner of my eye, and it wasn't long before he was calling out, 'Picture!' So I turned and gave him the picture, but I really wanted to dance with Pete. And I thought, *Please just take the bloody pictures, I don't want to pose all the time!*

Next up on the entertainment front was Rowetta, from *X Factor*, who I think has got an awesome voice, but even as I was enjoying her singing Claire came up to me and said they wanted to take more pictures.

'Claire!' I exclaimed. 'Please let me watch Rowetta first and enjoy the entertainment. Pete and I booked her because we wanted to watch her!' Rowetta was followed by some amazing drummers who led us all outside the marquee, where we had another surprise for our guests. I had been really looking forward to this part of the entertainment because I knew it was going to be stunning. Opposite the marquee the entire wall of the castle was lit by an amazing projection show – planets and stars appeared as the drumming gave way to a different soundtrack, and everyone gasped as a trapeze artist appeared, suspended from a great white heliosphere and looking like the lady in the moon, from where she performed her acrobatics. All I wanted to do was watch the show, but as I tried to stand outside the marquee with everyone else and enjoy it the security guards shouted, 'Stand back! Someone will get a picture!' They insisted that Pete and I stand inside the marquee, which didn't give us the best view. I was fucking pissed off – Pete and I had paid all this money and we couldn't even watch the show properly, and it was amazing. The trapeze artist was followed by fire jugglers and the projection show turned to brilliant orange flames moving up the castle wall. The finale was a projection of photographs of Pete's and my childhood, careers, first meeting, how our romance progressed and our life together with our children. It really was something . . .

But then it was off to do more pictures, which seemed like such a waste of time to me as they were with the same people we'd been photographed with earlier. And I couldn't help noticing one of my relatives looking at me as if to say, 'Aren't the rest of the family good enough to be in your wedding pictures?' And I found myself shouting, 'Quickly, go and get the rest of the family together and we'll do one now, otherwise there will be no time.' And I thought, *God, I'm shouting at my family. What am I doing?*

*

I could hear the band Pete and I had chosen but I didn't get to see their set or dance to a single song because I was in my dressing room, taking off my dress and putting on my tutu skirt. I even missed Pete singing 'Ain't No Sunshine', which I would love to have heard. My long skirt was so heavy it had really dug into my skin, leaving it scratched and bruised, and it was such a relief to take it off. Then I had to take the crown off because that was so heavy as well. My neck was really hurting from where I'd had to keep bending it, with the weight of the crown, to double kiss all my guests. It's not easy looking like a fairy-tale princess, you know! So then Nick and Royston had to rearrange my hair and Gary had to touch up my make-up, and instead of it being a quick change I was gone for forty minutes.

'I need a drink!' I said, discovering to my complete surprise that it was midnight. The time seemed to have flown by. I'd only had one dance with Pete and I'd hardly talked to any of my guests.

I walked back into the marquee. By now the music had switched to an eighties disco and everyone seemed to be going for it on the dance floor; they also seemed pretty merry from the champagne and cocktails, and as I was stone-cold sober I felt a bit out of it. I heard that one of my guests had collapsed and an ambulance had to be called. Also, one of Pete's relatives passed out and had to be rushed to hospital. Suddenly I felt absolutely exhausted. I had wanted to go round to all the tables earlier and greet my guests, but I would have had difficulty squeezing past the tables. Now I felt too drained and I didn't think I was up to it either. It all stemmed from when I had Junior and felt so emotional and low, from the huge build-up to the wedding, from working constantly, and even from the fact that I'd done a shoot the day before the wedding. I wanted to find the quietest spot I could, so I went and sat by my nan. Unfortunately she had taken the table cock-up very personally and she moaned to me, saying she was appalled about where she had been sitting.

'Thanks a lot, Nan,' I said. 'Now you're ruining my day as well!' I had asked earlier if the tables could be swapped round, but it was too late as everyone had already sat down and it would have delayed the meal even further. I suspect my real dad thought that I had meant him to be sitting so far away and that I had pretended that he was on the wrong table, as we don't see each other any more, but that really wasn't the case.

I'd hardly seen Pete and I didn't have the strength to mingle. All around me I could see people I wanted to talk to, but I knew if I went over to see them it wouldn't just be a quick, 'Hi, how are you?' They would have to be in-depth conversations and I really didn't have the energy. Also there's nothing worse than talking to people who are a little the worse for wear when you are sober. I was watching everyone else enjoying themselves and having a fantastic time, and I couldn't help wishing that I was too. All I wanted to do was go to bed. I only stayed up because I knew Pete would wonder what was wrong with me. He had already asked me why I was stressing but it wasn't that I was stressed – I was just so physically exhausted from everything that had happened before the wedding.

But even tucked away there was no peace for me, and every five minutes it seemed that people would come over and introduce themselves to me. 'Are you alright?' they kept asking, obviously wondering why I was sitting in a corner.

'Yes,' I assured them. 'I'm just having a rest,' thinking, *Please go now and leave me alone*, but they would keep asking me if I was alright.

The party was supposed to finish at two but people were still having such a great time that we ended up extending it for half an hour, which cost us more money. But I had to go. Taking a deep breath I shouted out, 'I've got to go to bed, I'm exhausted. I haven't got the energy to say goodbye to you all individually, but please don't think I'm being arrogant and thank you very much for coming!'

Pete wanted to stay but I thought I would collapse if I didn't get into bed.

'Stay if you want to,' I said to him.

'I don't want to let you go up to bed on your own on our wedding night!' he exclaimed. 'Plus, we've got to say goodbye to everyone.'

'You can, I can't,' was my answer.

'Why are you being like this?' he asked me.

The last thing I wanted to do was have an argument on our wedding day, so I simply told him I was exhausted. I knew he had the hump with me, even though he did come up to bed.

Given my state of complete exhaustion, it

shouldn't surprise you that we didn't consummate our marriage that night. I actually ended up on the bed, eating crisp sandwiches and having a cup of tea with my mum, Paul, my brother Daniel, his wife Louise and Pete, chatting about the day – who says I don't know how to have a good time!

Your wedding day is supposed to be one of the happiest days of your life, and don't get me wrong, I will always remember it. Everything was stunning – it completely matched my dreams and I couldn't have been happier that I was marrying Pete. But I would have enjoyed the day so much more if I hadn't had to spend so much of it being photographed. Probably if I had been more myself, and physically and emotionally stronger, I wouldn't have let it bother me. As it was, I was still feeling vulnerable and everything got to me.

We didn't rush off on honeymoon – mainly because we hadn't known until the last moment whether Harvey would be out of hospital – and so we had a week to recover from our big day. I was so pleased that the press didn't manage to get any pictures of us – after all, someone had even managed to sneak a picture of David and Victoria Beckham's wedding. Our security was so tight that nothing got out. But I have to admit that I wasn't happy with some of the pictures from the *OK!* shoot. I am a perfectionist when it comes to photographs – I'm photographed for a living, so I know exactly what looks good. They hadn't been airbrushed for a start, as it was such a rushed turnaround. Claire, my manager, had to go to London the day after our wedding to go through all the pictures, and they were printed that night, so I appreciate that time was really tight and I know how hard everyone worked to get them out in time. But I still think some of them should have been airbrushed. Usually the other shoots we do with the magazine are airbrushed, and as the wedding day was supposed to be the ultimate shoot I would have thought they could have done it. I also thought the lighting should have been better. I had spent a fortune on my dress, and I wanted the lighting to pick up on the crystals and really sparkle in the pictures. But I thought the lighting made everything look too flat and it didn't accentuate the sparkles enough. Everyone else thought the pictures were great, but I can't help having such high standards.

Pete and I were also really disappointed when we discovered that our wonderful wedding cake had been thrown away and we hadn't even had a piece of it! We were hoping to freeze some of it and have it at Junior's first birthday. And then we discovered something even worse. Our wedding was being filmed for ITV and one of the other reasons why Pete and I paid so much money for the entertainment that night was because we knew that people at home could watch it and we wanted it to be a big show, something that people would never have seen before at a wedding. Then we were told that they were ending the film at our dance because the lighting inside the marquee was too pink and it made everything look fuzzy on camera. Well I'm sorry, but that's not Pete's or my fault – that's down to the production people. And even if that was the case inside, I really don't understand why they couldn't have filmed what happened outside, with the trapeze artist and the projection show. I'm sure people would love to have seen the entertainments because they were so special. And we can't get that evening back, so we would have loved our own film of it . . .

* * *

'Oh God, here we go again!' I groaned to myself as I arrived at Heathrow with Pete and the children to find the film crew ready to start filming me. It had seemed such a good idea at the time to agree to have the wedding and some of the honeymoon filmed, but now all I wanted to do was escape from the cameras. 'Just try and make it a laugh,' Pete told me. But straight away the crew were in my face, asking me questions, and that's what I hate. I wanted the documentary to look natural. The minute I'm inter-viewed I know my voice changes – I stop feeling relaxed and I stop being myself.

'Look,' I said to Claire, 'you've got to tell them not to ask me questions. And what's the point of them asking me where I am? Isn't it pretty bloody obvious that I'm at the airport?!'

Fortunately the crew weren't going to be able to film me on the flight, as they were in economy and I was in first. But if I thought I would have a chance to relax, I had another thing coming. Usually Harvey is really good when we fly and he'll play, have his bottle and sleep. Not this time: he didn't sleep for the whole nine hours and neither did Junior; both of them cried and moaned throughout the flight. I had brought my mum with us, to stay for the first week, as a thank you for helping with the wedding. Not many people can afford to go to the Maldives, unless it's a package, and I wanted to give her a first-class, luxury stay at the six-star Hilton Maldives Resort and Spa, which is amazing. So I really didn't want her to have to help out on the flight – I wanted her to relax and Pete and I would look after the children. But it was such hard work and I knew that everyone was looking at us, thinking, *Shut those children up!*

We had to change at Dubai, and by then Pete and I were feeling very frazzled. We had the double buggy to negotiate and the two bags for the kids, plus our own hand luggage. The final straw came when the lift to take us to departures didn't work and we had to unload all the bags off the buggy, take out the children and carry them upstairs. That's when the film crew did come in handy, helping us.

Our next flight was four hours and I prayed that the children would finally go to sleep, but they didn't, and by now Pete and I were bickering at each other because we were so knackered. In the end I told him to sleep and I would deal with the kids. When we landed at the Maldives we had to get a small seaplane to our island, and only then did the children finally fall asleep – after Harvey had a massive tantrum in the first-class lounge while we were waiting for the plane, throwing himself on the floor and screaming.

And I came close to having a tantrum myself when the film crew insisted on filming me when I came off the plane. 'Please do something, Claire!' I exclaimed. 'I don't want to be filmed now. I haven't slept at all and I look like shit!' I had thought that the crew might give us one day off, but no; they wanted to make the show look real by showing how tired we were . . .

'Thank God we're finally here!' I exclaimed, looking out at the stunning view from our water bungalow – miles and miles of dazzling blue ocean and behind us a beautiful white sand beach. Luckily the children were still asleep and Pete and I collapsed into bed, totally exhausted.

For the first four days of our honeymoon we were filmed for our documentary. Mostly I was fine about it, but I lost it one day when they wanted to film me swimming underwater. Before we came away my hair extensions had been taken out, and I really wasn't happy about showing my hair – it's only shoulder-length and it doesn't look glamorous enough for me; I can't bear being filmed or photographed with it like that. Claire suggested I wear my hairpieces for the shot, but I replied that there was no way I was ruining them. So in the end I wore a pink swimming hat!

Once the film crew had finished filming they flew back and we were photographed for our *OK!* shoot. Luckily that was with the team of people I know and get on with so well, and the whole experience was relaxed and a laugh. When we weren't working we all went swimming or fishing and had dinner in the evening and played mad games of Articulate. One fishing trip nearly ended in disaster for Pete. We were all mucking about, pretending we had something on our lines. I was shouting, 'Oh my God, I've caught Jaws!' And then suddenly Pete shouted, 'My finger!' At first we all thought he was winding us up, then we realised he was in agony. I rushed to get a knife, to cut the line, but was beaten by the guy who was looking after us. He reckoned that Pete had caught a giant stingray, and if he hadn't cut the line when he did it would have pulled Pete over the side of the boat and into the water. Poor Pete was very shaken – he was in agony where the line had wrapped so tightly round his finger. I made him sit down and put his head between his knees because I was worried he was going to have a panic attack. Luckily he was alright, though his finger was numb for weeks afterwards and it's put him off fishing for life . . .

Pete wasn't the only one who suffered an injury. One day I had taken Harvey swimming in the sea – he loves water and is very confident in it – but suddenly he started screaming. When I got him out of the water I saw that his big toe had a nasty cut on it. Immediately we called the doctor out – because of Harvey's cortisol deficiency we have to be very careful if anything happens to him, as it could lead to his temperature getting so high that he might have a fit. The doctor said that he had probably stood on a rock fish or a sea urchin and we had to immerse his foot in hot water to draw the venom out – no easy task with a screaming three-and-a-half-year-old, but luckily he was okay.

Once the *OK!* shoot was done Pete and I were

alone with the children. This was our time to relax and unwind – well, as much as you can with two children! Because we were on our own as a family I started to feel that I was bonding with Junior; I felt that I was connecting with him in the same way I did with Harvey. And we finally discovered a way of getting him to go to sleep – he likes to be rocked on a pillow – a major breakthrough as before that he would just cry whatever you did. I felt in control again; the anger and pain I had felt seemed to have gone. I felt physically and emotionally so much stronger. The doctor had been right: I just needed time. And it was so wonderful being with Harvey again. I had missed him so much when he was in hospital and was sure that had added to me feeling so low after Junior was born. Of course it was hard work, because Harvey was walking around more than he used to and so had to be constantly watched as our water bungalow was actually over the sea. I got the hotel to drain most of the water out of our Jacuzzi, which was on the balcony, and Harvey had a great time splashing around in there in his armbands.

*

We had a wonderful time. We were staying in what must be one of the most beautiful, unspoilt places in the world, in the lap of absolute luxury. We even had our own butler, who would get us whatever we wanted and take us wherever we wanted to go. Every day we'd have a treatment – massages, body wraps, facials – and we'd lie on the beds and look at the fish swimming through the glass floor. In the evening we would have two babysitters looking after the children, leaving us free to have dinner in one of the amazing restaurants.

Early on in our stay I had noticed that the hotel had a new gym and there was a juicing machine. In a fit of enthusiasm Pete and I ordered new trainers and new kit, thinking that we would work out and follow the juicing diet. Did we bollocks! The kit took two days to arrive and remained untouched, and I pigged out on the delicious food every single night – one night we even had a twenty-seven course feast! *I'll get back into shape when I get home*, I thought. Whilst I had been feeling so low I had decided to sell my horses, something which made me feel even more depressed as I love them. But now I was stronger I decided to keep them and to look after them myself.

Mucking them out twice a day would be good exercise – I've realised that gyms aren't really for me.

Unusually for us, we made friends with two other couples – normally we like to keep to ourselves on holiday, but they were so friendly that we met up for dinner with them several times. They told us they couldn't believe how down to earth we were. And it was lovely hearing their stories about how they met – one couple had made contact on the Internet and exchanged pictures, and then by complete coincidence recognised each other on the Tube one day but didn't say anything. When they got home and emailed each other they realised they had seen each other and they've been together ever since.

Even though we had the children with us we still had such a romantic time. But I decided that I would definitely treat Pete to a weekend away in Venice when we returned home – just the two of us – because as everyone who has children knows, sometimes you need some time when it's just you and your partner. Every morning we'd wake up and exclaim, 'Wow! We're married!' It felt so good to say that. And we managed to make up for the lack of action on our wedding night with lots of passionate and spontaneous sex. Pete had his hair cut short after the wedding, and I have to admit that I found him a lot sexier with his hair like this. I thought he looked gorgeous and clean-cut. Although his long hair had gone well with his wedding outfit, I much preferred it short.

We had just one tiny row over Pete's mobile phone. Two days into our honeymoon we were having breakfast with everyone and Pete got out his phone to make a call. When I asked him who he was calling he told me it was his mum and dad. *Fair enough*, I thought. But then the cheeky bastard phoned his mate, which didn't best please me, and I went off in a bit of a huff. I really don't think you should have your mobile on during your honeymoon. But that was the only thing that annoyed me. Apart from that I felt so close to Pete and so in love that I felt so totally myself with him and so relaxed. It may sound like a little thing, but I think all you girls will understand – Pete is the only man I have ever let see me without my hair extensions in. I know that he loves me for myself, not just what I look like.

As if he hadn't treated me enough with my gorgeous wedding ring, one day when I was sunbathing Pete gave me two more necklaces – a heart-shaped one with a pink stone to match my engagement ring, and one in gold which matched a ring he had bought for me last time we were in the Maldives. Every night we would sit on the hammock on our balcony and look out at the stars – the sky is so clear out there you can see them so clearly. One night I actually saw three shooting stars, which was just awesome. I thought, *That's a star for Pete and one for Harvey and Junior, and I'm the luckiest girl in the world to have them all . . .*

* * *

It's been such an incredible two years since I first met Pete – I've experienced such highs and lows. I have never felt so happy before or at times so unhappy – those few months after Junior was born were some of the hardest of my life. There were times when I felt as if I was never going to feel better, that I was never going to feel bonded to Junior. I am just so relieved that I am out of that dark place now. I know Pete would love more children, and I would too, but I'm not ready yet, so just after we were married I went back on the pill.

'How come all the time we've been together you weren't on the pill, and now we're married you're on it?' Pete asked me, quite upset about my decision.

'Because if I don't take it, I'll get pregnant again!' I replied.

'Yes, but we're married now!' was Pete's answer.

I told him I needed to wait until Junior was at least two before we tried for another baby. That way I will be able to spend time with him and Harvey and enjoy them, not be totally stressed out.

'Seriously Pete,' I said, 'if we had another baby now do you really think we could cope with Harvey and Junior, who would only be just over a year old?'

He saw my point.

I've also got my career to think of. The fact that I'm a married woman with two children is not going to stop me from pursuing my glamour-modelling career and my pop career – it's made me even more determined to carry on as Jordan. And on that score, by the time you read this I might have been for boob job number four – this time I am going for a reduction. I want my boobs to be smaller and more pert – having two kids has done nothing for them, as any mum will tell you!

In November 2005 I had the chance to put Eurovision well and truly behind me when I sang live on Children in Need and I finally proved to everyone that I could sing and that I hadn't just been bullshitting! Not only was I doing it for a good cause but I was also singing a ballad live – something that I had always wanted to do. It also meant so much to me because 'A Whole New World' was our wedding song, and I was singing it with the love of my life.

Now we're married I feel complete, and I know that Pete is with me because he truly loves me. Just before we were married we signed a pre-nup agreement. If we ever split up I wouldn't have to give Pete anything, he would just have what was his, nor would he have to give me anything. His solicitor apparently questioned him, saying, 'Are you sure about this? She's made a lot of money.' But Pete was absolutely clear, he didn't want anything from me. The pre-nup just confirmed what I already knew – he's with me for love, as I am with him. We have to see what the future holds, but at the moment I couldn't be happier and as far as I am concerned I am with him for the rest of my life . . . Though I will say this: Ladies, when you think you've found the right man, never trust him one hundred per cent because you never know what's round the corner . . . And as I've always said: Never underestimate the Pricey – *just wait to see what's coming up in every way . . .*

If you enjoyed *Jordan: A Whole New World*, you'll love *Crystal* – the brilliant new novel by Katie Price coming this summer. Read an exclusive sneak preview here!

There was already a queue of people outside *Max's* in Covent Garden. Crystal walked to the front and spoke to the doorman with more confidence than she felt.

'Max is expecting me, tell him it's Crystal.'

A phone call later she was inside the club and walking towards the bar in the VIP area where she knew Max would be.

'Hey Crystal!' Max had seen her. Immediately he

walked over to her and kissed her on each cheek.

'So glad you could make it,' he murmured, his hand lightly touching the small of her back. 'I'll get us some champagne. We can celebrate.'

'What are we celebrating?' Crystal dared herself to ask.

Max couldn't keep the naughty little glint out of his gorgeous brown eyes, 'Oh I don't know, we just are.'

A few minutes later they were sitting at one of the private tables, screened off from the rest of the club and Crystal was doing her very best not to stare at Max. God she wanted him so much. It just wasn't fair. Why had Belle met him first? *He's much more my type,* she thought wistfully, loving his unpredictable, slightly dangerous edge, and if she was honest, she couldn't help being attracted to him because she knew he was a bit of a bastard.

'You said you needed to talk to me. Is it about one of the record deals?' Crystal asked, trying to cover up the surge of attraction and adrenaline he always provoked in her. He nodded, 'All in good time, first tell me how the rehearsals have been going?'

Crystal shrugged, 'Good I think. The others are being pessimistic, but I reckon we've got a chance.

We're sounding better than we ever have.'

'There's definitely interest out there for you. I've had another meeting with the label; I'm just waiting for the paperwork to be drawn up.'

'We'll need to go through it together,' Crystal said quickly. Infatuated as she was with Max, she knew she couldn't trust anybody in the business she was in. The group had worked so hard to get to where they were and she wasn't about to let anyone take that away from them.

Max lit a cigarette, 'You're right to be cautious babe, but you know I'd never rip you off.'

Crystal covered her face with her hands and groaned, 'Max, you're smoking in front of me, and you promised you wouldn't.' She'd given up a month ago, at her manager's insistence and she was finding it extremely difficult, even with nicotine patches and gum.

Max gave her one of his sexy smiles, blew a perfect smoke ring at her face, then held out the cigarette, 'One little puff won't hurt will it? I won't tell Dallas if you won't.'

For a few seconds Crystal hesitated, then reached out for the cigarette, took a deep drag, immediately getting the nicotine hit that she'd been missing, 'Oh my God you're such a bastard!'

'And that's exactly why you like me isn't it?' Max said quietly, staring directly at her, his brown eyes serious for a change.

She quickly looked away, half loving what was happening, half knowing it was wrong. Max was off limits, she should leave. Right now.

'How do you know I like you?' She challenged, 'I only put up with you because of Belle.' She tried to sound as if she believed her words, but knew they lacked conviction.

Max gave that sexy smile again, turning her will power to dust, 'Okay Crystal we can play this game if you want or you can admit that you like me as much as I like you.'

Crystal looked down. *This was definitely the moment to leave.* But still she didn't. 'It's not fair to make me say that, you're the one who's going out with someone.' She couldn't bring herself to say Belle's name.

'Shall I tell you why I like you then?' Max said softly.

Now Max had Crystal's full attention. She raised

her face and he was looking at her, definitely not in the way you were supposed to look at your girl-friend's friend.

'For your eyes, that know more than you let on, for your sexy laugh, for your ambition, for being the sexiest woman I've ever met, for your mouth.' And here Max reached over and gently traced round the outline of Crystal's lips. She closed her eyes, willing herself to be strong but it was a battle she was fast losing. She couldn't stop herself, she kissed his finger and then his mouth was on hers, he was kissing her and she was kissing him back. No kiss had ever felt so good. Crystal forgot everything apart from the feel of his lips, the taste of him. She closed her eyes again but Max was pulling away, whispering, 'Let's go upstairs.'

He stood up and held out his hand. Crystal hesitated, torn between desire and guilt. She knew that upstairs meant Max's office, where he sometimes stayed the night, she knew there was a bed. Somehow she managed to say, 'No, I can't.' And before Max had a chance to try and stop her she got up and ran for the door, pushing her way through the clubbers and out in to the cold November air.

* * *

'Christina, get up! You've got ten minutes before the car picks us up.' Belle was standing by the side of Crystal's bed. Crystal knew she was pissed off, people only called her by her real name when they were annoyed with her. 'Dallas will go ape if we're late.'

Groaning, Crystal sat up. She picked up her watch. Eight o'clock. 'Okay, okay' she muttered, hardly able to look Belle in the face. She was the very last person she wanted to see this morning.

Belle walked over to the door. She looked pretty and fresh in her tight white cashmere cardigan and denim mini, her long blonde hair pulled back into a sleek pony tail. 'And don't think I don't know what you did last night,' she called out as she opened the door.

Crystal's stomach lurched, *Oh my God, how could she know?*

'You were smoking!' Belle called out, 'I can smell it. For god's sake, Crystal, you promised you'd given up.'

Crystal collapsed back on the bed, feeling a mixture of guilt and relief, 'I know, Belle, I'm a bad person.'

Belle laughed, 'You've got no will power, just like Max. Now get your arse into the shower and put some slap on, you look like shit. What did he have to say by the way?'

'Oh, it's still a bit vague, he's hoping for some news in a couple of days,' Crystal lied, hating herself for doing it.

* * *

Kathy their singing coach was rehearsing with them. The girls adored her, she was laid back and had been in the business for years. Crystal tried to push what had happened out of her mind and concentrate on singing. But she couldn't stop the images flooding into her head, the feel of Max's lips on hers, the feel of his body against hers . . . *It was just a one off,* she told herself sternly, *It's never going to happen again.* But when she checked her phone during a break there was a text from Max asking her to meet him again that night, which triggered the all too familiar feeling of desire. She wanted to text back *No,* to tell him to leave her alone, instead she ignored the text and turned her phone off.

Don't fuck up, she urged herself. Winning the competition could change her life and she couldn't allow herself to be distracted like this. For as long as she could remember all she had ever wanted to be was a singer. Singing had always been her escape. When she sang she was at her most happiest; she knew she was doing something she was good at. She could block out the pain of her dad leaving her, her mother's lack of interest, the responsibility of looking after her brother, her money worries, and lose herself in the music. It made her feel alive like nothing else ever had and she loved every minute in front of the mic. Someone like Belle wanted to win the competition because she longed to be famous and to live the life of a celebrity, to be photographed in the celeb mags, to go to the parties, to hang out with other stars. But to Crystal, winning the competition wasn't about fame; it was about being a singer.

After rehearsal, it was straight back to the hotel to be interviewed by the TV channel that was showing the competition. She was dying to check her messages to see if Max had called again, but couldn't risk doing it in front of Belle. Crystal dreaded these interviews more than the live show itself. Having a camera stuck in her face and feeling nervous made

Tahlia even sweeter than she usually was, Belle came across as bubbly and fun but it had the opposite effect on Crystal and she worried that she came across as a right hard bitch. Belle had agreed to do most of the talking and Crystal did her very best to sound sweet and humble, when really she was thinking, *vote for us, we're the bollocks!*

'So how's this week been for you girls?' asked Hadley, the young good-looking presenter. Crystal and Belle were convinced he fancied the pants off Tahlia, but she wouldn't have it.

'It's been great Hadley,' answered Belle, as Crystal worked her sweet look.

'Because it was a tough one last week wasn't it when you and *Trick or Treat* came last and had to sing your songs again?'

'Yeah, thanks for reminding us,' Crystal couldn't stop herself blurting out.

'It was hard,' Tahlia added, 'and we felt really sorry for the guys.'

Like fuck we did, thought Crystal, now doing her best to look sympathetic.

'How about you Crystal?' Hadley was now pointing the mic at her.

'We've been working our arses off and the song's sounding shit hot.'

Hadley frowned, 'Crystal, I did ask you not to swear if possible, this programme goes out before nine. So same question again.'

Crystal tried not to giggle, he was so serious. And yes he was very good looking, but not in a sexy-get-your-kit-off kind of way, more like a clean cut member of a boy band – definitely not Crystal's type.

'Sorry Hadley. We've been working really hard and we're really hoping that everyone's going to like the song. We've put everything we've got into it.'

Hadley seemed happy with that and the cameras stopped filming. As the girls were filing out of the room, Hadley walked over to Tahlia and looking a little awkward asked, 'Um Tahlia, I was wondering if you fancied going out for a drink sometime?'

'Okay,' Tahlia said shyly, 'but it might have to wait until after the competition.'

Belle and Crystal gave each other meaningful looks and walked out of the room, giving Tahlia and Hadley the chance to swap numbers.

'Lucky Tahlia,' Belle said outside, 'he's fit.'

'What are you up to now?' Crystal asked, longing to

get to her hotel room to check her mobile.

'Oh I'm meeting mum and dad for dinner. What about you?'

'Having an early night,' Crystal replied, faking a yawn, 'see you in the morning.'

She was just opening the door to her hotel room when Tahlia walked along the corridor, a smile on her face.

'Well?' Crystal asked, raising her eyebrows.

'What do you think of him?' Tahlia asked

'Very sweet, you should definitely go out with him. Do you want to come in and talk?' she asked, praying the answer would be no as she thought she might explode if she couldn't check her messages.

'Thanks, but I'm going to babysit for mum,' Tahlia answered.

Tahlia was always babysitting her little sister and Crystal had given up telling her that her mum should bloody well pay for her own babysitter.

'Okay, see you in the morning then.'

Finally Crystal was alone. She reached for her phone. There were five texts from Max and ten voice mails. All of them begging her to call him, begging her to come and see him. Crystal knew she wouldn't be able to do anything until she'd called him.

'I can't see you Max,' she said, her voice sounding more certain than she felt.

'*Please* Crystal, I've got to see you babe.'

Crystal took a deep breath, 'I can't. You're with Belle.'

There was a pause and Max said, 'So if I wasn't with Belle you'd see me?'

Crystal hesitated, 'Yes, no, I don't know.' She felt so torn, wanting Max, not wanting to hurt Belle.

'We can't do this over the phone, please come to the club. We'll talk, that's all.'

* * *

An hour later Crystal was once more sitting at one of the private tables next to Max, smoking – her will power on that score had crumbled – and sipping her drink, trying hard to play it cool.

'You know I can't finish with Belle until after the competition, I don't want to do anything to jeopardise the group's chances but I will as soon as it's over. I want to be with you Crystal,' Max said urgently. 'I want you Crystal, I wanted you the first time I saw you and I haven't stopped wanting you.'

He reached over and took her hand in his, 'We could be so good together, I know we could.'

Crystal felt something inside her give, hearing the words that she'd been dying to hear Max say for so long. She looked at him, 'So after the competition, you promise?'

He nodded, and Crystal continued, 'And you won't tell her it's because of me? I don't want to hurt her.'

'I won't babe, I promise,' and he put his arms round Crystal and pulled her to him, kissing her deeply.

'No running away this time,' he murmured. As Crystal lost herself in the kiss, she had never felt less like running away. And this time when Max suggested they went upstairs, she didn't resist.

She held his hand and the two of them walked quickly through the bar and up the private staircase. Max had brought the bottle of champagne with him and as soon as they were in the room he poured them each a glass and locked the door. They both drained their glasses and then they were in each other's arms, and they were kissing. He was running his hands over her body, unbuttoning her jacket and letting it slip to the floor, caressing her breasts, kissing them. He led her to the bed, taking off her jeans, 'No underwear Crystal, you are a naughty girl.' He pulled off his t-shirt revealing his toned chest, his tanned perfect skin; he unbuttoned his jeans and slipped them off. He pinned Crystal to the bed kissing her all over, caressing her with his tongue, sending shivers of pleasure through her. And she was kissing him, moving down his body, slipping off his black Hugo Boss shorts, teasing him with her mouth. And then they were fucking, and Crystal wasn't thinking about anything except how good it felt, how it felt the best ever. And when she came she cried because it had been so good and because she knew she should have waited.

She closed her eyes, not wanting Max to see the tears, but he already had and was kissing them gently away, 'Oh Crystal, what have you done to me?'

* * *

The next morning when she woke up she couldn't help feeling guilty even though Max had told her that he was going to finish with Belle. What if Belle really loved him? It was admittedly hard to tell what Belle thought of Max – she definitely seemed to enjoy the glamour of the relationship, going out with a famous ex-racing driver, hanging out in all the hip clubs, being taken out to expensive restaurants. Crystal tried to remember if she'd ever actually heard Belle say that she loved Max. She never had, had she?

She spent the rest of the day in a loved-up haze.

Angel

Katie Price

A sparkling and sexy tale of glamour modelling, romance and the treacherous promises of fame.

When Angel is discovered by a model agent, her life changes for ever. Young, beautiful and sexy, she seems destined for a successful career and, very quickly, the glitzy world of celebrity fame and riches becomes her new home.

But then she meets Mickey, the lead singer of a boy band, who is as irresistible as he is dangerous, and Angel realises that a rising star can just as quickly fall . . .

'The perfect sexy summer read' *heat*

'A page-turner . . . it is brilliant. Genuinely amusing and readable. This summer, every beach will be polka-dotted with its neon pink covers' *Evening Standard*

'The perfect post-modern fairy tale' *Glamour*

arrow books

**Order further Arrow titles
from your local bookshop, or have them delivered
direct to your door by Bookpost**

☐ **Angel** Katie Price   0099497867   £6.99

Free post and packing
Overseas customers allow £2 per paperback

Phone: 01624 677237

Post: Random House Books
c/o Bookpost, PO Box 29, Douglas, Isle of Man IM99 1BQ

Fax: 01624 670923

email: bookshop@enterprise.net

Cheques (payable to Bookpost) and credit cards accepted

Prices and availability subject to change without notice.
Allow 28 days for delivery.
When placing your order, please state if you do not wish to receive any
additional information.

www.randomhouse.co.uk/arrowbooks

arrow books

THE POWER OF READING

Visit the Random House website and get connected with information on all our books and authors

EXTRACTS from our recently published books and selected backlist titles

COMPETITIONS AND PRIZE DRAWS Win signed books, audiobooks and more

AUTHOR EVENTS Find out which of our authors are on tour and where you can meet them

LATEST NEWS on bestsellers, awards and new publications

MINISITES with exclusive special features dedicated to our authors and their titles

READING GROUPS Reading guides, special features and all the information you need for your reading group

LISTEN to extracts from the latest audiobook publications

WATCH video clips of interviews and readings with our authors

RANDOM HOUSE INFORMATION including advice for writers, job vacancies and all your general queries answered

Come home to Random House

www.randomhouse.co.uk